The Occupation of the Factories

Paolo Spriano

The Occupation of
the Factories: Italy 1920

Translated and introduced by
Gwyn A. Williams

1964

 **Pluto** **Press** 1975

First published 1964 as
L'Occupazione delle fabbriche
Copyright © 1964 Giulio Einaudi Editore Spa, Torino
This translation first published 1975 by Pluto Press Limited,
Unit 10, Spencer Court
7 Chalcot Road
London NW1 8LH

Copyright © Pluto Press 1975

ISBN 0 902818 67 8 paperback
ISBN 0 902818 68 6 hardback

Printed in Great Britain by
Bristol Typesetting Company Limited,
Barton Manor, St Philips, Bristol

Designed by Richard Hollis, GrR
Cover photographs, Collection Moro, Rome

Contents

Translator's Introduction

In Gibbon's *Decline and Fall*, the footnotes are entertainment; in Paolo Spriano's *The Occupation of the Factories*, they are essential.

This uncertainty in the placing of historical evidence reflects the curious indeterminacy of the crisis itself. The occupation of the factories in Italy in 1920 exploded out of a 'normal' wage agitation. Central to it was the utter intransigence of the employers. Organized in their mighty federation Confindustria, they had already inflicted a severe defeat upon the factory council movement in Turin, the only dynamic and institutional force to emerge from the turmoil of the populist revolts of 1919. Isolated and scorned within the socialist movement, the Turin 'communists', inspired by Antonio Gramsci's journal *L'Ordine Nuovo*, had been broken by a lockout supported by 50,000 troops. During the summer, the communist presence in the socialist movement shrank and the reformists grew stronger. Popular militancy, denied expression in socialism, found outlet in anarcho-syndicalist modes and styles. Confindustria, secure in its strength and in its expectation of an unemployment crisis, totally refused even to discuss the wage claim of the metalworkers' union federation FIOM: 'Since the war, we've done nothing but drop our pants. Now it's your turn', said its spokesman. This basilisk intransigence threatened FIOM's very existence; with the syndicalist unions claiming 800,000 members and breathing on its neck, it slid into the exasperated militancy of its rank and file. The newly installed government of Giovanni Giolitti, prewar master of the art of popular manipulation and the reconciliation of opposites, who had appointed an ex-syndicalist as Minister of Labour, was committed to a reformist solution of the Italian crisis: it was alleged that a Giolittian bank, the Banca Commerciale, guaranteed the loan FIOM raised to finance the occupation. In September the crisis exploded. Half a million metalworkers and others occupied their factories; in Turin and on the railways, an anti-state began to take shape; the establishment panicked and its leading spokesman called for power to pass to the socialist trade union federation, the CGL. The Italian state seemed about to crumble in the most vivid and traumatic crisis of the postwar period. The climax was anti-climax. In solemn ritual, the 'assizes' of the socialist movement met in Milan and formally debated whether to have a communist revolution or not. They rejected the proposal by 591,245 votes to 409,569 with some 93,000 abstentions. This decision, as Giolitti and the CGL pressed forward with schemes for 'union control' of industry on an employer class infuriated by government 'betrayal', initiated the process in which capitalism disengaged itself from democratic order in Italy and the working-class movements slithered into demoralizing rout, as fascism rode to power in monstrous and tumultuous growth, and a small communist party struggled out of the wreck.[1]

The immediate, human and psychological obstacle to revolutionary action is the rooted *sense of the normal*, that 'normality' which makes tolerable an objectively intolerable predicament, the return of which one senses and awaits even as rubbish piles up in the strike-bound streets and a torrent of unprecedented talk breaks over the paralysed city. In September 1920, the socialists of Italy, confronted by a situation become 'intolerable', reverted to 'normal': they put the issue of revolution to a democratic vote: an overt act of historic renunciation. But in that same September, the 'communists' of the vanguard city of Turin created a directive committee to coordinate the action of occupied factories: exchanges between different branches of the same firm, they decided, did not require committee authorization; exchanges between different firms did. Under workers' control, they preserved the 'normality' of the capitalist definition of industry: a covert act of historic renunciation.

One neglected factor in the crisis, which Spriano fully documents, is the objective resilience of Italian capitalism. At the height of the crisis, Agnelli, director of Fiat, offered in despair to turn the

---

1. For a fuller treatment of the social context see my *Proletarian Order: Antonio Gramsci, Factory Councils and the Origins of Communism in Italy 1911-21*, published by Pluto Press as a companion volume to this; John Cammett, *Antonio Gramsci and the Origins of Italian Communism*, Stanford University Press, 1967; Martin N. Clark, 'Factory Councils and the Italian Labour Movement 1916-21', Ph.D. London, typescript, 1966 and *The Failure of Revolution in Italy 1919-20*, University of Reading, 1973.

firm into a co-operative: 'How can you build anything with 25,000 enemies?' Albertini, editor of *Il Corriere della Sera*, the *Times* of Italy, 'offered power' to the socialist leaders; there was a widespread feeling that the transition to a socialist economy had begun. These subjective reactions masked a reality. In a very real sense there is a logic in the arc of capitalist development in Italy which curves from 1900 into the fascist regime. It is the logic of imperialism, state monopoly capitalism, mass industrialization and mass mobilization. Fiat was established in Turin in 1899; by 1914, 44 firms with a capital of 67 million lire were in the vanguard of the European automobile industry. In the war, there was a colossal expansion into trucks, submarines, aircraft, railways, weapons; Turin became an industrial monolith, Fiat's capital rose from 17 to 200 million lire. It weathered the postwar crises and settled into the Mussolini regime, with a virtual monopoly by 1927. Electrical production mushroomed from 100 million kilo-watt hours around 1900 to nearly 5,000 million during the war. Chemicals grew into the monster Montecatini enterprise, stimulated growth in photography, dynamite, rubber, as Pirelli and its kin moved to predominance. Steel and engineering experienced parallel growth. At every stage the process was powered by the state, with its control over coal and water rights, and by the precociously developed banking system.

After the failure of a first abortive thrust into mass industrialization and imperialism in the 1880s, capitalist industry in its most advanced forms mushroomed around the traditional Milan-Turin-Genoa triangle from the 1890s. Its very rapid growth in the 1900s developed breakneck speed during the war itself, when Ansaldo and the other trusts became monsters. The postwar crises were certainly severe, but it was the totally unprecedented temper of the new popular mobilization which gave them their quasi-revolutionary dimension; in strictly 'economic' terms, they were fairly 'normal' crises of adjustment. It was in the midst of the 'anarchy and exaltation' of 1919 that the Perrone brothers led Ansaldo and the rest into their breath-taking stock-exchange exploits, and the hardening of Italian capitalism into a form of state monopoly capitalism in the early years of the Mussolini regime seems the logical terminus of its trajectory of growth since the 1890s.

This logic is deceptive, since the curve was fixed, of course, by the outcome of the head-on collisions of 1919-20. What has to be grasped, however, as central to the postwar crisis, is the underlying strength and resilience of capitalism, manifested in the toughness and self-confidence of its leaders in 1920, and, even more central, the power of its associated ideologies, particularly the reformist, radical and social-democratic. For they played upon and informed mass populist revolts which were utterly disparate, unco-ordinated and, in some basic senses, contradictory. The vote in the socialist assembly in Milan in September was decided by the powerful rural unions allied to the craft federations. The fascist offensive was to reveal, in all its stark horror, the isolation of the industrial working class and the factory proletariat at its heart. That isolation registered first and foremost within the socialist movement itself.

The most striking feature of the postwar crisis was the entry of the rural classes into history. Of the nearly six million men conscripted, 46 per cent were peasants or rural workers; 1,300,000 were killed or disabled. Agricultural prices doubled while industrial prices trebled. There were requisitions and controls. On the other hand, the black market flourished, and many peasant households fought through to some security from debt and mortgage. In northern Italy the proportion of peasant proprietors rose from 26 to 36 per cent. After the Caporetto disaster of 1917, government was lavish in its promises of land reform. The net effect was an explosion of rural militancy and land-hunger. Catholic trade unions, authorized by the Pope in 1918, mushroomed into the federation CIL which, with over one and a half million members rivalled the CGL; while a Catholic Popular Party (PPI, *popolari*) won over 100 seats at the general election of November 1919, second only to the socialists themselves. In some rural areas there was a revolutionary temper.

But the movement was both contradictory within itself and divorced from the mass rally around the socialist party and trade unions. Of an Italian population of about 37 million, some 57 per cent were dependent on the land on the eve of the war, as against some 28 per cent on industry, but there was a very wide range of predicaments. In the industrialized agriculture of the Po Valley, a bitter triangular struggle developed around socialist-controlled labour exchanges among rural proletarians and small farmers proletarian in condition; Tuscany and other centres of tenants and share-croppers were swept by anti-landlord feeling; among the big, under-employed estates of the South, peasant ex-servicemen led ritual land-occupations. The crisis was severe but the Popular Party, which tried to represent every class of the rural population, proved ineffective. A radical wing led by Miglioli, the 'white bolshevik', tried to work for socialist solutions, but by and large the rural movement, itself internally incoherent, was divorced from the socialists.

The central failure of the Italian Socialist Party (PSI) was its failure to exploit and develop this situation, in stark contrast to the performance of the Russian communists in 1917. G.M.Serrati, effective leader of the party, in practice accepted the division between socialist 'labourers' and catholic 'peasants' as structural, and resisted the policies of Lenin and the Comintern precisely on this issue. The PSI had its own difficulties. In the mass mobilization of the new industrial working class created by the war, and climbing out of the semi-military labour and trade union collaborationism of the war years, the socialist trade union federation, the CGL grew near to the two million mark by 1920; the PSI itself shot over 200,000 by 1920; it controlled over 2,000 local communes and, with 156 deputies, was easily the strongest single force in parliament. But it failed to channel the explosive temper of the people. A great wave of strikes broke over Italy and won the eight-hour day in the spring of 1919; in June-July popular revolt against food prices brought a collapse of authority in the North, when the CGL was compelled to act virtually as an alternative government in some areas, and when an insurrectionary coup might well have succeeded. Instead the PSI and the CGL fought desperately to control the upsurge and direct it towards radical democratic action. The stunning socialist victory in the elections of November 1919 virtually paralysed government, already subject to attack and insubordination from the right and the nationalist left, who cultivated chauvinist and pseudo-revolutionary hostility to the 'lost peace' and democracy. The socialist movement failed to break out of its immobilism after parliamentary victory, and stood by while the employers broke the Turin council movement in the struggle of April 1920, itself the climax of a wave of popular militancy in early 1920 which the bourgeoisie experienced as a strike frenzy. It was from that point that established order began to regain its nerve, the socialist movement to shuffle towards a 'labourist' solution, and the anarcho-syndicalists in their union federation USI to scoop up popular disappointment and exasperation.

This performance of the PSI, while critical in the heady

atmosphere of 1919, in fact rehearsed a practice which had become 'traditional', for a species of functional centrism was integral to the party's history. Born in the 1890s in sharp reaction to the Bakuninist tradition of populist and 'anarchoid' revolt, the PSI, under the leadership of Filippo Turati and the reformists, had defined itself in total rejection of anarchism and its communal tradition. Strongly buttressed by the reformism of the CGL, the PSI had become increasingly parliamentary and devoted to the necessary preliminary of democratization. Its leadership was essentially middle-class, and exposed not only to the attractions of liberal democracy, but to the exploits of meteoric demagogues of whom Mussolini was simply the most sensational example. From time to time, explosions of popular discontent, which the party failed to channel, by-passed it into semi-anarchist movements and provoked a radical reaction within, often ouvrierist and primitively anti-middle-class and anti-intellectual in character. Riding this permanent tension and trying to canalize its energies was the party directorate, a direct emanation of the party membership, which was committed to the party's maximum programme of socialist revolution. The directorate was constantly having to adjust and adapt to the relentless drive of the CGL leadership and the parliamentary deputies into reformism, and to the periodic explosions of militancy among the popular classes and the socialist rank and file.

The party entered its final crisis in 1911-12 as the imperialist crisis broke in Italy. During the decade of Giolitti's political predominance, the party leadership had beaten off a raid from anarcho-syndicalists and become essentially parliamentarian. Its ambivalent response to the immediate prewar crisis, initiated in Italy by the Libyan War and the granting of near-universal suffrage in circumstances of crisis-ridden but rapid industrial growth, precipitated the assault of an intransigent revolutionary fraction which radicalized the party, expelled the more right-wing reformists, and found expression in the near-insurrectionary leadership of Benito Mussolini, until his defection to the cause of intervention in the war. Virtually alone among the parties of the Second International, the PSI opposed the war and tried hard to rebuild an international. Its inner polarization, however, worsened. State mobilization of industry tended increasingly to incorporate the trade union and parliamentary wing of the movement, particularly in the national revival after Caporetto;

the radical democracy of Woodrow Wilson gave it a global perspective. The intransigents, scattered and repressed, moved towards a revolutionary defeatist policy and responded immediately to the Bolshevik revolution. Popular exasperation against the war, however, exploded in the summer of 1917, particularly in the Turin insurrection of August, before the revolutionary fraction achieved any effective coherence, and it was drowned in the almost tribal response to Caporetto from November. In these circumstances, Serrati, editor of the party journal, *Avanti*, succeeded in his heroic effort to maintain the unity of the party in the face of a polarization which appeared fatal.

He, and the 'maximalists' around him, persisted in this policy after the war. Convinced from his experience of the populist troubles of 1919 that the PSI needed to build an efficient striking force, he made the achievement of socialist unity in readiness for the 'revolutionary moment' the lynchpin of his policy. The party rallied spontaneously to the Third International in March 1919, but its leadership refused to turn the party into a communist party, even in name. At the second, the real founding congress of the Third International, Serrati, rejecting the agrarian policies of Lenin and the Comintern, refused to expel the reformists, and demanded the same degree of national autonomy as he claimed the International had granted the French. In the end, he rallied Italian national feeling and the 'glorious tradition' of Italian socialism against the 'red freemasonry' of the Comintern. In the process he attacked and in large measure succeeded in neutralizing both wings of the nascent communist movement in Italy.

The oldest was that associated with Amadeo Bordiga, of Naples, who had been developing a principled and intransigent marxist critique since the crisis of 1912, had been the prime leader of the revolutionary fraction during the war, and who in his journal *Il Soviet*, 1918-20, called for the formation of a strictly defined class party which would be the instrument of a narrowly defined proletariat, and would abstain from the parliamentary elections of bourgeois democracy. Abstentionism, conceived at first as a device complementary to the expulsion of the reformists for purging the party of all bourgeois influence, tended to harden into a self-isolating principle. The theses of the Bordiga fraction remain to this day powerful, cogent and often prophetic statements. Abstentionism tended to alienate much potential support, and the quality of the movement's marxism induced it to reject the other communist movement, that grouped around *L'Ordine Nuovo* in Turin.

The remote origin of this movement was the Turin youth section founded by Angelo Tasca in 1909. Tasca had been an opponent of Bordiga's in the youth movement, arguing for an intellectual regeneration of the movement and a modernization of marxism. Antonio Gramsci and Palmiro Togliatti had been drawn into his movement but dispersed in varying reactions to the war and Mussolini's defection. The group reformed around Gramsci and Tasca in 1919, after the former, overcoming initial uncertainty, had moved to the centre of the tough Turin working-class movement. Their journal *L'Ordine Nuovo* argued for the formation of factory councils, elected by the entire workforce by unit of production as the first cells of a new proletarian state, and achieved remarkable success within the Turin region, where some 150,000 workers were ultimately organized in councils. In party political terms, however, they were incoherent and remained prisoners of Serratian maximalism.

The break came after the party's election victory in November 1919, its continued immobilism during the popular upsurge of the winter, and Serrati's attacks, in the name of unity, on both the council and the abstentionist communist movements. It was after the national council of the PSI in January 1920 had rejected both communist wings in a welter of prophylactic and utopian schemes for 'councils' and 'soviets', that Bordiga tried to contact Lenin direct, identified Serrati and not Turati as a 'centrist', and decided to break away from the PSI, with a small minority, if necessary. The Turin council communists, whose movement had been unable to break out of isolation and was succumbing to reformist and, more particularly, syndicalist pressure, launched a campaign to regenerate the PSI from Turin, and to organize an emergency convention around a national congress of factory councils. What to Gramsci was 'indiscipline' brought down the state and capitalist counter-attack of April 1920, when the socialist party and the trade unions abandoned the council movement. In the summer of 1920 the *Ordine Nuovo* group disintegrated; first Tasca and then Togliatti broke away, to leave Gramsci isolated, and to form a left wing within maximalism, largely in response to the upsurge of syndicalist power, which mobilized a factory campaign against arms production after a mutiny among troops destined for Albania, and tended to capture the reviving council movement, and in opposition to the hardening intransigence of the Bordiga fraction. At the Second Congress of the Comintern, Lenin's praise of the manifesto of the Turin Left provoked violent attacks from all other sections of the Italian delegation, which forced him to withdraw his blanket commendation. On the other hand, Bordiga was induced to renounce formal abstentionism and to undertake to form a communist party on as broad a base as possible. The occupation crisis, therefore, broke on a divided party, and in response to the conflict with the Comintern and the PSI's conduct during the occupations, the PSI dissolved into fractions. Serrati carried the majority, largely by an appeal to nationalist and traditionalist instincts, and the communist party formed around Bordiga's fraction, to emerge from the congress of Livorno in January 1921 as a small, rigorous, exclusive fraternity of 40,000 militants, and to struggle for life and for its historical identity against economic recession, fascist offensive, Comintern incomprehension and the shuddering collapse of working-class morale and organization.

Paolo Spriano's study is to be located within this context. It is not perhaps the most cogent of his works but, in its evidence, is among the more valuable. At an immediate level, there appears to be a certain incoherence in the organization of the material. The distribution of material between text, references and appendix is sometimes confusing. For example, the material cited on the attitude of Turati and Treves in the appendix seems to warrant a considerably stronger comment than appears in the text; a more strictly chronological arrangement of the text material, supplemented by the incorporation of material from the references into the text would, I think, alter the balance of the argument, or at least the emphasis, in some instances. For this reason, it is essential that readers study the references and the appendix as closely as they do the text; they may reach different conclusions.

On closer examination, the reader will observe that these hesitations and qualifications refer almost wholly to matters touching the conduct and attitude of *the left*. On the complexities of response at state, government, bourgeois, capitalist, and liberal level, the book is superb. This is, indeed, its great strength. The close, documented analysis of variant attitudes among the established, in which text and appendix complement each other, presents a finely nuanced, compelling and convincing picture which is at times quite remarkable.

A closer examination still of the eccentricities in the treatment of the left reveal idiosyncracies which are not wholly those of craftsmanship. Notable is the lack of emphasis on the anarcho-syndicalists. In the build-up to the crisis, their *presence* is in fact essential. FIOM could never forget they were there; the actual occupation was, in a very real if limited sense, their triumph. At the other pole, Gramsci figures quite prominently. This is entirely understandable, but, however compelling his writing, it is important to remember that, at this point, Gramsci was in fact an isolated and marginal person. Less fashionable is the abundant use of Tasca, expelled from the Communist Party in 1929 and abused as a semi-fascist for dubious behaviour at one point during the Second World War. Tasca's book on the rise of fascism is still one of the best on the subject, and it is interesting to note that left historians who represent a quite different more rigid tendency from Spriano's, like Luigi Cortesi, are happy to make use of Tasca's work. What Tasca would represent in the 1960s of course is an *anti-Togliatti*. So would Bordiga – and there *is* a certain *opacity* in Spriano's book on Bordiga and his fraction: Giovanni Parodi, the hero of Fiat-Centro, and many of the militants cited were in fact abstentionists.

Bordiga, in opposition to the united front and what he saw as the degeneration of the Comintern, was displaced from the leadership of the Communist Party of Italy in 1923; Tasca offered a right-wing alternative, but it was Gramsci who, in molecular slowness and against the Italian grain, constructed a new leadership for the party during 1923-24, confirmed by his Lyons Theses of 1926. Gramsci was imprisoned late in that year and, in the sudden turn in Comintern policy against the united front from 1928, the leadership of the PCI was decimated. Tasca was expelled as a rightist, Bordiga as an unrepentant oppositionist, Gramsci withdrew in prison. From around 1930 the Communist Party, under Togliatti's leadership, began to write its own history. Directed essentially against both Tasca and Bordiga, it employed the writings (or to be more exact, some writings) of Gramsci to construct a 'tradition'. The effort was intensified during the years of the Popular Front, the war of liberation, and the turn of 1944, when Togliatti committed the movement to the construction of a mass party and the democratization of Italy. The 'Gramscian' tradition was central, to be seriously challenged in the 1950s and 1960s, firstly by the swift incorporation of a suitably denatured 'Gramsci' into bourgeois culture, secondly by the entry of Tasca and Bordiga into the historiographical struggle, and by the emergence of a group of forceful historians, leftist and doctrinal, the effect of whose work was to 'rehabilitate' Bordiga and diminish, indeed dismiss, Gramsci. The response of Togliatti's Communist Party reminds us that that party is not only the strongest but also the most intelligent communist party in Europe. To a large degree, it opened its archives to sympathetic but independent-minded historians. One consequence has been the finest history of a communist party yet to emerge from the vicinity of the communist movement.

Its author is Paolo Spriano. Now in its fourth volume, it is a magnificent undertaking and, to anyone accustomed to historical work by comrades, often quite staggeringly candid (particularly in the footnotes).[2] Spriano, of course, built on an already celebrated series of studies of Turin and its working-class movements and of the *L'Ordine Nuovo* enterprise.[3] It is the craftsmanship of these gem-like studies which makes Spriano a historian's historian, but, while the massive history of the Communist Party shows signs of transcending this condition, his work has been on the whole satisfying at a tactical rather than a strategic level. The same quality can be detected in this study of the occupation of the factories and it is important to remember that Spriano is an intelligent, sympathetic and often very effective historian who, in his occasionally indeterminate generalizations and his occasional reticences, is situated within the last of the Togliatti traditions.

In an indirect sense, this emerges in his concluding chapter, a masterly survey of opinion on the reality of the 'revolutionary opportunity', which is perhaps rather negative on the theme (a response intriguingly modified in the latest of his prefaces written after the experiences of 1968) but which is, essentially, indeterminate.

The indeterminacy is understandable, for we are ultimately

---

2. P.Spriano, *Storia del partito comunista italiano*, Einaudi, Turin, four volumes, 1967-to date.
3. P.Spriano, *Socialismo e classe operaia a Torino dal 1898 al 1913; Torino operaia nella grande guerra; L'occupazione delle fabbriche; L'Ordine Nuovo e i consigli di fabbrica*, Einaudi, Turin, 1958, 1960, 1964, 1971.

left with Lenin's question: during the occupation did one single communist put in an appearance? Which takes us back in the end to the terrible, gnawing agony of the central problem – the exact *quality* of the popular 'militancy' of 1919-20. During the great debate in the socialist movement, Bruno Buozzi, leader of FIOM, put forward a motion, intended to be intermediate between the communist and social-democrat motions, on which the FIOM delegates abstained. It in fact expressed a species of 'revolutionary reformism', which later experiences in France and elsewhere have made familiar. There is strong evidence in this book and others that Buozzi's motion may in fact have more accurately reflected the temper of *the masses* in occupation than any other. If this assessment (which in one sense was also Serrati's and in another Bordiga's) is correct, is the real 'revolutionary opportunity' to be located rather in the war years, or at least before that demobilization which meant that 'groups of armed men' were once more the monopoly of government and the right? This would not only call for a re-examination of Brest-Litovsk and Bukharin's 'revolutionary war', the interplay between the Russian sector of the revolution and the rest, but for a reconsideration of at least some of those communist thinkers, like Anton Pannekoek and Herman Gorter (and in his own distinctive way, Amadeo Bordiga), who were apparently so easily expelled from history by Lenin's *Left-wing Communism, an Infantile Disorder*. For their assessments were ultimately grounded in an appreciation of the European crisis of 1919-20 which does not seem dissimilar to that suggested by Buozzi's motion. If they were correct, that assessment called for communist policies and tactics in Europe radically different from those actually adopted from 1920-21.

These are large, speculative and possibly unanswerable questions. But they *are* the questions ultimately provoked by this little, 'technical' study of one incident written by a historian's historian. Read it, and see what questions it raises in your mind. For in reading it, you join comrades in the necessarily arduous process of creating a usable past for the working-class movement.

The author's Latin tags have been omitted and some liberties taken with his sentence and paragraph structure, but an effort has been made not to English him out of character. I thank Giuliana Parodi for her help with the Appendix.

Gwyn A. Williams

Preface to the 1968 Edition

In 1968 the subject of factory occupations became a burning issue in Italy and in France; what is more, factories themselves were once again occupied by workers in struggle and universities by students. Throughout, there was constant reference to similar experiences in the past: that of 1936 for France and, above all, that of September 1920 for Italy.

We therefore reissue this, our study of 1964, in the hope that it may furnish further material for reflection. We have added nothing to the first edition (except for some additions to the bibliography); nor does it seem necessary to alter the general tenor of its argument. Current experience alone, however, perhaps brings into greater prominence some points touched on in the analysis, above all the relationship between the initiative of the masses and their 'institutional' politico-social leadership. It is always a difficult relationship and the example of September 1920 suggests that the lack of a precise objective in the latter ultimately checks the thrust of the former. We see a dynamic of occupation which in itself drives forward to a choice: either an extension of the movement to confront the crucial problem of power, the 'dual power' of Lenin, or else a trade union adjustment of a wages dispute whose gains however are never realized unless the general situation is altered to the benefit of the workers.

But this is material for today's debate. The experience examined in these pages can nourish it; it certainly cannot settle or divert it; the differences in historical context are too obvious. The occupation of the factories of 1920 was in every way a fundamental experience in this sense: it shows what energies can be generated by a working class which does not restrict itself to a corporate struggle, but tackles a whole society, state order, the management of production. At that moment, everything changes rapidly, every day becomes precious; the terms on which the conflict ends are very different from those on which it begins. It is this order of things: force, presence, an energy which creates new institutions, which evidently must register today as the most important to investigate and develop.

P.S.

August 1968

Introduction

In the *Socialist Almanac* for 1921 there are some rare photographs of what the diligent compiler called 'the most striking episode in the struggle being fought in Italy between capital and labour': the occupation of the factories by the metalworkers in September 1920. These photographs recreate a legendary atmosphere; their images, bright or sombre, register in the memory as the very symbol of the *biennio rosso*, the 'red two years' of the blazing aftermath of the First World War. It was power which was at stake in this conflict 'between capital and labour' and for most people, whether they feared it or hoped for it, revolution loomed as the natural and imminent outcome of the great social upheaval precipitated by the war, the Russian October, the profound crisis in which all the nations and peoples of Europe were struggling.

In one photograph, before a closed gate emblazoned with the hammer and sickle, a red guard stands sentry, with helmet and fixed bayonet. In another, a red flag flies from the prow of a ship on the stocks, easily visible on its side the name under which the workers launched it: *Lenin*. In a third, workers sit at table in a long canteen; the caption reads: 'Communist kitchen during the occupation.' In others, there are 'occupiers' armed with clubs and rifles before a factory wall or behind rolls of barbed wire; women sitting in the workshop of an electrical engineering plant, posing as for a school photograph; proud youngsters giving the clenched-fist salute beside howitzers, serious trade union faces above flowing black cravats. The most famous of these images is also the most symbolic: a group of workers of the factory council sit at the desk of the director of the greatest motor-car factory in Italy.

What happened in Italy in September 1920 was in truth an exceptional event, and these images give us at least an immediate perception of it. Like Lenin far off, these hundreds of thousands of workers, with arms or without, who worked and slept and kept watch in the factories, thought the extraordinary days they were living through 'the revolution in action'. But was it really a revolutionary moment? Or must we set the episode in a more modest context? The questions pose themselves today as they did yesterday, forty years ago.

The occupation of the factories by the Italian metalworkers in September 1920 has been recounted time and time again in memoirs, in political polemic charged with symbolic reference and ideological schematization, but it has rarely been submitted to straightforward historical analysis. On first examination, a study of the different interpretations to which it has given rise, with all their different perspectives, is disconcerting. Not only do scholars and militants of the same ideological persuasion and the same political convictions differ in their judgment; very often an individual's assessment will vary in proportion to the distance which separates him from that crucial postwar month. The bibliography is very rich, even if, curiously enough, the only two specific historical studies of these events are French (one in 1920, the other in 1930, neither very significant). From Giolitti to Albertini, from Salvemini to Einaudi, Salvatorelli to Missiroli, Buozzi to Nenni, Gramsci and Togliatti, Tasca and Bordiga, Mussolini and Gioachino Volpe, Errico Malatesta and Armando Borghi, Arturo Labriola and Filippo Turati, from the president of Confindustria to the secretary of the CGL, major political figures, scholars, observers directly embroiled in the conflict itself, have left valuable testimony and often something more: a critical reassessment, a particular suggestion, a general definition, a key to interpretation. The knot, however, remains tangled, nor have the scholars who have confronted this problem in the context of a study of the *biennio rosso*, or made passing reference to it, managed fully to unravel it.

It is, perhaps, the very contradiction between the extreme complexity of the historical problem and the need to extract its essential traits within the framework of a particular interpretation of the postwar period which has ensured that the lineaments of the phenomenon remain blurred. If even today, and not by chance, the occupation of the factories of 1920 sets off flurries of controversy in the press (from time to time evoked as a spectre to be exorcized from the present), it is easy to visualize how much political sediment it has slowly deposited over the intervening forty years. From that month a whole series of questions has arisen. Was it the great revolutionary opportunity? Was it the high point of postwar social tension? Was it really the month of the great fear for the Italian bourgeoisie? How did the working masses see it? Was there any connexion between the occupation of the factories and the occupation of the land? Why did the movement suffer a heavy defeat? Who was responsible for taking the working-class movements, individually and collectively, to that point? What was the significance of the experience and its outcome for the schism in the socialist movement of 1921? What was the government's position? Giolitti's conduct is itself a very controversial subject; some see it as a masterpiece of the Giolittian art of government, a convincing demonstration of the old premier's understanding of the working class (with particular reference to his celebrated decree on union control); others dismiss it as mere necessity, a reflection of the impotence of public authority, neutral in the conflict because the coercive apparatus of the state was so fragile.

All these lines of enquiry run together naturally into the immediate sequel to the occupation of the factories: the outbreak of civil war in the country, the growth of fascist squadrism from the autumn of 1920. On this question, experience has engendered a virtually unanimous interpretation: the way the occupation of the factories ended was a severe blow to the revolutionary movement, signalled the end of the revolutionary wave and initiated the period of reaction. But it is precisely in this area, on the most delicate issues, that opinions are discordant or timid: for, to understand a process of cause and effect – a phenomenon whose features were more psychological than substantive, an almost 'excessive' response, in itself quite disproportionate to the workers' challenge, and one charged with 'a retrospective fear' – is not to comprehend a necessary relationship, determined by those very contradictions whose explosion the crisis precipitated.

It is appropriate to begin with a subject which is very controversial but an essential preliminary to a correct assessment of all these aspects: the nature of the metalworkers' movement, its development, its trajectory, its character as a 'revolutionary opportunity'. We begin with an analysis of this kind, but we cannot hope, in this study, finally to untie or decisively to cut this knot; more modestly, we hope to recreate in all its aspects and all its infinitely various components an event which has had a profound influence on the life of contemporary Italy. We will take up the thread of exposition again, in the light of a political and historical critique controlled by a precise reconstruction of the facts, based on the frequently revealing documentation of the police records, of the state archives, of other archives, of the great body of working-class recollection, and of the vivid evidence of the newspapers of the period.

To direct oneself to the atmosphere, the problems, the daily chronicle of the occupation means also to liberate one's judgment from the clichés, the generalizations, the myths and the apocalyptic visions which have encrusted it. It certainly does not mean giving up the right to express that judgment, correctly and in full.

Gramsci wrote, on the very eve of these events, that history is a teacher without pupils. And yet the history of the occupation of the factories, if it cannot give any direct sign to the present, embraces and examines issues about which the most passionate debate revolves in our own day.

It was no accident when Gramsci, writing in one of his prison notebooks on the climacteric moment of the *biennio rosso,* spoke of the 'great fear'. The emotions it evoked throughout the country were titanic: and not only at that moment, for, after decades, the occupation of the factories is still an obligatory point of reference in the social and political life of Italy.

Paolo Spriano
April 1964

We would like to thank the directors and officials of the central state archives for their assistance in searching the archives of the Ministry of the Interior, pivot of this investigation. We are no less grateful to the directors of the Istituto Giangiacomo Feltrinelli, of the Istituto Gramsci, and to Professor Aldo Romano for their suggestions and their general assistance in the discovery of sources on the working-class movement of the time. Finally, our thanks go to the presidency of the Banca Commerciale Italiana for having granted us permission to consult some documents in the archives of the central management touching on a particular point in these events.

1.
The Protagonists

The metalworkers of Italy won the eight-hour day in February 1919. Their numbers had increased dramatically during the war, which had brought hundreds of thousands of working men flooding out of the country districts into the factories. The historic conquest of the eight-hour day (principal demand of the Rome congress of the Federazione Italiana Operai Metallurgici (FIOM)* held in the last days of the war) was the climax of a complex process, an inter-action of many factors, which was opening a new era in the relations between capital and labour, between ruling classes and labouring masses.

There is no need to evoke once again the climate of 1919, the waves of recruitment to the Socialist Party (PSI) translated at the general election into 1,834,000 votes and 156 deputies in the Chamber, the thrust of trade unionism into the urban and rural proletariat, which involved 3,800,000 workers, five times the prewar total. The Socialist Party, 200,000 strong, took control of 2,800 communes (24 per cent of the total), directed thousands of co-operatives, opened over 2,000 local sections throughout the country. And the great majority of organized workers were federated in syndicates, leagues, *camere del lavoro*** led by socialists. The growth of the Confederazione Generale del Lavoro (CGL) was impressive: in

---

* FIOM: Italian federation of metalworkers, founded 1901; headquarters Turin. Led by able Bruno Buozzi, claimed 160,000 members.

** Camera del lavoro (literally, chamber of labour): Basic labour institution, centre and focus of local unions, leagues, co-operatives, savings banks etc. Set up from 1890s in imitation of French syndicalist model, basically as worker-controlled labour exchanges, pre-dated craft and industrial federations. While often minutely sub-divided by craft, used local 'general strike' as weapon and sometimes bred more of a communal, sometimes class, spirit than the unions. With its headquarters the *casa del popolo* (people's house/home), prime target for fascists.

September 1920, it numbered 1,930,000 members, of whom over half were industrial workers.[1]* Other trade union federations were active, but they carried much less weight, particularly in the world of industrial labour. The anarcho-syndicalist Unione Sindacale Italiana (USI), despite the schism caused by the secession of interventionist militants in 1914,** had 300,000 members and offered a serious challenge in particular localities, this city, that region, districts where the revolutionary-syndicalist tradition had struck deeper roots (Emilia, the Romagna, Liguria, Tuscany – Piombino, Pisa, Viareggio – in the Marches and Apulia).[2]

The other two trade union federations were much less weighty. The Catholic Confederazione Italiana del Lavoro (CIL or white union) claimed an impressive membership (1,823,491 in 1920)[3] but its influence was largely restricted to country areas; agriculture supplied 80 per cent of its members. In the industrial movement, its strength lay in 131,232 textile workers, most of them women.*** The weakest union organization was the Unione Italiana del Lavoro

---

* CGL: Major union federation, founded in 1906 in reaction against revolutionary syndicalists, as confederation of trade unions and *camere*; complicated confederal structure with much local autonomy, rising to a national council and small directive council which emerged from union leaderships rather than from general congresses. Close relations Socialist Party, in terms of decisions of Stuttgart congress of International 1907, reaffirmed by Pact of Alliance 1918, which assigned leadership of 'political' strikes to the party, 'economic' strikes to the CGL. Leadership generally reformist socialist; organ *Battaglie Sindacali* (Union Struggles). The largest single group were the rural workers, whether landless or not, organized in their federation Federterra, which was approaching 900,000 at this time, a factor of significance in the voting on 11 September; see below.

** USI: Revolutionary syndicalist federation founded in 1912, committed to class war, fought on 'class terrain', scorned 'politics'. Most militant of labour organizations, its secretary Armando Borghi, was an anarchist. Rapid, if ephemeral growth; claimed 800,000 supporters summer of 1920; headquarters and journal *Guerra di Classe* (Class War) moved from traditional Parma to Milan, March 1920.

*** CIL: Catholic union federation which, after papal recognition in March 1918, grew very rapidly. Committed to profit-sharing and co-operatives, could be militant in union terms; politically ambiguous.

(UIL) with fewer than 200,000 members and a handful of republican *camere del lavoro* in the Ravenna region, Forlí, Jesi, Lugo and Rome;* its political attitude was determined by the interventionist past (syndicalist, republican, nationalist) of its leaders. To these should be added the railwaymen's union, the Sindacato Ferrovieri, 200,000 strong and independent of the CGL, as were the maritime workers, the Federazione Lavoratori del Mare.

Among metalworkers, FIOM (the metalworkers' federation led by Bruno Buozzi) was vastly superior to the other unions in its power and influence, its ability to lead the workers. After the first phase of the dispute, the presentation of union memoranda, UIL and CIL practically disappear. The metalworkers' union affiliated to USI did preserve some independent power (particularly in Sestri Ponente, Verona and Brescia) but the real enemy of the employers was the federation. Its membership was significant (160,000); even more significant was the fact that its orders were accepted and carried out by the great majority of the labour force, apart from a few factories where nuclei of revolutionary syndicalists were very vigorous.

Since the beginning of the century, FIOM had lived through a long period of organizational weakness in the 'red' workers' strongholds during the Giolitti decade** and a wretched moment of ideological division during the war, when its participation in the committees for industrial mobilization, increasing the temptations of 'collaborationism' and corporatism, provoked bitter attacks from more intransigent militants, particularly in Turin and Milan. The federation, however, 'built some muscle' during the war, greatly strengthened its bargaining power and equipped itself with cadres under the young and bold secretary-general Bruno Buozzi – a staff whose striking technical competence, powerful personal prestige and

---

* UIL: Union federation formed by republicans, syndicalists, radicals of nationalist temper who supported Italian intervention in the war, 1914-15. Much of initial leadership supplied by revolutionary syndicalists and itself supplied some of fascism's original cadres, though its temper was generally radical-democratic.
** Giovanni Giolitti (1842-1928): The major political figure in the prewar regime. First premier in 1892, he dominated the prewar decade as Prime Minister and Minister of the Interior. Master of *trasformismo*, the art of manipulating parliamentary interests, his aim was to incorporate the socialist movement into the parliamentary system. Withdrew from office early 1914 and opposed Italy's entry into the war.

experience of leadership made it, in the circumstances, almost irreplaceable.

The mentality of these unionists, their ideological formation, was very similar to that of the reformist political leadership of the party and, generally speaking, to the prototype trade union leadership of the classic social democracy of the Second International, the German in particular. This did not mean that they could not respond to the masses' lurch to the left, sympathize with the Russian revolutionaries (FIOM like the CGL promptly rallied to the call for a red international of trade unions after the war) or appreciate the need for a battle over principle. To understand these men and their limitations, it is necessary to grasp the concept of trade unionism which was rooted in them. It was a very rigid conception, which erected centralized organization – the discipline, authority, contractual power of the union – into a kind of fetish. Buozzi, Guarnieri, Colombino, indeed all the leaders of FIOM, had fought their most formative struggles against anarcho-syndicalism. They had seen the havoc that provocative 'revolutionary syndicalists' had inflicted on the trades in Turin and Milan in 1911-13. They had rebuilt the federation around a patient labour of strictly legal, 'trade union' agitation, painful argument around the negotiating table. Their natural tendency towards a bureaucratic perspective on the problem had been reinforced by their wartime experience.

The attitude of FIOM towards the Turin movement of 'factory councils' was typical: deep suspicion of an experiment in workers' democracy which broke the hold of the traditional union over the masses, which shifted the focus of organization inside the factory, made the productive unit the fulcrum of a new proletarian union structure and gave voice and representation to the unorganized. The national leaders of FIOM feared all this as a new version of anarcho-syndicalism. They were afraid that the intellectual attractions of the *ordinovisti*,* with their impulsive experiments, would

---

* Ordinovisti: Name applied to group around journal *L'Ordine Nuovo*, Turin, founded May 1919 by Angelo Tasca, Antonio Gramsci, Palmiro Togliatti and Umberto Terracini, which became organ of revolutionary factory council movement of which Gramsci was the major theorist. By the summer of 1920 the group had disintegrated as a cohesive faction, but its influence was important and helped make Turin a highly distinctive region; see below.

undercut the union's authority.[4] Hence the condemnation of the factory council movement at the Genoa congress of FIOM in May 1920.

This is not to say, however, that FIOM rejected mass struggle or simply lost itself in the more general gradualist tendencies of the CGL and the reformists. It drew a line to its right as well as its left. Experience of bitter industrial conflict buttressed its tough stance in the dispute which escalated into the occupation of the factories in September. Although the metalworkers secured a reduction in hours without loss of wages through fairly peaceful negotiations with the employers' association in February 1919, it was a very hard fight for FIOM in Lombardy, Liguria and Emilia during the summer of 1919 to win 'minimum pay' rates and an adjustment in cost of living bonuses to meet the continuing rise in the price of 'commodities of prime necessity'. In those districts the strike lasted for two months; it demanded harsh sacrifices from the workers. The agreement, so wearisomely wrung out, was repeatedly broken by their opponents. Tension was thus so acute, crucial economic problems so real, that in the spring of 1920, as workers' living conditions worsened, a new campaign loomed imminent.

The working-class sector, then, was complicated. There was a mass movement into unionism, belligerent passion in every conflict; expectations rose with the revolutionary wave. But the weaknesses were no less significant. Within the trade union world, for example, mass recruitment did not lead to unity. There were deep divisions between the different federations – USI, CGL, CIL, UIL – in ideology and tactics, in inter-union rivalry, in needling polemic bristling with personalities. FIOM, for example, refused to have its claims discussed in common with those of unions affiliated to the other workers' organizations.

The trade union movement was living through a crisis of unforeseen growth, for which the leadership was unprepared in organization, still less in psychology. At the end of the war the CGL had 250,000 members; within two years they were two million. When the confederation held its Fifth Congress in February 1921, delegates and executive members raised lament after lament over this 'excessive' growth, which is revealing of the inner contradictions of the movement. The CGL chiefs were trained in the trade union practice of the Giolitti era, not to mention the Giolittian perspective on the relations between capital and labour; after the occupation of the factories, Giolitti was to say that he had always had faith in the CGL and that the latter had fully merited that faith.[5] These men suffered all the more from their inability to direct and control the postwar wave of often chaotic strikes.

It was the CGL leader D'Aragona, at that congress in 1921, who was most revealing on the confederation's inadequacy. On innumerable occasions, he complained, the CGL had been forced to intervene, to take over the job of appeasing and resolving all sorts of ill-considered agitations provoked by craft federations or workers in particular factories.[6]

Throughout 1918 and 1919 the CGL worked to win the whole socialist movement to the idea of a 'constituent assembly of labour', the programme which best corresponded to its own reformist and gradualist bent.[7] But the socialist movement as a whole rejected it, adopting a revolutionary programme to which the great majority of the party and the more militant union nuclei seemed totally committed. In exact parallel to Turati and Treves in *Critica Sociale*, the men and press organs of the CGL, *Battaglie Sindacali* in the van, ran a continuous polemic, a veritable campaign against the 'war socialists', the adventurist and amateur spirit of new converts who were trying to throw over the policy and techniques of progressive economic and political advance. This obsession mastered the CGL congress, when recrimination against 'latecomers' became the dominant theme of the debates.

A similar psychology, of course, was at the root of a choice and interpretation which became visible only at critical moments: the belief that in Italy there could be no immediate and violent solution to the revolutionary crisis, that, on the contrary, the conditions for a successful revolution simply did not exist. Hence the search for solutions which could pre-empt rash action and guarantee a gradual advance for the world of labour.

The CGL leaders' response to the soviet experiment under way in Russia was characteristic: a verdict which day by day became more ponderous and negative. A commission of enquiry led by D'Aragona himself visited Russia in the spring of 1920.[8] Even before their reports were published as a book, D'Aragona, Colombino, Bianchi and the others were making press statements which were circumspect, charged with reservations and reticence – which the conservative press was shrewdly to exploit during the occupation of the factories as admissions of the experiment's failure.[9]

No assessment of the CGL would be accurate, however, unless it took account of its general ambiguity and 'availability'. For example, when even the more traditional reformists were singing the praises of the Russian revolution and the young soviet republic, the CGL joined the international general strike of July 1919 in solidarity with the proletarians of Russia and Hungary. As the PSI delegates to the Second Congress of the Communist International reaffirmed their 'revolutionary will', so D'Aragona and Baldesi signed at that congress a resolution which preached the dictatorship of the proletariat and invoked 'the triumph of the social revolution and the universal soviet republic'.[10]

There was a similar ambiguity over programmes. If, among the conflicting doctrines of Bombacci, Serrati and Bordiga, the party seemed to oscillate between a bureaucratic conception of soviets as an alternative to parliament[11] and an interpretation of the dictatorship of the proletariat as a dictatorship of the socialist sections, the CGL in turn oscillated between an advanced democratic programme (progressive wealth tax, universal suffrage, disarmament, gradual socialization of the soil and subsoil) and a demand for power for 'consultative syndical bodies' which was frankly corporatist in spirit. Implicit in the latter was 'the right of control by workers' representatives over factory management', a demand which took practical form during the September struggle.

This aspiration, so powerful during the occupation of the factories, ran right through the whole of this two-year period, 1919-20. As it took increasingly elaborate shape, it brought CGL doctrine into line with Turati's (particularly in his famous speech, 'Rifare l'Italia')[12] and, ultimately, with the reformist and anti-plutocratic notions of Giolitti himself, a drive towards an incorporation of the working masses and their *legitimate* representatives into the structure of the democratic state, towards an organization of production which would register the increased weight of those masses and broadly co-opt them into the effort to rebuild the country's economy, towards a power which, in Turati's words, would take over management and 'in one sense, anticipate the advent of the proletariat, in another, prolong the rule of the bourgeoisie'.

Even on the subject of union control, this profoundly

gradualist and corporatist spirit took the form of proposals for 'councils' which were the negation of those of the *ordinovisti* and which should be emphasized because they reappeared during the broadening controversy over the occupation of the factories. The Baldesi project of 'company councils', for example,[13] was wholly inspired by the will to create organizations at the workplace recruited from union men only, which were narrowly dependent on craft federations and *camere del lavoro*. They were to exercise powers wider than those of the internal commissions*, to defend trade union rights and enforce respect for agreements, to undertake research into industrial production methods ('exploring those changes which can benefit the collectivity') and to conduct 'propaganda to convert the mass of the workers to the socialization of the means of production and exchange'.

The hostility of the CGL to new forms of direct democracy (quite apart from the bitter controversy with *L'Ordine Nuovo*) was obvious in the suspicion with which the CGL looked on the handful of council experiments which workers tried in some plants in the course of desperate conflict. In isolated and dramatic episodes, workers occupied several factories during the spring of 1920: the Mazzonis cotton-mills in the Canavese (February-March),[14] the shipyards of Ansaldo, Odero, Piaggio, Ilva and San Giorgio in Sestri Ponente (February)[15] and the Miani-Silvestri plants in Naples (March).[16]

Every one of these episodes had its own history and represented the spontaneous reaction of workers to intolerable con-

---

* Internal commissions: Grievance committees elected by union men within a factory to handle everyday problems of discipline, arbitration etc. First officially recognized in Fiat-FIOM agreement of 1906, enjoyed sporadic existence before the war, multiplied greatly during the war. Forms of election varied; in Turin area, generally five workers elected for fixed periods, elections dominated by FIOM officials and 'leading workers'. Became focus for autonomous shop-floor action and were chosen as essential instruments for campaign for revolutionary factory councils conducted by Gramsci and *L'Ordine Nuovo* which called for election of workshop commissars by all workers, whether union members or not, who were then to elect the internal commission as the executive of the factory council. Leading organizations of the council movement, they survived defeat of councils, in emasculated form, for several years.

ditions. The welcome the CGL reserved for them was negative. Over the Mazzonis mills, the CGL was content to support the Nitti government's requisition order and to accept the subsequent 'derequisition', but in Sestri Ponente, the mere suspicion that the workers had been inspired by anarcho-syndicalists was enough to bring down a CGL condemnation on their heads. The occupation of the Sestri Ponente dockyards ended in a few days with a big police action, and in Naples, too, a harsh repression hammered the 1,800 workers of Miani-Silvestri.

The real test for the CGL, however, was the April strike in Turin, when the city's metalworkers came out for a month and its whole working class for ten days, over the principle of recognition of factory councils. The inspirers of this resistance, the theoreticians of the councils as new revolutionary institutions, organs of power, the men of *L'Ordine Nuovo*, who had already been accused of anarcho-syndicalism by the bureaucracies of FIOM and the CGL, and of economism and corporatism by Bordiga and Serrati, were now denounced as adventurist dilettantes and intellectuals. And the very issue at stake, power in the factory, which in Turin precipitated the most bitter conflict of the whole period, evoked no response in the national organizations. So the Turin movement went down to defeat, left in total and hopeless isolation to confront the offensive of the local employers and a massive mobilization of the repressive forces of the state. What has to be remembered, because it is directly relevant to the occupation of the factories, is that the April strike opened an abyss between the CGL and the leaders in Turin, where the FIOM section had been won over to *ordinovista* doctrine. And it dragged with it a train of mutual suspicions and rancour which exploded at the critical moment of the factory occupations. The issue of workers' control, officially buried in the rubble of the Turin defeat, once more became crucial and the men of *L'Ordine Nuovo* were able to assert, with some reason and much bitterness, that this principle, for which the Turin men had fought a lonely and savage battle in April, was central to the entire September agitation.

Furthermore, the April strike raised much wider questions than those of trade union and class organization. The relationship between the union and the party came into focus, a relationship which was codified in a written agreement fixing spheres of action.[17]

To the CGL fell the leadership of economic struggles, to the party, leadership in struggles which might acquire political meaning. But how was this boundary to be drawn in a situation in which every agitation rapidly took on a political colour, but was still charged with that 'wage claim' spirit generated by the deepening economic crisis itself? And what direct contacts did the party have with the worker and peasant masses? This was perhaps the cruellest contradiction in the socialist movement at that time.

For the men who really had the capacity and the organizing power, the men who exercised leadership over the labouring masses, over the working class in the authentic sense of the term, were the union chiefs – the D'Aragonas, Buozzis, Dugonis, Baldesis. They directed that working class towards unashamedly trade unionist, practical objectives. The men of the party, however much they might want – as ideologically they had to want – to direct the masses towards a violent rupture of established order, the seizure of power and soviet construction (as the phrase ran), were in general remote, lacked levers of command, experience, cadres, a rapport with the class which permitted effective leadership. The *Ordine Nuovo* group, at that moment, had no roots in the masses outside Turin.

The working-class and socialist movement, then, confronted what was to be one of the critical moments of the revolutionary crisis of the *biennio rosso* in a state of division between party and unions, a division which was not merely a division of duties and fields of action, but something deeper, a configuration of two sovereign entities, each operating in its own orbit. In fact the action, the perspectives of the party were purely propagandist and electoral. Antonio Gramsci, on 21 August, eve of the struggle, unerringly put his finger on the spot. He wrote in *L'Ordine Nuovo* that the problem of the relationship between party and union was fundamental and that the party had done nothing to solve it. The metalworkers' federation, he said, had set the vanguard of the proletariat moving into 'a new phase of agitations and strikes of a national character' and yet 'the central organization of the party has not thought it worthwhile, so far, to express a single opinion or launch a single slogan'. The agitation might at any moment transform itself from a corporative into a political movement; 'how could and how can the party remain a stranger to, be present as a simple spectator of, such an agitation?' Yet so it was despite the maximalist rhetoric it was still using, 'rolling around the mouth with acrobatic tongue' the expression 'the present period is revolutionary'. The party did not lead, did not intervene, was not present in the factory, appeared heedless of the fact that 'the workers' revolution is either a movement of the deepest masses or it is nothing'.

'So today,' concluded Gramsci,

> as the metalworkers' movement opens a phase of intense agitation, when the *revolutionary period* might, from one moment to the next, precipitate the party into action, the Italian movement has not only failed in practice to solve the problem of the relations between party and union, it has never even raised it; the Italian proletarian movement is the battleground of two political parties, the one official, the other formed by the union bosses.[18]

On the other side of the barricades, the situation was less contradictory from the viewpoint of class organization. In the action of the employers there was a thrust for centralized discipline and direct political intervention, in factory and in kingdom, which was one of the most interesting (and unexpected) elements in the postwar period. The Confederazione Generale dell' Industria (Confindustria) was born, *de facto* if not *de jure*, in 1919-20. Only in March 1920, with the first national conference of Italian industrialists, did it really constitute itself a national industrial organization with its own general political line, its tactics, its unified corporate policy. Seventy-two associations were federated, with 11,000 industrialists. Confindustria established itself on the dual basis of regional and national organizations by trade and of industrial unions (the first at Turin dating from 1905) which grouped the employers of a province or district.

The regionalist tradition had retarded the process of national unification, but had given entrepreneurs in the more advanced regions a peculiarly combative, disciplined, bellicose spirit in industrial conflict. Pressure on government, lockouts, the 'capture' of press organs, 'defence' organizations based on blacklists of undesirable workers: all the devices they employed in response to the national metalworkers' agitation were nothing new to the big employers, to AMMA (the Association of Metallurgical, Mechanical and Affiliated Industrialists), which had its base in Turin, to the Lombard consortium of the metallurgical and engineering industries, the analogous group in Liguria, or to the various associations of employers on the national, regional, local level, in their 'syndical' organizations.

Nevertheless, the capacity for political independence in the teeth of government was new. Relations between Giolitti and the Italian employer class before the war had been harmonious, since Giolitti interpreted and mediated the deeper interests of the ruling classes; but these relations had not always escaped conflict, sometimes severe conflict. What was novel was the ability which employers demonstrated, spurred on by working-class pressure, to perfect their organization, centralize and discipline their membership, present a common policy to both the Nitti and Giolitti governments; to think of themselves as a *national political power* in their own right.

Indeed at the Milan conference in March, the resolution passed by 'the industrial class' called for government intervention to restrain the exorbitant demands of the workers, but at the same time, 'affirms the necessity for the working bourgeoisie, fully convinced of the utility of its functions and its organization, itself to create the means for energetic action against illusions and deviations'.[19]

The first opportunity for energetic action was the lockout which Turin metal industrialists proclaimed in April, to launch the battle for 'factory power'.[20] On this issue of principle (the refusal to share management with workers' representatives), Olivetti, secretary of the industrial confederation, had been explicit at Milan. It was an issue central to the two great conflicts in which Italian employers were engaged in 1920: in Turin in April, in all Italy in September. It was the issue on which the class first gave battle, first went over to the offensive. The *reaction* of industrialists during this year was characterized by an *offensive spirit* so powerful that it must have been the product of either exasperation or calculation. This, contrary to much current interpretation which underplays it, was one of the most significant factors in the postwar crisis.

The homogeneity of the industrialists' political front, its class spirit ('The future lies with the organized classes,' cried Olivetti in Milan) did not however, rule out division and group rivalries which were to be decisive at crucial moments.

One major cause of disequilibrium and dissension was the process of intense interpenetration of financial and industrial capital, which was punctuated by devastating shocks, notably the celebrated assault by the Perrone group on the Banca Commerciale Italiana in the spring of 1920.[21] The failure of this raid, and its after-effects, indicate a moment of weakness and uncertainty on the capitalist front. To be more exact, it reflected the differentiation of rival groups and the struggle between them. On the one hand, there were those which were 'newer', more aggressive and adventurous on both the productive and financial terrain (the steel firms of Ilva and Ansaldo in the van); on the other, those more 'traditional', more closely bound to the prewar economico-political system of Giolitti. It is no accident that the political and ideological instincts of the former were classically nationalist (and duly reflected in the newspapers they controlled) while the latter were liberal, tending towards radicalism, particularly around the influential Banca Commerciale (with its Italo-German capital).[22] This was a divergence which was to prove crucial during the occupation of the factories.

These financial powers based their hopes on Giolitti's return to office in June 1920,[23] as a guarantee of social pacification, political restoration and cautious economic reform. And it was the pervasive unity of the industrial world, no less than the cracks which the tumultuous expansion and mushroom fortunes of wartime had opened in it, which were to be reflected in September.

Among these conflicting forces, Giolitti seemed destined to play the role of mediator. There is no need to mull over yet again the problem of Giolittism as a system of government during this, its last phase, the administration which lasted to the end of June 1921. More interesting is the fact that its policy was two-faced. Carocci describes the programme with which Giolitti returned to power as 'conservative in politics, reformist in economics',[24] and observes that Giolitti emphasized the reformist aspect up to the autumn of 1920, the conservative after that date.

On his return to power, Giolitti in fact proposed a very full programme of legislative and financial action: measures against speculation, the taxation of excess war profits, an extraordinary property tax, the compulsory registration of shares in the owner's name, steeper death duties, tariff reform. It is true that many of these measures (only partly realized) ran into resistance from industrialists which amounted to assiduous and ultimately successful sabotage (particularly over the compulsory registration of shares, introduced by Giolitti on 24 September 1920 and abolished by Mussolini). But it cannot be said that Confindustria and its most influential groups and newspapers took up arms against the new Giolitti government. Some were suspicious, like *Il Corriere della Sera*, but others were full of confident expectation, including the conservative *Giornale d'Italia* and the organs of Confindustria itself.

Bourgeois circles, at least the more traditional, expected from the skill and prestige of the old statesman, from Giovanni Giolitti Minister of the Interior, a restoration of that order they felt to be brutally menaced, and a curbing of socialist 'subversionism' (which they bitterly denounced Nitti for failing to master). The PSI, for its part, seemed to fear above all the conservative and 'corrupting' nature of the last Giolittian experiment: hence their hostile vote in the Chamber on 9 July 1920, though it was a vote which many reformists registered more out of respect for the generic 'intransigence' of the party than from inner conviction.

Gradually, however, day by day from June to September, a certain Giolittian style in labour conflicts began to emerge, which worried industrialists and, vice versa, put heart into reformist circles (notably the CGL and Turati's followers), which remained organically bound to the Giolittian system. The anti-plutocratic tone of Giolitti's speeches at the end of the war, their onslaught on exploiters, stock exchange speculators, war profiteers, was visibly shaping into a conscious policy, a tendency for government to sponsor a reformist development of the country, in which workers' organizations would play an increasingly important role.

Giolitti chose as Minister of Labour Arturo Labriola,* a man who in interviews and statements talked openly of a phase of transition from a capitalistic to a socialistic economy. The premier, if he did not share this, to say the least, confused attitude of his minister, did hold scrupulously to the principle of non-intervention

---

* Arturo Labriola: Remarkable Neapolitan leader of revolutionary syndicalist upsurge within socialist party in 1900s; moved from Naples to win powerful position in Milan 1902 and became a force within the PSI. After general strike 1904 and struggles of 1907-8, experienced 'intellectual and moral crisis' of his generation of syndicalists, moved towards political action, pro-war and nationalist positions. But retained quasi-revolutionary attitudes and styles. According to reformist Treves, Labriola's speeches as Giolitti's Minister of Labour were a contributory factor to crisis of September 1920; see below, Appendix, no. I p.177.

in industrial disputes, in the teeth of protests, abuse and threats from employers.

During the summer of 1920, suspicion and hostility began to displace the original sympathetic expectation in Confindustria. When conflict finally broke out, the protagonists clashed head-on, while the state seemed unwilling to throw the weight of its intervention to one side or the other. This was the final preliminary factor which determined the original nature of the crisis, its character as a 'frontier crisis' in the global context of established state, political and social structures.

2.
The First Phase of the Dispute

The occupation of the factories followed four long months of weary and sterile dispute, stretching from May to August and ending in a breakdown in negotiations which had never really begun. The dispute, classically 'economic' in style, ground down to an exasperated confrontation of diametrically opposed points of view. Employers claimed they could not grant a shilling, union men replied that, on the wages they got, metalworkers could not stand the continuous increase in the cost of living. And on and on it went, from May to August.

FIOM discussed its memorandum at the Genoa congress of 20-25 May, and worked out a series of demands for the naval, steel, engineering, metallurgical and railway supply industries. The memorandum was presented on 18 June to the National Federation of Engineering and Metallurgical Industrialists, who promptly threw it out. Ignoring the workers' case completely, the employers, through Jarach, president of their syndical federation, demanded from FIOM 'a realistic look at conditions in industry which rule out any increase in pay'.

Into this dialogue of the deaf entered the other workers' organizations (USI, UIL, the 'white' union), each presenting its own memorandum. This multiplicity of claims was exploited in employers' demands that the different memoranda should be taken together on every point, and that the final agreement should be binding on all unions. FIOM refused to submit to this condition and specifically rejected any association with the anarcho-syndicalist USI; it cited 'moral reasons' in explanation, in other words, the abyss of mutual insult and slander which had opened up between the two organizations before the war and deepened during the troubles of 1919: ulterior motives certainly complicated the dispute.

The claims tended to converge on wages and diverge on other points. The FIOM proposal ran:
An increase in piecework rates, 50 per cent in steel, 40 per cent in other industries.

A new classification of personnel into five groups. For the first group (women and apprentices) an increase of 50 per cent in basic hourly pay; for the others, a smaller increase.

The formula for hourly pay increase to be

$$NP = 5/7 \, (TW + A - C)$$

where NP = new pay, TW = total present wage, A = increase of 0.90 lire per hour, C = 0.15 lire per hour cost of living bonus not included in global total, or a new bonus.

There were further demands for increased percentages (30-100 per cent) for overtime and night work, higher 'minimum pay' rates, twelve days' paid holiday a year and new rates of compensation for dismissal.[1]

In practice, the average increase in pay would have been 7.20 lire a day on the current rate of 18 lire.[2]

More important than arguments over norms and technical points was FIOM's basic line of reasoning. Even these increases would not meet the increase in weekly costs on the budget of a five-person family recorded in the bulletin of the commune of Milan.[3] Furthermore, many other trades in Italy got higher wages than the metalworkers[4] and the comparison with the metalworkers of other European countries was still more unfavourable.[5]

On the quantitative side, the demands of the other unions ran parallel to FIOM's. The USI, however, was opposed to any national settlement and argued for systematic negotiation firm by firm, in the hope of introducing a general argument for workers' control over production.[6] The white union, CIL, also opened up a more general perspective: profit-sharing. But the common and crucial point was the wage claim. The industrialists did not in fact contest its essentials. There were ferocious wrangles, certainly, over how much take-home pay metalworkers actually got, over the productivity of their labour in an eight-hour day, over the real ratio between wage increases and increases in the cost of living. The employers maintained that this ratio had not seriously worsened in recent months, but did not persist in this line of argument. Instead they painted a picture of ever-worsening conditions in industry which ruled out any possibility of a wage increase, except at the cost of a total breakdown in the Italian economy.

When the first meeting between the contending parties took place on 29 July, the industrialists' commission, in substance, simply developed their arguments about the economic crisis and its causes: increased foreign competition, lack of market demand, the difficulties of 'conversion' from war to peace, the coal shortage, the weight of taxes and the growing restriction on credit. Any acceptance of the workers' demands would mean an insupportable increase in production costs.

USI's reply was a punch in the face: it was not up to the workers to take account of conditions in industry but to defend the purchasing power of their wages; if industrialists did not know how to run production properly, let them stand aside. FIOM, on the other hand, went into the argument and raised all manner of objections. It disputed the scale of the crisis officially lamented by the employers. Railway, automobile, naval, electro-mechanical and precision industries had plenty of orders. The financial troubles stemmed from the speculative mania rampant in the financial world, from grasping credit firms, the appalling efforts by industrialists to monopolize banks, from stock exchange trickery. Needless to say, this was all reinforced by that permanent theme in FIOM polemic: a stress on the exceptional profits made by industrialists during the war and the financial resources accumulated then. The real issue was the basic one: whose shoulders were to carry the burdens of the crisis, of the difficult transition from 'the years of fat cattle to the years of lean'?

In statistical tables[7] as in workshops, outbursts of mutual abuse over the past repeatedly reinforced conflicting visions of present and future; a situation summed up by Rodolfo Morandi in these terms:

> The trial of strength between capitalist circles and labouring masses grew more fierce in every particular. Both sides went into battle on the offensive, bursting with energy, ready for any violence. The industrial class blatantly indulged an adventurist spirit and arrogant instincts which the war had nourished and which now manifested themselves in fantasies of resistance to the authority of the state and the law. At the same time, the mass organizations reached a fever pitch of combativity. The semi-serf labour of the war years transformed itself into a hammering shock-force intent on disorganizing the economic structure of the nation in its capitalist form and smashing class resistance to proletarian demands.[8]

Every country in postwar Europe was in serious trouble. Italy was particularly hit by a fall in the production of grain (52 million quintals in 1911-13, 45 million in 1919, 38 million in 1920) and maize (from 25 to 22 million). Imports of food accounted for 40 per cent of the trade deficit. It is well known that Giolitti, in his preparatory sequence of social and fiscal measures against the plutocracy, was trying to open the way, in political no less than economic action, to that increase in the price of bread which Nitti had tried and failed to effect and which had caused the fall of his ministry.

Industrial production also fell: by 15 per cent in mining, 40 per cent in engineering, 20 per cent in chemicals. The whole productive apparatus was blocked; masses of immobile capital were frozen in investments which the ending of the war made unprofitable. Naturally, strikes too ran parallel to the shrinkage in production: in 1920, there were 1,881, with 1,267,953 strikers and 16,398,227 lost working-days, the highest figure ever recorded. These, however, were largely a response to the increased cost of living and the endless rise in the price of 'commodities of prime necessity'.[9]

The pressure which workers could exercise, thanks to the increase in their political 'specific weight' after the war, enabled them to resist this devaluation of their purchasing power with wage increases which partly compensated for the rapid price rises. The inflationary spiral, however, accelerated month by month. Monetary circulation increased by 4,000 million lire in the second half of 1919 alone. The exchange rate against the dollar leaped from 6.34 at the end of 1918, to 13.07 in 1919, 28.57 at the end of 1920; against sterling, from 30.27 to 50.08 to 99.96.

This hit imports of fuel and raw materials and had a direct impact on heavy industry. In 1920 the price index for coal reached 1,666, pig-iron, 1,036 (base: 1913 = 100). Supply proved increasingly difficult. England sent 300,000 tons a month against a demand for 800,000. The internal public debt was 74,496 million lire in 1919, 86,432 million in 1920. The state was placing orders with heavy industry at prices well above the international market level.

Many economists argue that, in these circumstances, Giolitti's fiscal policies made matters worse. This may be partly, though by no means wholly, true. But any discussion of 'subjective' factors in the crisis has to take account of the policies adopted by major industrial groups in steel and engineering at the end of the war. They had in fact amassed enormous profits during the war. Steel production between 1914 and 1917 rose from 5.2 per cent to

10.8 per cent of total manufacturing production, engineering production from 21.6 per cent to 31.8 per cent. Automobile production rose from 9,200 in 1914 to 20,000 in 1918. The capital of joint-stock companies increased by 56 per cent, that of metal and engineering firms reached 252 per cent of the prewar level. Ilva's capital jumped from 30 million lire in 1916 to 300 million in 1918; Breda's from 14 to 110 million; Fiat's from 17 million in 1914 to 200 million in 1919; Ansaldo's, a colossus which in its myriad enterprises employed 110,000 workers, from 30 to 500 million; Terni's from 27 million in 1916 to 137 million in 1919. Steel profits rose, on average, from 6.3 per cent on the eve of war to 16.55 per cent in 1918, automobile profits from 8.2 per cent to the same figure. There was a parallel intensification of industrial concentration in Piedmont, Lombardy, Liguria.[10]

In the years after the war, these leading groups launched into breakneck vertical and horizontal expansion and above all, into an assault on the banks. During 1919-20 this spectacular assault gave rise to many scandals, involving in turn Ilva, Ansaldo and Fiat. The Ansaldo complex of the newspaper-owning Perrone brothers (whose growth was thought the most 'audacious and adventurous')[11] seized majority shareholdings in the Banca Italiana di Sconto and seemed about to swallow the Banca Commerciale as well. It has been said, with justice, that 'into this disorderly expansion were sucked most of those profits which, reinvested in steel and engineering, would have solved many of the real problems of costs and production in those sectors.'[12]

This tendency towards stock-exchange and financial speculation blended with old protectionist attitudes, translated into highly lucrative supply contracts with the state. There was a total failure to redirect production and accept marginally lower profits (which fell on average to 7 per cent during 1920). This failure was one reason for some groups' aggressiveness in labour disputes, particularly in steel. Without doubt, this was one cause of the recession which exploded in spectacular bankruptcies during 1921-22: the fall of the Banca di Sconto and Ilva, the disasters of the Credito Italiano (which the Agnelli-Guarini group were trying to take over) and of Ansaldo, which broke in 1923.

The boarding of banks to turn them into the monopoly of a few powerful private speculators caused serious friction with the

Giolitti government. Industrialists, after the strike on the secondary railway network (when authority proved very tolerant), began to denounce that government for its flexibility in the face of working-class agitation.

Through July and August 1920 the economic crisis got worse. By this time, trade union leaders were being presented with a bill which the endless increase in the cost of living made all the more pressing. At the same time, precisely because of the difficult economic situation, they were compelled to devise a form of action which would be most damaging to the adversary but least costly for workers. The industrialists, in turn, were strengthened in their intransigence by the prospect of economic disaster. Riccardo Bachi accurately traced the process of polarization in his annual review:

> So both parties moved into battle without full awareness of the consequences of such a large-scale conflict: the industrialists maintained an intransigent front perhaps because of the outcome of the Turin struggle and from fear of economic trouble; they failed to appreciate the power of the workers' organizations, forgot the lesson of the past year's struggles and were blind to political realities.

That the workers' side, too, did not foresee the consequences of the agitation is largely proven by events. This, however, was the moment at which the leadership of the metalworkers' organization decided to accept a trial of strength. After they had vainly offered to discuss their demands with the industrialists, they realized that this was much more than a wages dispute. At stake was the very bargaining power of the union itself. The moment came during 10-13 August, when the inter-regional commission nominated by the industrialists, after a long speech from the advocate Rotigliano, finally told the workers' representatives that 'given the state of the industry, no demand for economic betterment can be entertained at this time'.[13] It was the breakdown of negotiations. Bruno Buozzi often recalled, and a few years later singled out as the determinant element in the rupture, the episode which put an end to three days of argument in Milan city hall:

> When the workers' delegation had finished refuting the argument of the employers, the latter's leader, Rotigliano, then a nationalist, later a fascist, put a stop to all argument with this provocative statement: 'All discussion is useless. The industrialists will not

grant any increase at all. Since the end of the war, they've done nothing but drop their pants. We've had enough. Now we're going to start on you.' The challenge was clear.[14]

FIOM took it up, says Buozzi, because on so vital a principle it could not yield. An extraordinary congress of the federation was summoned for 16-17 August in Milan, and delegates of the CGL and the PSI leadership were invited. The congress unanimously decided to adopt a policy of obstructionism (ca'canny) from the 21st, in every engineering and metallurgical factory and every naval dockyard. Obstructionism implied a slowdown in all work processes (pieceworkers taking a cut in pay as a result) and a demand for the most rigorous observance of all safety precautions.[15] There was to be no sabotage.

Why choose this form of struggle? The explanation was strictly 'trade unionist':

> The application of obstructionism must hit the industrialists in that production will fall while general costs remain unchanged. As for the workers, though their earnings will fall with production, they will always have enough wages in hand to enable them to keep up the struggle for some time.[16]

They decided, further, that if any industrialists tried to counter obstructionism with a lockout, then the workers would have to take possession of the factories: by all the means at their disposal, added Buozzi, if necessary by battering in the gates.

The USI metalworkers' union thought obstructionism an inadequate response to the crisis, but fell into line 'in order not to divide the forces of the working class'.[17] In the opinion of the anarcho-syndicalist organization, obstructionism could not hold for more than a few days; the USI's policy, scorning the defensive vocabulary of FIOM, was altogether more combative.

> The expropriation of the factories by the metalworkers of Italy must be simultaneous and speedy, before a lockout shuts them out, and must then be defended by all necessary measures. We are determined, further, to call the workers of other industries into the battle.[18]

There is evidence that some within FIOM itself favoured an immediate seizure of the factories, but it was the more 'possibilist' policies of Buozzi which prevailed.[19] Plausible evidence from working-class sources[20] suggests that, among the industrialists, it was the steelmen led by the Ilva directors who were the most committed to intransigence and who overcame the moderates. Events were to confirm this assessment of the relative strength of the factions. Public opinion, in the meantime, was distracted. Newspaper headlines were full of the battles in Poland, the Albanian problem (settled by Giolitti on 3 August) and the Second Congress of the Third International which opened in Moscow in the last days of July.

The Italian socialist movement was entering a new phase in the summer of 1920: its internal disarray got worse and there was a certain weakness in its response to the reactionaries' first street sorties. After the Ancona riots (26 June to 1 July)* both party and CGL gave up the idea of a general strike, even if they went on talking about a revolution if a new war broke out. In Moscow, where the Third International explicitly demanded the expulsion of Turati and his friends, Serrati resisted, and the maximalists of the party leadership supported him. Was it so that the party could go united into the revolution? Or was it, on the contrary, because they thought the revolution unlikely? *Avanti* was very guarded on the point. For the time being, they were dodging the issue.[21]

At this moment, only the reformists spoke clearly. The issue of *Critica Sociale* which appeared on 15 August carried a significant editorial article with the title: 'Shorten the range!'[22] Significant for a number of reasons: because it detected an important shift in the distribution of power between classes and because it foreshadowed a no less important shift in the position of the party's right wing, which within weeks would be urging the movement to change direction. Behind all the thunder of sonorous words, said *Critica Sociale*, twenty months after the end of the war there had been no preparation whatsoever, of men or measures, for the revolution. Not a single step had been taken towards revolution:

> The masses are becoming confused and disillusioned; at any moment, they might disperse and abandon us, to run, blown by

---

* The Ancona riots: On 26 June 1920, troops massed at Ancona, an anarchist stronghold, mutinied against an expedition to Albania. This action precipitated a popular rising and a campaign against arms production (the Russo-Polish War was at a critical moment) led by syndicalists, which revived the factory council movement, but disrupted unity negotiations between the PSI and USI.

chance, into the breakers of anarchism or the swamps of selfish corporatism. The bourgeoisie is regaining its strength. It has built more solid defences, in the *carabinieri*, in the royal guards; it has a white guard of volunteers against the proletariat which has nothing like a red guard of its own.

What then? Take another road, aim at less distant objectives, with more hope of success.

Was the reformist group, shortly to organize a fraction calling itself 'socialist concentration', the only group to think in this way? Yes and no. The maximalist leadership itself, as early as April, after its national council,[23] had been forced to recognize the impasse it had reached on 'the problem of making the revolution', and the bourgeois press had talked about 'adjusting sights' and 'moderate extremism'. However, in Moscow at the Second Congress of the Communist International, the Italian delegates went on talking about imminent revolution,[24] and extremist formulae, plans for soviets, went on filling the party press. So, while passivity, a waiting upon the 'natural death' of the bourgeoisie, characterized socialist politics, and while 'the masses take the game seriously'[25] there was a moment of historic paradox: caught in the grip of the conflict between the metalworkers and the most combative sector of this 'dying bourgeoisie' were men like Buozzi and with him D'Aragona, Baldesi and the rest, men who fully shared the political opinions of *Critica Sociale*, who on 3 September were to sign, in the name of the 'socialist concentration' fraction, a manifesto which codified them.[26] The maximalist leadership, on the other hand (the top men still in Moscow at the congress) were left standing on the sidelines, virtually indifferent to the course of events. And a final irony: the group which was considered the most 'breathless', the group so harshly castigated over the Turin troubles in April, the *Ordine Nuovo* group, was in fact sceptical and pessimistic, fearful of the oncoming conflict, worried over its timing and the manner of its inception.

In its trouble, however, this group simply reflected the travail, the uncertainty of the whole socialist movement, racked by centrifugal impulses and by severe controversies which were driving it to the brink of schism. And this internal conflict conditioned the response of every group and fraction to the struggle of the metalworkers.

As for the spirit and morale of the workers themselves, it is difficult to be sure. We know that the Turin section of FIOM voted for 'a decisive struggle',[27] but we also know that elsewhere there was uncertainty. Buozzi at the Fifth Congress of the CGL recalled that 'the mass was hesitant' about obstructionism, which seemed a novel and unfamiliar method. He added, however, 'through obstructionism we succeeded in galvanizing the masses'.[28] It was in truth this 'galvanizing' process which filled the last ten days of August.

3.
From Go-Slow to Lockout

When FIOM ordered the slowdown and the other unions reluctantly followed,[1] it looked as though the employers meant to make the best of a bad job. In Turin, on 19 August, Boella, president of AMMA, said in an interview 'that the struggle will develop in a peculiarly peaceful manner'.[2] An Association circular told members to 'react to this crisis with maximum calm and serenity and face it in the most peaceable spirit; do nothing to exacerbate or aggravate it by ill-considered action'.[3] They were urged to fine culprits, however, if work was done excessively slowly and were to see to it that leading workers of the internal commissions did not leave their posts. Obstructionism seemed to be a form of workers' action that industrialists could get something out of: this was a commonly-held opinion.[4]

The government, however, was very worried from the start. The prefects of the great cities were the first to express alarm. As early as 18 August, Taddei at Turin was afraid that the dispute would turn violent; he reminded the Ministry that 'there are 800 foot and 35 horse in the security forces facing about 72,000 metalworkers'.[5] Poggi in Genoa expressed the same fears and called for reinforcements of *carabinieri* and royal guards.[6] The richest source is the correspondence of the prefect of Milan. This documents, on the one hand, the government's cautious but urgent pressure on both sides to resume negotiations, on the other, the development of the crisis in the opposite direction. Corradini, under-secretary at the Ministry of the Interior, was afraid that the industrialists in both Turin and Milan had already decided to force a lockout at the first opportunity. He telegraphed the prefect of Milan: 'It is essential to contact all the most influential industrialists to talk them out of taking precipitate action which could have the most serious effects on future events.'[7]

Government appeals had little effect, though the union was sensitive; Buozzi went to Rome on 25 August. The Minister of Labour, Labriola, saw the parties separately on 26 August, but ran into further evidence of the industrialists' intransigence. His testimony on the point is precise and has not been contradicted.

'I made the following proposal,' he said in his report to the Senate,

> I said: you workers promise to suspend obstructionism and I in turn will urge the industrialists to resume negotiations on the basis of the memorials. I repeated the proposition to Jarach and Rotigliano. The workers accepted it and Bruno Buozzi agreed to suspend obstructionism on 27 August, on condition that the factory-owners promised to resume negotiations on the basis of the memoranda alone; naturally they had to recognize their essential principles. But it was precisely this condition which the industrialists refused to accept.[8]

Did the industrialists really want a lockout? This was what workers suspected at the time and what the government increasingly came to fear. Labriola said so openly to Giolitti; he thought the industrialists, with their threat of a lockout, were trying to saddle the government with 'the necessity to resort to force, as if to compel it to take up a position against the workers'.[9]

Luigi Einaudi, writing as an historian, implicitly admits the possibility; he says: 'The occupation, coming when the wind changed (from the economic point of view) did not turn out to be wholly undesirable to the industrialists, to whom it gave an opportunity to stop unprofitable production and to throw on to agitators the blame for what they themselves wanted, but did not dare, to do.'[10]

At all events, between 24 and 30 August, there was a swift radicalization of the conflict. The employers' intransigence toughened obstructionism, which in some factories quickly escalated into a sitdown strike; the fall in production was substantial in some places. Tempers were inflamed on both sides. Reports from prefectures grew more and more alarmist. Conservative newspapers began to talk of outright sabotage in the metal industry.

On 24 August work was suspended at the Romeo plant in Milan. *Il Corriere della Sera* quoted a communiqué from the Federation of Engineering and Metallurgical Industries which claimed that 'workers do not work, they lounge about smoking, they even play cards, they are insolent to foremen'; it was already talking about 'the adoption of such measures as may become necessary'.[11] Tension was in fact high in all the industrial centres. By 24 August, the prefect of Turin was reporting that in the foundries and steelworks obstruc-

From Go-Slow to Lockout / 51

tionism 'has taken a form which borders on sabotage' and that, on the other hand, 'industrialists have said they are being driven towards an immediate lockout'.[12] According to *Avanti*, production at Fiat Centro (15,000 workers) fell by 60 per cent in a single week. Similar reports from Pistoia and Genoa singled out the activities of leading members of USI.[13] Milan reported on the 26th that industrialists 'have already decided to close the steelworks and forges of Sesto San Giovanni, the Romeo and Tosti plants in Milan'; only on the insistence of the prefect Lusignoli had there been 'a postponement which, however, cannot be stretched beyond 48 hours'.[14] The next day, the prefect's telegram was even more pessimistic:

> The industrialists are resolved on a lockout. I will pursue the action taken in the last few days and today, to prevent the execution of this decision, but I cannot conceal the fact that, if it proves impossible for minister Labriola to bring the contending parties together, my pressure will not be very effective.[15]

We already know that the industrialists' delegation which had gone to Rome (Jarach, Rotigliano, Questa and Boella) answered with a blank 'No'. From 27 August, when news of the final rupture became public, the slowdown grew massive. The Sunday break did nothing but reinforce battle positions. FIOM complimented itself on the workers' discipline, and all its sections prepared for an occupation of the factories as a riposte to the lockout which was looming. A significant note appeared in the Piedmont *Avanti* for Monday, 30 August. It stated that obstructionism was the prelude to a sharper phase of battle. What would follow?

> A moment will come and it cannot be far off, when either the workers or the industrialists will have to shift the action to a different terrain. The workers will hardly be the first: the slowdown is an effective measure of fairly simple application. The industrialists, how can they resist? Will they resort to a general lockout?

While *Avanti* put this question in Turin, the crisis was precipitated in Milan. On that same Monday morning, the 2,000 workers at the Romeo plant found the gates closed and the factory guarded by troops. The lockout began with this action. At that moment, it could have looked like the arbitrary act of a single employer in a factory which *Il Corriere della Sera* called one of the most turbulent. It looked that way to the prefect.

His dismay, however, was obvious. Lusignoli telegraphed,

> While the federation of metallurgical industries, just after their return from Rome, promised to defer the lockout for further talks which were to take place on 31 August, this Romeo, although begged repeatedly not to do so, this morning closed his factory, in breach of every agreement with the federation. As a result, the workers in all plants have decided not to abandon the plants but to occupy them. The Romeo plant has been put under guard. Security patrols have been ordered in the city.[16]

Controversy has raged over Romeo's action: whether it was really arbitrary, taken without the knowledge or consent of the employers' organization. The working-class press consistently and flatly denied it, employers' spokesmen like senator Conti, on the other hand, solemnly affirmed it.[17] Government sources, on the evidence of what happened between 30 August and 1 September, tend to emphasize the irreducible intransigence of the employers, that attitude which Giolitti in his memoirs defined as 'an ill-timed threat of a lockout by some industrialists who had not fully appreciated the dangers of the situation'.[18]

The fact is that the situation, at least in Milan, was already hopelessly compromised by 30 August. As soon as it heard of the Romeo lockout, the Milan section of FIOM, 'bearing in mind that the example would have been followed without fail by the other factories',[19] ordered its members to take possession of about 300 metallurgical factories in and around the city of Milan. At that point, it was simply a matter of carrying into effect those proposals, those 'ripostes' which had been decided on in the event of a lockout. Was the application of the order too extensive, disproportionate? Several observers, aware of Buozzi's prudence and moderation, thought so, then and later, but there is no evidence that the Milan section went further than the national organization wished. Certainly the central committee of FIOM, meeting in Turin, voted on that same 30 August to commend the energetic behaviour of the Milan comrades and took pains formally to warn 'both the employers' association and individual industrialists against committing acts of provocation and reprisal which would authorize the proletariat to resort to every measure of defence against the new oppression which the employers are contemplating'.[20]

The union, in effect, did not want to take action which might prejudice the national situation: the decision, as it were, was left to the adversary. But by this time, it is clear that the spark struck at Romeo's was bound to ignite a great conflagration. In Milan, the metalworkers learned of their organization's decision to occupy the factories during the lunch break. Members of the internal commissions warned the managers who, to quote *Il Corriere della Sera*, wore themselves out in futile efforts to prove that the Romeo lockout was an isolated action. The workers prepared to stay overnight in the factories. The managers on the other hand left, and with them, said *Avanti*, 'the girls and office personnel'. Only at Breda did the workers lock up two civil engineers, who were 'treated with respect', in the words of *Il Corriere*.

Albertini's* paper is rich in detail on this improvised beginning to an occupation which was to last for a whole month. The picture its journalist paints deserves full quotation ; its essential characteristics were to reappear in other cities during the next few days.

'From outside,' the Milanese paper reported on 31 August,

> the factories yesterday evening presented a singular spectacle. One reached them through crowds of women and children, coming and going with dinners for the strikers, voluntary prisoners of the factories. Nearer to them, here and there, on the pavement or on the grass, were the debris of the day's bivouac. Entrances were strictly guarded by groups of workers. Not the ghost of an official or police officer in sight [the paper did not fail to note]. The strikers were complete masters of the field. Whoever passed, in car or cab, was subjected to control as if he were crossing the frontier, control exercised by vigilance squads of workers and their enthusiastic companions.

A French visitor to Milan conveys a similar impression:

> The spectacle could not fail to be impressive, above all towards evening, when the red guards, straddling the walls, weapon in hand, were silhouetted against the night sky and the wail of the sirens rang the whole length of the Adda to echo in the Resegon.[21]

---

* Luigi Albertini: editor of Italy's most influential newspaper, *Il Corriere della Sera* of Milan; liberal, constitutionalist of open but conservative temper; senator; interventionist, initially supported Mussolini, but after Matteotti murder, turned his paper into major anti-fascist organ and was driven out of editorship. In September 1920, at climax of crisis, called for socialists and CGL to assume power; see below, Appendix, no. V pp188-93.

Everywhere the scene was the same: a peaceful occupation carried through by workers not only in discipline but with enthusiasm (all observers agree on this), and a total *laisser faire* by the security forces who abandoned not only the factories but also their access roads to the vigilance (which soon became an armed vigilance) of the occupiers.

Prefects and questors (chief constables) followed the precise instructions of the government; evidence on this point is abundant. For twenty-four hours the Milan events had little echo; most of the dailies, including *Avanti*, referred to them casually, as if they were of only local significance. But at Milan on 31 August, the industrialists' national organization put an end to all delay and decided that all federated members should 'move to a closure of factories in a manner to be decided by individual consortia'.

Lusignoli's report to the Ministry of the Interior is a precious indication of the employers' will, of their tenacious resistance to the urgent pleas of the government's representative to pull back from so serious a measure.[22] Nothing moved them, not even a government statement that it could not mobilize adequate forces to protect the plants. They were not convinced or affected by 'dark forebodings' of violence and disorder. One detail cited by Lusignoli as he listed possible explanations of the employers' intransigence is therefore significant. 'To my protest against the decision they had taken, the reply was that Agnelli had talked to the Prime Minister that morning in Turin. They inferred from this that the Prime Minister himself was not far from their way of thinking.'

This is significant, because the Turin talks between Agnelli and the Prime Minister, who was passing through on his way to Cavour and then Bardonecchia for the vacation, showed nothing of the kind. Giolitti recalled them tersely, in the Senate: 'The industrialists told me, as I passed through Turin, that they intended to resort to a lockout. I advised against it in every possible way and gave them to understand that they could in no way count on the intervention of the security forces.' His statement was confirmed by Agnelli and other industrialists.[23] Giolitti's friends added an anecdote which brilliantly captures the psychology of the man.

The anecdote, now famous, concerns a talk with Agnelli a week later, when in Turin, too, the occupation had assumed massive proportions. Senator Frassati says that Agnelli went to Bardonecchia to ask again for government intervention. Giolitti listened attentively and patiently. Then he spoke at length on his policy.

> Giolitti: Only time can solve the problem. Otherwise there is no policy but force.
> Agnelli: Precisely . . .
> Giolitti: Maybe. But let us understand each other. I will not allow the security forces to stay in the streets, defenceless if the red guards open fire from above. To drive the workers out of the factories, we need artillery . . .
> Agnelli: I agree . . .
> Giolitti: We are in a position to supply it immediately. At Turin, there is the 7th regiment of mountain artillery. I will give the orders at once. At dawn tomorrow, Fiat will be bombarded and liberated from the occupiers.
> Agnelli: No! No! . . .
> Giolitti: Well, then?
> Agnelli: no reply.[24]

The episode precisely mirrors the premier's attitude, which was shaped by many factors – choice, necessity, opportunity. And if the political outlines of his policy became clearer during the next few days, from the crisis moment of national lockout and occupation, one essential fact emerges: Giolitti could not stop the occupation except with a bloodbath, at the risk of civil war.

Because he was not ready to run that risk and therefore trusted to the end in a trade union solution to the conflict, he clung to the most rigorous neutrality. He told the Senate:

> How could I stop the occupation? It is a question of 600 factories in the metallurgical industry. To prevent the occupation, I would have had to put a garrison in each of them, a hundred men in the small, several thousand in the large. To occupy the factories I would have had to use all the forces at my disposal! And who would exercise surveillance over the 500,000 workers outside the factories? Who would guard the security of the country? Once the occupation had happened, should I perhaps have cleaned out the factories by force? It would have been civil war.[25]

Giolitti's logic, matured in an incomparable experience at the Ministry of the Interior, was so compelling that in the very heat of controversy, not even the partisans of the strong arm dared to criticize his initial conduct. Mussolini himself was compelled to admit that Giolitti could not have acted otherwise.[26] And, to go back to those first days of 31 August and 1 September, the orders flowing from the premier and his loyal colleague Camillo Corradini faithfully followed the line laid down by the government.

The decision of the national industrial federation became public knowledge only in the morning of 1 September. The hour of decision had struck for the employers' regional organizations. They had the power to proclaim or defer the lockout. The metallurgical consortia of the greater cities showed no hesitation. During the night of 31 August-1 September, the executive council of AMMA decided on a lockout in Turin; it was proclaimed in Genoa, La Spezia and lesser centres. In a Rome already in lockout after the closure of the Bastianelli plants in Porta San Paolo, metalworkers moved into the handful of metal plants in the capital. During the next few days the lockout was proclaimed virtually everywhere, and promptly followed by the workers' occupation. This relationship was constant and characterized the very tone of the movement from the beginning: occupation as a response to lockout.

It was not only the workers who insisted on this correlation, but the government itself. Corradini, surveying the situation on 1 September in a telegram to Giolitti in Bardonecchia, caught the rhythm of events in a few lines:

> Industrialists persist in their intransigent attitude. Rejection of negotiation. Public denunciation of the slowdown which they say has degenerated into sitdown strikes, acts of sabotage, violence against managers. They proclaim a lockout. Workers in retaliation to lockout occupy factories. Declarations made to me personally by industrialists reveal a will to go to extremes. I confirm that government does not intend to intervene in conflict, responsibility for which is almost exclusively theirs. Industrialists' order of the day shows their intentions.[27]

These 'intentions' masked considerable complexity and divergence in the very heart of the industrial class. It was by now clear that the employers meant to 'force' things. They were determined to go to extremes even though they knew that the government would not defend the lockout. They had in mind, as they had told Buozzi himself, that a settling of accounts with the workers could no longer be postponed; many were exasperated by the atmosphere in the factories, the effects of the slowdown. And if we probe deeper? Was there a tendency as tension built up, to shuffle on to the state the economic difficulties of the sector, to squeeze out those tax exemptions, that tariff protection which the government was refusing? Was there perhaps a conscious will to force the fall of the ministry and strangle the promised legislation on the registration of shares and the taxation of war profits? Many said so at the time[28] and these rumours ran as a constant descant to the conflict. In any case, as Corradini said, there was the will to go to extremes.

Giolitti preached the utmost calm to the public powers: no intervention unless requested by both parties, abstention from unnecessary initiatives.[29] The behaviour of FIOM was also transparently prudent. The call to occupy the metal plants was accompanied by exhortations to discipline, to continued production within the fixed limits of obstructionism. 'We hope that the tenacity of the workers in remaining at their posts of struggle and sacrifice will finally persuade the industrialists to take other steps towards a solution.'[30]

They stayed, then, within the most narrow trade union boundaries. But for FIOM, too, the target was double not single: industrialists and government. If the employers used the lockout to put pressure on the government, the same can be said of the workers' federation. The occupation was used as an instrument to pre-empt and obstruct the lockout and even to escape exposure to a strike, which ran the risk of lasting several months. It was, in essence, a defensive measure, a cheaper method.

'The occupation of the factories,' Angelo Tasca justly observed,

> which is often represented as a kind of culminating point of a revolutionary fever, was in its origin a simple substitute for the strike weapon, which had become too difficult to use; it was a low-cost method to enforce a new collective labour contract. The leaders of FIOM had chosen the line of minimum force. They thought the occupation of the factories would provoke government intervention and some of them also cherished the hope – without daring to admit it – that the occupation would find a political solution in the participation of the socialists in government.[31]

We are here, however, still in the realm of 'intentions'. Nobody, neither one side nor the other, industrialists or unionists, appreciated the new character which the dispute was about to assume. Not only because of its scope and its bitterness, but because it had come to a focus within the factories themselves, with the workers as protagonists, workers who were about to undergo an experience not at first envisaged: themselves to produce, to manage and organize work, production, distribution; to use their new economic power and new political weight. It is no accident that it was a man like Gramsci, theorist of the producer consciousness of the worker, who immediately seized on this 'qualitative leap' in the struggle.

'A new fact,' he wrote on 5 September,

> was suddenly created by the new method of struggle. When workers struggled to improve their economic condition through a strike, the duty of workers in struggle was limited to a faith in remote leaders, to the building of a morale of solidarity and resistance grounded precisely in this generalized faith. But if workers in struggle occupy the factories and decide to go on producing, the moral position of the mass abruptly assumes a different form and value. Union bosses can no longer lead. Union bosses dwindle in the immensity of the perspective. The mass must solve the problems of the factory itself, with its own means, its own men.[32]

The union bosses were not to disappear, nor were the political leaders. 'Divergences' were therefore to condition the dispute in a decisive manner, and in Gramsci's excitement, there is certainly an illusion typical of the *ordinovisti*, product of a certain lack of interest in those decisive instruments of class organization, the party and the union.[33] Yet Gramsci, in his perception of the spontaneous movement of the masses, grasped from the beginning that a radically novel situation had emerged from the flux of events. The first days of struggle clamorously confirmed it.

4.
The Occupation of the Factories

Between Wednesday, 1 September and Saturday, 4 September, the metalworkers of Italy occupied their factories throughout the peninsula.

One exception was Venezia Giulia, where there was a very tense political situation, with the first clashes between socialists and fascists and a general strike in Trieste. In some small centres, the employers surrendered at once and workers won a new agreement based on the FIOM memorandum.

Otherwise the occupation was total. The occupiers numbered over 400,000. The total reached half a million when the labour force of non-metallurgical plants in some cities moved into occupation.

This universality was itself a basic reality of the crisis. Not only in the industrial triangle, but in Rome, Palermo and Florence, the plans of the unions were at once activated. From the great urban centres to the country districts of the Veneto, Liguria, Tuscany, the Marches, wherever there was a factory, a dockyard, a steelworks, a forge, a foundry in which *metalos* worked, there was an occupation. The universal character of the phenomenon is remarkable. It demonstrates that workers, whether unionized or not, agreed with the union programme and made it reality. It also demonstrates that local authorities and security forces left every road open to the occupation, which was in fact carried out in an extraordinarily peaceful manner.

Reports from the prefects of the kingdom flowed into the Viminale (Ministry of the Interior) in massive unanimity. A rapid geographical survey gives the measure of the movement. In Piedmont, not only Turin, Alessandria, Asti, Novara and Vercelli, but Acqui, Arquata Scrivia, Novi Ligure, Casale, Tortona, Gallarate. In Liguria, not only the whole Genoa district, Savona, Vado, La Spezia, but Porto Maurizio and Oneglia. In Lombardy, from the industrial complex of Milan to Bergamo, from Cremona to Crema, from Pavia to

Legnano, from Como to Lecco, Varese to Brescia. In the Veneto, Verona, Udine, Padua, Venice, Treviso, Castelfranco Veneto, Battaglia. In Emilia, Bologna, Modena, Ferrara, Reggio, Piacenza. In Tuscany, Florence, Pisa, Siena, Pontedera, Piombino, Portoferraio, Livorno, Arezzo, Pistoia, Grosseto, San Giovanni Valdarno, Castelfiorentino, Lucca. In the Marches, the naval dockyard of Ancona. In Umbria, Terni and Perugia. In Campania, Naples, San Giovanni a Teduccio, Castellammare, Torre Annunziata; in Sicily, Palermo.

As for the density and consistency of the movement, the basic structural factor is immediately obvious. Only in Turin, Milan and Genoa did the occupation assume a character so massive as to constitute a major historical event: in those cities hundreds of thousands were in occupation. But the movement elsewhere was also remarkable. In Piombino, for example, 5,000 workers were involved. In Portoferraio, the blast furnaces were occupied and railwaymen sent eight loaded trucks down the feeder track into the plants. In Livorno, at the Orlando shipyard occupied on the 2nd, the destroyer *San Marino* was launched. 'The launching,' telegraphed the prefect, 'was carried out without incident, without red flags and without changing the name of the ship.'[1]

In Florence on the afternoon of the 2nd the Galileo (1,200 workers), the Pignone (600 workers) and six other factories with a hundred workers each were occupied. At the Galileo, where technicians also stayed at their posts, red flags sprouted everywhere and an improvised band played the workers' anthem.[2] At the foundry of the Terni blast furnaces, the occupation was celebrated with a 'magnificent casting'. According to *Avanti*, 'a very large, very delicate cylinder was cast for the railways'. In the Valdarno the labour force of the San Giovanni forges was joined by miners who occupied the pitheads. In the Trevigiano, the forty workers of a factory in San Maria della Rovere moved into total occupation. The red flag rose over the naval dockyard of Palermo and the red and black flag of the anarchists over the roofs of Verona, where the supremacy of USI syndicalists made the occupation peculiarly incendiary.

In Naples the first to move on the morning of the 2nd were the 2,500 workers of the Vasto and Bufola plants, the workshops of the southern railways. The occupation went ahead everywhere during the day, encompassing the dry dock basins from Naples to

Castellammare (metallurgical dockyards) to Torre Annunziata (the Vesuvius railway). The trans-Atlantic liner *Mafalda* was shut into the port of Naples by the workers. Only at Miani-Silvestri, which was under guard, was there conflict: an attempted occupation was repeatedly repulsed by the security forces during the 2nd and 3rd.[3] In Venice, the naval dockyards of the Giudecca and the Arsenal were occupied.

In Rome at the Tabanelli, the Soviet emblem was raised over the factory entrance. And while tramway men sent in four cars for repair, railwaymen 'supplied the occupiers with cushions of the best quality to make their night's rest less uncomfortable'. The director was locked up and only released after the intervention of the quarter's police commissioner. With the Tabanelli, the Roman metalworkers occupied the Auer, Contini, Fatme, Focis, Sascher, Lori and Rocco Bonaldi factories.

A report by an *Avanti* correspondent on the Fatme plant captures the spirit of the movement – which took possession of workers in Rome no less than in the great industrial centres. 'In every corner, there were slogans clearly socialist in inspiration: *he who does not work shall not eat; honour and labour, our objective; chains and fetters we break; we want not wealth but freedom.* The factory commissars preach economy in the use of material and electricity.' In the evening after eleven, the advice is 'to sleep not in the open but in places allotted by the factory committee, to pay attention to personal cleanliness, to devote the evenings to reading, not useless pastimes'.[4]

Generally, in all areas where metalworkers were not overwhelming in number, the occupation rolled forward in impeccable order. Incidents were rare; the few directors and technicians who were locked in were soon released and suffered no violence. There was much enthusiasm. For the most part, technicians stayed on the job under workers' control. Production was low, partly because of the inevitable confusion, partly because of material shortages, mainly because the slowdown continued, on union instructions.

The newspapers on Sunday the 5th reported festive scenes and an atmosphere of euphoria. At the Galileo in Florence, the picture painted by *Avanti* was idyllic: 'The day passed peacefully in songs and jokes, symptoms of the enthusiasm of masses of workers. Gramophones, mandolin bands and other assorted entertainments enlivened the drowsy Sunday hours.'[5] *La Nazione*'s report was no different.

But it was in Turin, Milan and Genoa that the occupation grew into a mass popular movement. Here it captured, riveted, alarmed public opinion. It bubbled with novelty. It gave rise to episodes full of vivid life, and in some cases as at Genoa, of drama and suffering. Here in short was the full power-charge of a great working-class action pregnant with political potential.

In Turin within a few days the occupation embraced nearly 100,000 workers. After the lockout of the night of 31 August-1 September, masses of workers poured into the factories on the morning of the 1st. There was no violence.[6] The watchmen opened the gates, the workers went to their stations. 'Because of the new situation,' noted *La Stampa*, 'work, still subject to the slowdown, was not resumed. The workers stood idle before their machines while members of the internal commissions and the workshop commissars decided what to do.'[7]

At Fiat-Centro, Giovanni Parodi, secretary of the internal commission (here an organ of the factory council), spoke to the workers. He urged them to maintain discipline and armed vigilance and to work to union rules, which implied perseverance in the slowdown. What happened at Fiat-Centro was the product of council organization, of the workshop commissars. All power was assumed by the council which promptly published its first communiqué:

> The workers' internal commission, in agreement with the technicians' internal commission, calls upon all workers to remain at their workplaces and to carry on work as in the past (obstructionism) in reciprocal respect. Workers! Show that you can run this factory without employers! Your internal commission will watch over your interests and will summon you at the opportune moment.[8]

In the other factories (185 were soon occupied) it was the same story: from Itala to Lancia, Dubosc to Westinghouse, Diatto to Garavini, from the Sub-Alpine foundry to the factories of Moncenisio, from the Ansaldo San Giorgio to the aircraft shops. On the role of clerks and technicians, working-class sources are not very reliable. There was an obvious obsession with stiffening the resolve of the nervous and securing a majority of them (backed later by threats of dismissal for absenteeism),[9] but desertions were in fact large-scale and tended to increase rapidly. Some individuals were held by force, but such instances were very rare and were played down by both *La Stampa* and the prefect.[10] The industrialists sent the latter an open letter of protest at an occupation 'effected with the connivance of local authority which although formally warned several times and again late last night, made no attempt to avert the occurrence or to mitigate its consequences in any way'.[11]

The first day passed peacefully. The labour force did two shifts of 12 hours (8 hours' work, 4 hours' rest). In the evening, 'at the gates, on the factory walls, the new sentries kept watch, but there were no alarms or incidents to speak of'. Only at Fiat-Lingotto did the police force an entry to seize machine-guns left there earlier; but the workers had already distributed them to other plants and the mission failed.[12] On the arming of workers the most contradictory rumours circulated. There were accounts of preparations in the larger factories, 'not only for defence, with electrified wiring, barbed wire, ranged machine-guns, but also offensive preparations for an eventual conflict with the security forces and a resort to violence'. There was exaggeration in plenty, 'but we are watching the situation closely', reported the prefect.[13]

The central feature of the occupation in Turin, visible from the earliest days, was the effort to organize a 'system' of workers' management which would co-ordinate production, control the movement of material and ensure supply. An action committee and various labour commissions were created at the *camera del lavoro*.[14] Discipline was very rigorous and in the early days, to Sunday the 5th, production in the shops continued, though slowly.[15] Public order remained largely unaffected; in the vicinity of the factories this was 'guaranteed' by the red guards. Sometimes trucks shuttling between occupied plants were stopped by *carabinieri* or royal guards; all of them, however, with their loads, were allowed to proceed. Yet more obvious was the 'tolerance' of authority in the face of rail trucks loaded with coal, fuel and ferrous material which workers liberated from depots and railwaymen in solidarity despatched along tracks and sidings feeding the steel plants.[16]

That the atmosphere was relatively calm and free from bombast was confirmed by the well-known union leader Emilio Colombino of FIOM, who wrote in *Avanti* on 4 September:

The first thing which strikes you in Milan are the red flags flying from every stack and chimney. In Turin, even today on the fourth day of our occupation, around the workshops of the periphery, external symbols of the achievement are rare. An occasional red flag, the odd sentry on the parapet, but energies are concentrated inside. What the workers prefer to concentrate on is the technical organization of labour, both in the individual plant and in the industrial complex of the city.[17]

Given a certain rhetoric proper to the occasion, it was in truth this 'concreteness' which characterized 'automobile city'. Already some workers in the factory councils and the union were calling for a sales organization to dispose of production. FIOM was opposed. 'Production,' ran a communiqué from the Turin section, 'is for the collectivity and as such ought to be administered by superior organizations which represent the interests of all.' It called for an inventory of production.

A detail illustrates their state of mind. The inventory was proposed 'above all, with a view to possible direct trade with Soviet Russia which, it is not inconceivable, may supply the means to consolidate the workers' gains'. *La Stampa* ironically described a curious telephone conversation. The representative of a transport firm which was to supply some truckloads to Fiat phoned the plant, in the hope of getting some guidance from a manager:

> 'Hello, Who's there?'
> 'This is Fiat Soviet!'
> 'Ah! ... pardon ... I'll ring again ...'

A 'communist' style, in full moral rigour, ruled the factories. No one could enter or leave without permission. Workers were searched at the exits and thieves severely punished. Alcohol was strictly forbidden.[18] The corps of red guards kept watch inside the plants to check possible troublemakers.

Giovanni Parodi tells an apt story (common to other towns and factories) from the early days at Fiat-Centro.

> Three gentlemen were strolling around the factory at nine in the evening. The red guards approached them: 'What are you doing here?' 'Oh, we just wanted to see what work you were doing.' 'Oh, you want to see what work we're doing? Come along in!' The three put up a bit of a fight but were carried inside, searched, found to be festooned in revolvers and cartridge-belts like a combat squad. 'Now then, if you want to see what work we do, you'd better go and work with the workers.' All three were up-

ended and frogmarched to the furnaces. They yelled that the metal was scorching. The workers replied, 'For us, it burns all our lives. For you it's burning only tonight, so get on with it.' On the face of the furnace someone had inscribed *Labour is Noble*.[19]

The police, who generally stayed well back from the factories, limited their action to mounting guard over the banks, the offices of AMMA and the newspapers, and throwing a cordon around the notoriously 'red' quarter of the Barriera di Milano. Meanwhile, to make sure of oxygen, FIOM ordered the occupation of the gas plant: the workforce obeyed at once. The council of the workers' leagues voted a resolution which promised that if other industrialists went to the aid of their colleagues in metal, the occupation would be extended. And it added: 'The struggle of the metalworkers opens a new era in the class struggle which will close only with the establishment of workers' control over all production.'[20]

As Sunday approached – the first Red Sunday – a communiqué from the factory council of Fiat-Centro on the eve warned: 'Sunday, no playing around, no going on the spree. The workers must prove their seriousness.' At Fiat-Brevetti they decided to work. 'Show that you can scorn weariness, suffering, danger,' said the factory council, 'in the cause of the emancipation of the human race from capitalist gangs.'[21] In many factories there were meetings. The most famous socialist leaders, young and old, spoke to assemblies: Gramsci at Garrone Fiat, Pagella and Pastore at Fiat-Centro, Tasca at the Ansaldo yards and Fiat-Brevetti, Montagnana and Boero at Savigliano, Togliatti at Dubosc. The Piedmont *Avanti* that day opened with the editorial by Gramsci we have already quoted. It underlined the historic significance of the event:

> The social hierarchies are broken, historic values overthrown. The *executive* classes, the *instrumental* classes are become *directive* classes. They have taken possession of themselves, they have found within themselves representative men, men to invest with the power of government, men who will undertake all those tasks which will transform a primitive and mechanical human aggregate into an organic brotherhood, a living creation.

And he ended: 'Today, Red Sunday of the metalworkers, the workers themselves must build the first historic cell of the proletarian revolution which thrusts through the general crisis with all the irresistible power of a force of nature.'[22]

In the heat of conflict, the initial diffidence of the *ordinovista* group had evidently disappeared. The workers' Turin of September was the climax of their movement.

In Genoa and its hinterland, 100,000 *metalos* worked. The economy of the city was dominated by Ansaldo, whose directors also controlled the Consortium. The Genoese proletariat, particularly combative at this time, had already experienced go-slow, occupation and workers' management during the dramatic days of February 1920 in Sestri Ponente. To a degree it is possible to detect a tendency towards council organization by factory, at least as the USI syndicalists interpreted it.

However, in contrast to the Turin comrades, the workers of Genoa were less unionized. Moreover their organized vanguard was much more divided. There were three *camere* in Genoa – in the Nervi district, Sampierdarena and Voltri. The division was not simply territorial. In Nervi the 'autonomous' socialists of Genoa, strongly reformist, were dominant; maximalists were in control of the others. In Sestri Ponente the *camera*, with 14,000 members led by Antonio Negro, was in the hands of the anarcho-syndicalists who also had a journal, *La Lotta Operaia*; syndicalist influence was also strong in Savona and La Spezia.[23]

The workers' occupation rolled through all Liguria on the morning of the 2nd. There was serious conflict outside the Odero shipyard which was defended by royal guards. Workers circled the walls and tried to force an entry into the stocks, climbing over ships under construction. They ran into a fusillade. Three were seriously wounded. One, the coppersmith Domenico Martelli, aged 35, died on the way to hospital. Elsewhere, *Il Lavoro* noted, 'the troops offered only a token defence of bourgeois property' and there was no trouble.

It was peaceful in Sestri Ponente, where workers marched in columns into the workshops at seven in the morning, in Cornigliano at the Ciampi steelworks, where an infantry lieutenant and a warrant officer were taken hostage and later released, in Voltri where at the naval yard of Campanella, a squad of young men climbed the locked gates and opened them from inside. At the Voltri foundries, it was the night shift who broke the padlocks to admit their morning comrades, as at the aircraft and naval yards of Ansaldo, the Multedo foundry, at San Giorgio, Piaggio, the Grandi Ferrieri Giorgio Fossati.

The incident at the Odero yard did not precipitate a general strike. The prefect worked hard to prevent it and the idea was also rejected at the Genoa *camera* because the Minister of the Interior insisted on the arrest of some of the royal guards who had opened fire. This provoked a near-riot among the guards who demanded, and obtained the next day, the release of their comrades. On the 3rd the funeral procession of the dead workman was huge.

The occupation in Genoa, up to the 5th, passed peacefully in a fervour of organization, as at Turin (workshop commissars were elected everywhere). Symbols of the movement's politics and its military vigilance were flamboyant. *Il Giornale d'Italia* recorded them:

> All along the line from Sampierdarena to Voltri, there is a lavish display of red and black flags hoisted over machines, gates, ships under construction. On the great gate of the Ansaldo shop in Sestri Ponente there is a placard, *Communist Factory*. On another, the notice: *Workers! if the security forces try to break in, take to sabotage!* . . . In the Ansaldo plants, at the Giano pier, everything is ready to repel the security forces if they attack. Access points are solidly blocked, defence works built out of vehicles and scrap iron. Even the three steamships under construction, the *Duilio, Ansaldo VIII* and *Cesare Battisti*, are isolated and manned by worker guards . . . Access points are guarded by squads of workers who refuse entry to strangers. At the warehouses select men of the internal commission are in charge and nothing can be taken out without a chit from the departmental commissariat.[24]

As for Milan, according to the same sources, 'it is confirmed that prisons have been created everywhere to hold workers taken in possession of stolen property or neglecting their work'. The workers' weapons, as in other cities, seem to have been mainly revolvers and pikes, 'sometimes model 91 rifles or cavalry muskets'.[25]

In Milan, newspaper reports are abundant but not noticeably different from those on factory life in Turin and Genoa. Barin, director-general of Lombard Steel, who had been immediately 'sequestered' outside his house, was released after he signed a statement that 'during his sojourn in the factory he was treated with every respect and courtesy'.[26] *Il Corriere della Sera* reported on the 2nd that the workers at Isotta Fraschini had kicked out a comrade who tried to steal a magnet. The prefect reported on the 4th that 'everything goes on normally', and he summed up the situation:

The workers who are occupying the metal plants continue to arm themselves and to reinforce the defences. The labour force in other industries are pressing their leading organizations to extend the movement. I have called on Buozzi and others to resist this pressure. Turati, at my request, will do his best to help find a settlement.[27]

That evening Lusignoli was insisting on the urgent need to settle the dispute quickly before the movement spread to other industries. That the atmosphere in Milan, despite the fact that its working class was dispersed in a myriad small and medium enterprises, was essentially the same as in Turin and Genoa is proven by a characteristic episode involving Benito Mussolini. The director of *Il Popolo d'Italia* was enormously impressed by the spectacle, and he went to find Bruno Buozzi to make him what was virtually an offer of help. 'Mussolini declared,' recalled Buozzi, 'that it mattered little to him if the factories were in the hands of the workers rather than the industrialists and that if the occupation developed into a constructive revolutionary movement, he would be on the side of the revolutionaries.'[28] Gaetano Salvemini commented that this was typical of Mussolini's tactics of 'keeping a foot in two shoes'.[29] Towards the end of the occupation, an offer of help from Mussolini would go in a very different direction. But however personal the opportunism which drove him to tail along behind the movement, it shows how powerful the thrust of the workers' attack was in the early days and how total was the paralysis in conservative circles. A *squadrista* reaction in the great cities of the triangle was still utterly unthinkable.

5.
The Government's
'Non-Intervention'

When the factories were occupied, Giolitti did not budge from Bardonecchia. He did not interrupt his holidays, did not postpone the meeting with the French premier Millerand fixed for the 12th at Aix-les-Bains. Press attacks on him began at once, to grow into shocked and furious denunciation as social tension sharpened. Was he trying to demonstrate the government's calm, to reassert its neutrality? Giolitti was certainly not indifferent. His biographer Gaetano Natale visited him in Bardonecchia at this time and paints the Giolitti of September 1920 as a man of strength and solitude. 'He did not seem particularly worried, but talked less than usual. When I saw him he was carrying some blue-covered handbooks which he told me were code-books, explaining that he preferred coded telegrams to telephone calls.'[1]

What is known of the coded telegraphic correspondence between Giolitti and Camillo Corradini documents the coherence and perseverance of the premier in his policy of official non-intervention. He did not rule out contact with the two parties, but insisted on extreme caution. It was Giolitti's colleagues who made the first moves, but without official mandate. Arturo Labriola seems to have acted entirely on his own initiative,[2] though without success. In his view (though the Minister of Labour was the last person to win the trust of either side) chances of a settlement were still remote; both sides were still testing each other's strength.

The first, extremely circumspect, attempts at mediation in Milan by the prefect Lusignoli in consultation with Corradini and Porzio (Under-secretary of the Presidency of the Council) and supported at Rome by the ministers Labriola and Meda, got nowhere. The Milan group of industrialists which, through the personal ascendancy of Rotigliano, director of Ilva, was most influential in Confindustria, wanted no compromise, nor had they yet to face any current of opinion opposed to their own intransigence. On the other side, control of the movement seemed day by day to be slipping from the hands of Buozzi and D'Aragona. A fever was beginning to grip the factories and an inchoate demand to intensify the struggle was rising from socialist and anarchist groups in the working-class movements.

The tireless prefect of Milan clearly saw the need to come quickly to some kind of agreement, no matter what, lest the crisis break. So in the early days of September he tried endlessly to find the basis for such an agreement; he thought he had found it in an effort to reduce the workers' cost of living with the help of the employers. Through the financing of big co-operatives, consumers' stores etc, the workers were to receive, even before the co-operatives were fully operative, a daily 'quid' (food voucher) in supplement of wages, which would diminish proportionately as these organizations began to register a profit.[3]

FIOM was ready to accept an increase of 5 lire instead of 7, subject to these reductions[4] and at one point, the industrialists seemed to be moving towards a compromise of this order. But just as the prefect was reporting that 'it looks as though the proposal is making some headway',[5] the talks broke down. The industrialists would grant no immediate wage increase; they still saw no need to give way on this point. The prefect and the ministers had probably been drawn too deeply into the intricacies of mediation, as Giolitti was quick to tell them.[6] The creation of consumer co-operatives seemed too complicated, their effectiveness too hypothetical – indeed Giolitti himself was to drop this scheme when he imposed his own solution.

On the other hand, there can be no doubt about Buozzi's desire to speed things up, to escape somehow from a campaign whose prospects seemed to him to be getting gloomier. He said so on 3 September in *Il Corriere della Sera*,[7] and even more urgently, to the prefect of Milan.[8] Turati[9] and Treves were no less worried. They were afraid that the conflict would spread, that the movement in the factories would break free from union control. The document, credible enough in itself, which claims to record the unquiet thoughts which Treves shared with a friend in the government, is symptomatic.[10] His fears of insurrection by masses in ferment and of possible incitement by maximalists encouraged by the government's passivity, are very evident.

The threat of an imminent trial of strength grew daily more

menacing. In the factories, with money now getting very tight, not everyone could go on 'spinning it out'.

Demands to extend the movement multiplied. Anarcho-syndicalist agitation was proving effective in the great northern cities,[11] where by no means all the FIOM sections and *camere* had been won to Buozzi's moderate line. They had not been in Genoa, in Turin, or in Milan, where the president of the executive commission of the *camera*, Schiavello, was one of the most intransigent maximalists.

It would be an exaggeration to say that the working class was mobilizing *on the left* around a common revolutionary programme. On the contrary, connexions between the different centres were still weak, perspectives anything but clear. The *ordinovisti* in the Piedmont *Avanti* between 2 and 5 September certainly took up a position distinct from that of the Milan edition (its editor absent throughout), which scrupulously followed the instructions of FIOM and the CGL and contented itself with a celebration of the solidarity and discipline of the workers. But even the Turin analysis was more interesting in theory than effective in practice. In an editorial of 2 September Gramsci warned the workers against the illusion that a simple factory occupation could solve the problem of power.[12] He was well aware of Giolitti's intention, through government neutrality, to wear down the proletariat 'to the point when it will itself fall to its knees'. He urged the workers to form 'a loyal armed force, ready for any eventuality'.

On the question of principle and method, the Piedmont *Avanti* reached the point of saying:

> A permanent establishment of the workers in the factories as self-governing producers rather than wage-earners is not possible unless other forces enter into play, forces which will completely displace the focus of the present struggle, which will carry the battle into other sectors, direct the workers' power against the real centres of the capitalist system: the means of communication, the banks, the armed forces, the state.[13]

Gramsci himself on 5 September stressed the problem of military defence. He argued the case for passing to the formation of an urban soviet.[14] His was certainly the most revolutionary voice, even in comparison with the anarchists, whom in fact he denounced for failing to understand the importance of this 'new hierarchy'.

Lucid analysis, bold proposal – but no decisive deed. All these arguments were to be the starting-points for criticism and self-criticism when the battle was over and inquest into defeat began. At the time, however, the search for national co-ordination and common direction ran into very serious difficulties, which virtually paralysed it.

The first opportunity was, so to speak, an interior dialogue. On 4-5 September, the 'States-General' of the proletarian movement assembled. The directive council of the CGL, the party directorate and representatives of the most important *camere* met in Milan.[15] After a thorough study of the situation, they decided that 'if, because of the obstinacy of the employers or the government's violation of its neutrality, no satisfactory solution is found', then the proletarian organizations would have to direct the struggle towards 'the objective of control over industry, to achieve collective management and the socialization of the means of production'. Furthermore, since the national council of the CGL had been called for 10 September, the party and union leaders decided to 'sit in permanence' at Milan and to call the leadership of the socialist parliamentary group there, 'thus summoning all the forces of the political and the trade union movement to come to a more precise decision on the objective of this decisive struggle and to adopt means adequate to ends'.[16]

Even though the proposal for revolution was conditional on the rejection of the trade union demands, criticism at once focused on the disproportion between the original union claims and the threats made at this meeting. This document, which was later denounced as a dodge, an evasion, and which largely deserved the accusation, in fact used control over industry, still more collective management, as a blackmail weapon, a bogey. The point, naturally, was not made only by historians! *Il Corriere della Sera*, for example, at once raised the obvious objection. Will you then make the revolution, Albertini's paper asked the socialists, as a reprisal for a failure to accept the wage demands of one category of labour? Will you subordinate an ultimate programme like the socialization of the means of production to the settlement of this dispute in the metal industry?

Albertini's paper, in influential articles written by Luigi Einaudi,[17] Giovanni Amendola[18] and himself, took its stance in the front ranks of the mobilized conservative press. Around this central point, it drew up an indictment of the entire socialist movement, which began to strike the government as well.

'Where do they want to go?' wrote Albertini on 5 September,

> To the revolution? There is no one, not a reformist, not even a maximalist, who seriously believes in the possibility of a revolution, in which a good third of the population of Italy would perish from poverty and hunger. And so? What ill-omened war is opening between aspirants for the favour of the working classes? We will not hide our fears. They are made worse by the apathy of the bourgeoisie and the weakness of a government whose leader thinks fit, in the present state of the country, to husband his strength in the golden mountains. No, the government must take a line and lay it down to the country. We fear that its tactics are to stand aside and look on, without compromising itself. It does not want the occupation to succeed, so does not press home its intervention. But if tomorrow things become more gross, then it will sacrifice everything to a temporary truce.

The 5th saw an important shift in the situation. At that point, only the nationalists of *L'Idea Nazionale* and the fascists of *Il Popolo d'Italia*[19] followed *Il Corriere della Sera* in sounding an alarm. The government had not yet lost faith in a settlement. The prefect, Lusignoli, issued strong orders to local security forces to avoid any measures which might provoke incidents with the occupiers (who passed the first 'Red Sunday' in the factories virtually in euphoria).[20] Giolitti, on the same day, sent a message to Corradini:

> I see talk in the papers of the possibility that the government will requisition some metal factory or other. I would never agree to such action. Whenever some proposal of this nature crops up, I ask you to see to it that it is immediately ruled out in the most categorical manner. Please advise Porzio, Labriola and Alessio of this.[21]

The industrialists were perfectly aware of this attitude. On the same day, their president Ettore Conti wrote in his diary:

> There is no hope of any government intervention to put a stop to this essay in revolution. Giolitti, apart from his motto of 'let them try it in practice', claims that he does not command enough power to expel the rebels from the factories. I do not believe the second reason. As for the first, we shall see whether the workers can learn their lesson. Brawn alone is not enough to run a firm.[22]

In a certain sense, then, the industrialists, too, like the

government, seemed ready to let the workers wear themselves out. At the same time they stepped up the pressure on that government even as they stalled on the negotiations which so occupied Labriola and Meda[23] as well as Corradini and Porzio.

On Monday, 6 September, however, the crisis got more serious. The government could not ignore, for example, a sharp increase in the land-occupations which for months had troubled many provinces in the South.[24] This movement was in no sense co-ordinated with the occupation of the factories; it did not in any way follow it. But it existed and it made the turmoil worse. To such an extent, indeed, that the Socialist Party chose this moment to launch a manifesto to 'peasants and soldiers' steeped in that maximalist rhetoric which was its public style.

This called on the peasants to support the metalworkers' struggle, 'because if the workers succeed in eliminating the sharks' profits of the owners, it will be possible to sell you machines at better prices'. It continued:

> If tomorrow the hour of decisive struggle strikes, you, too, must rally to the battle against all the bosses, all the exploiters! Take over the communes, the lands, disarm the *carabinieri*, form your battalions in unity with the workers, march on the great cities, take your stand with the people in arms against the hireling thugs of the bourgeoisie! For who knows, the day of justice and liberty is perhaps at hand.[25]

The manifesto urged 'proletarians in uniform' to join the workers' struggle, to refuse to resist the occupation of the factories, to refuse to storm the workshops if their officers gave the order.

This clearly looked like a pre-insurrectionary document. Not a single order was given to strike the 'decisive hour', but revolutionary fever visibly increased in the factories. The anarcho-syndicalists, also meeting in Milan, were talking of a simultaneous occupation of industries, mines, fields and mansions.[26]

In the week now beginning, tension reached breaking point. It was the arming of workers and the increasingly open support given by railwaymen which most worried the government and brought out the whole non-socialist press in swelling and noisy chorus. It is difficult, if not impossible, to establish the truth about workers' arms. Working-class memoirs are vague on the point or too sparse and localized. Papers of the Ministry of the Interior yield no precise information, and one often feels that prefects simply re-echoed press rumours about machine-guns, tanks, even aircraft in the hands of the workers, or else relied on dubious informants who were soon discredited. In Turin, Milan, Genoa, Florence and some lesser centres, as the strike moved into its second week, the air was thick with rumour.

According to the Turin correspondent of *Il Giornale d'Italia*, for example, 'the workers number former military pilots in their ranks who yesterday (6 September) brought aircraft into action. Two AVS machines took off from the Ansaldo airfield, manoeuvred over the field and part of the city and showered Turin with maximalist propaganda leaflets.'[27] This episode, real enough, was cited by other papers, but it was not this kind of exploit which worried the prefect, but other much more serious symptoms. On the 5th, Giolitti received a telephone message which reported, among other things:

> It seems the occupiers have machine-guns. They claim to have armed a tank, built at Fiat for the state. If this kind of thing goes on, the crisis will become extremely grave. In the factories, the most exalted elements begin to feel that the moment of triumph for their ideals approaches and there is a very real fear that the working masses, in strong armed detachments, might invade the city for more criminal enterprises.[28]

That projects of this nature were beginning to circulate in the factories is certain, a product of that restlessness and anxiety which were beginning to grip the workers in occupation. Gramsci recollected their state of mind in a private letter some years later:

> I retain a vivid memory of one scene in Turin during the occupation of the factories. The military committee was discussing the necessity, which might arise at any moment, for a sortie of armed workers from the factories. They all seemed to be drunk. They were on the point of coming to blows. Responsibility crushed them, chewed them to a pulp. One of them who got to his feet, who had lived through five years of war as an airman and had brushed death many times, staggered and seemed about to collapse. With a tremendous effort of will, I intervened and made them smile with a witticism, and led them back to normal and profitable work.[29]

If the security forces were alarmed, so were those workers. In many factories they were afraid that the army or the royal guards were going to drive them out. On the evening of 5 September, a rumour to that effect ran through the Barriera di Milano. Factory sirens sounded the alarm. Women and children ran out of their houses and rushed to the factory gates to protect their men and block the attack. Such incidents show how swiftly the atmosphere had changed. On 6 September in Turin, cannon with guard shields were wheeled into the Piazza Castello in front of the prefecture and machine-gun nests manned by infantry and gunners appeared at the entry points to the square.[30]

That 'military committee' which Gramsci spoke of did exist. In Turin it was the more effective in that it had been making preparations for months, since the April strike. The essential point, however, which became clearer minute by minute, was this: the whole military organization of the workers, the weaponry, the red guards, were essentially, indeed exclusively, defensive in purpose. It would not be easy for the security forces to storm some plants, but it would be very difficult for the workers to make a sortie from their fortresses unless a general popular insurrection had altered the balance of military force.

A Turin worker, Vincenzo Bianco, has left precious testimony on this point.[31] It confirms the defensive spirit and also laments a certain 'factory patriotism' which made co-ordination and plans for joint action (themselves never expressed in *offensive* terms) arduous and difficult. Angelo Tasca confirms Gramsci's assessment of the military position in the Turin factories:

> Armed insurrection was impossible because nothing was ready. The masses felt secure behind the walls of the factories not only because of their weapons, which were actually primitive and inadequate, but because they thought of the factories as securities which the government would hesitate to destroy by artillery fire in order to expel the occupiers. Between this 'defensive' attitude and open struggle in the streets, the difference is great, and the workers sensed it in more or less confused manner. In Turin itself, even where there was a bold vanguard better armed than elsewhere, communist leaders refrained from every initiative of this type and restrained those groups which at Fiat had prepared trucks for a sortie.[32]

The most serious incidents from the government's point of view were taking place not only in Turin but at the depots and marshalling yards of the railways. From 6 and 7 September, railwaymen, on the orders of their union,[33] saw to the regular supply of truckloads of raw materials and fuels to the occupied plants. On 6 September, Fiat-Lingotto got 21 trucks, 14 of diesel and 7 of various materials. Between the 7th and the 8th, 14 trucks of dolomite, pig-iron, and steel billets were sent into the Ferriere. Dramatic telephone conversations between the traffic manager and the central office of the state railways testify to the crisis.[34]

In Milan, the workers' military preparations were much less serious, although *Il Corriere della Sera* began to talk of arms channelled into the factories through Schiavello's *camera* organization.[35] On 6-7 September, the prefect was seized by fear of a workers' sortie against the banks and he drew up a veritable war-plan for the military defence of the city based on the line of the Naviglio; he called for a further 5,000 troops and royal guards, tanks and armoured cars.[36] Moreover the active presence of Errico Malatesta was reported in Milan, at meetings in Sesto San Giovanni. True, he seemed to be 'preaching discipline'[37] but the return to action of the famous anarchist agitator who for years had been the very symbol of subversive menace to all the prefectures of the kingdom was hardly reassuring.

From Genoa, Florence, Brescia, demands for more police, *carabinieri*, arms, flowed into the Ministry of the Interior. The situation on the 7th was 'more dangerous than ever' to the prefect of Florence.[38] The inspector in charge of the prefecture in Brescia warned that in that place 'arms and bombs are being manufactured in the factories themselves'.[39]

The workers should have found arms deposits in the armament factories at the moment of occupation. Official information about these is very scarce. From the second week of the occupation, they were certainly worrying the government. Telephone reports reaching Giolitti from Corradini, Porzio, the prefects of the industrial triangle and from Bonomi, Minister of War, seem to have seriously alarmed him. For on the morning of the 6th, Giolitti approved a suggestion from Corradini that it was time for the Ministry of the Interior officially to make those urgent approaches to the industrialists through the medium of the banks, which Labriola and Meda had unofficially and vainly tried.[40]

Giolitti suspected that the industrialists knew all about the arms deposits but kept the government in the dark in order to compel it to use force. On 7 September, he openly admitted his suspicion to the prefect of Milan and added the peremptory sentence: 'In that case, we have the right to compel the industrialists to come to an agreement.'[41] The prefect of Milan thereupon took up his contacts again.[42] This time, however, it was Buozzi who had to reply that nothing could be done immediately. The latter had for days been arguing, and with reason, that they had to come to a quick decision before the problem slipped out of FIOM's control. He reported:

> In the days after the meeting of 4-5 September, the prefect of Milan in the name of the government, Toeplitz of the Banca Commerciale, Bondi of Ilva, told the leaders of FIOM that the industrialists were ready to resume negotiations and to make big concessions. To all of them FIOM replied that the movement had now so developed that it involved not only the metalworkers but the whole Italian proletariat and that therefore any resumption of negotiations would have to wait upon the decisions which would be taken by the national council of the Confederation of Labour called for the 10th.[43]

Buozzi similarly resisted renewed personal appeals from D'Aragona and Bianchi.[44]

Was this the eve, then, of an extension of the movement throughout the working class? The industrialists, though beginning to retreat from intransigence on the strictly 'trade union' front, were still firm on the point of principle: refusal to accept an unlawful situation in the factories. On 7 September their leading organs solemnly affirmed that they would not negotiate until 'the dispute returns to the economic terrain and hierarchical discipline is restored in the factories.'[45]

These were the government's most difficult days. It kept up the pressure on both parties but got ready to face the worst. Corradini, in continuous contact with the most accessible agencies, was preparing a defence plan for the cities most threatened by insurrection.[46] Bonomi was to describe the agreement he reached with Giolitti on a more general plan for the defence of the state.

> In the telephone conversations I had with him in those dangerous days, I concurred in the means and methods to be adopted for dealing with the crisis. In substance, with the meagre forces at our disposal, we had to concern ourselves not with clearing the factories but with preparing to repel a possible attack by our bolsheviks, of whose movements and intentions we were informed. The essential pre-condition for a timely defence was the

control of communications. To that end, I prepared for the militarization of the railways, getting the signatures of Giolitti and the king, who was then at San Rossore, to the decree of mobilization, which remained for a long time in my hands and which I returned to the king, in a constitutionally correct manner, some months later.[47]

Bonomi's evidence bears witness to the difficulties local authorities found themselves in; on every possible occasion, they did not fail to complain about the weaknesses of the forces they disposed of in defence of public order. Massive deployment of the army, not yet demobilized but largely immobilized in the armistice zone, certainly seemed risky, after the incidents at Ancona. 25,000 royal guards and 60,000 *carabinieri* seemed manifestly inadequate to meet the threat of insurrection.[48]

The government's best weapon, in spite of the intolerable tension, remained the influence it was capable of exercising on the 'moderates' of both camps, on those most intimately committed to the existing system of government, existing ideologies and conceptions of economic and social change. This does not mean that the government could not conceive of using troops as the 'ultima ratio'. The gulf between soldiers and ex-combatants on the one hand and socialist workers on the other was now even wider than it had been in the months past,[49] and some vague appeal to the military from the PSI was not enough to bridge it and bring them over to the other side of the barricades.

6.
Revolution by Ballot

The week which culminated in the 'assizes' of the socialist unions on 10-11 September was a week dominated by the fear of revolution. A host of fears, suspicions, utopian impulses and recriminations, invaded the proletarian as well as the bourgeois leadership. Each was afraid that the other would take the first step beyond the point of no return. Neither of them did. No wonder the inquest lasted for decades.

On the eve of the national council of the CGL, the dispute narrowed to a single focus. The workers' organizations wanted to negotiate while maintaining the occupation as a surety.[1] They could do nothing else. Not only were the workers unwilling to abandon the factories without an economic victory, but also almost everywhere they were demanding to be paid for the working days of the two weeks of occupation. The industrialists did not intend to give way. By 10 September, Ettore Conti was noting the theme which dominated their discussions: enter into negotiations only on the pre-condition that factories would be evacuated and legality restored.[2]

The employers, as the crisis evolved, suffered a series of shocks. They went through agonizing reappraisals, savage reversions to intransigence. Giolitti mastered their resistance in the end only by a diktat linked to a new politico-financial manoeuvre. But at that point, it was the contradictions within the workers' movement which became crucial.

When the national council of the CGL opened in Milan, the occupation movement was still massive. Moreover, it was growing. In two ways: on the one hand, it was beginning to affect minor centres till now foreign to the struggle, on the other, there was a tendency in the great northern cities to invade the plants of other sectors, notably chemicals and textiles. To give only a few examples, between 6 and 8 September, occupation extended to the Fratte foundry of Salerno, the lignite mines of Castelnuovo Magra, the Oblach factory of Pontevicordazzere (Padua), the Piaggio di Finalmarina and all the engineering factories of Reggio Emilia, Oneglia, Rapallo. In Livorno, at the Orlando shipyard, a cargo ship was launched on 8 September by the wife of Pietro Mascagna, the master, in a speech delivered on the occasion hailed 'the collapse of joint-stock companies, the curse of Italy'.

In Turin, by this time, practically the whole working class was taking part in the occupation. Not only the small, medium and large metalworking firms (cars, coaches, foundries, service factories, railway material, marine engines, machine tools, bolts, precision instruments, typewriters) but rubber firms, Spiga, Michelin, Walter Martiny, Tedeschi, Saiga, the de Luca tannery, footwear plants, textiles from four important wool-factories to four hosiery firms, from the Hoffmann cotton-mills to Giordano's, from the Viscosa della Venaria artificial silk industry to hides – and not only in the city but in the province. The number of Turin workers directly or indirectly involved in the occupation has been put at 150,000.[3]

In Milan, too, the novelty of the second week of occupation was its extension into non-metallurgical establishments. Pirelli with 20,000 workers in the plants of Milan and the Bicocca, the Erba (at Milan and Bergamo), the Campari distillery, the Italia beer plants, the Hutchinson rubber firm, were all occupied.

On 10 September, *Il Corriere della Sera* reported that 'from what they say in the *camera del lavoro*, the occupation of the principal chemical plants will be proposed. The aim is to establish workers' control over production to make sure of supplies for the striking metalworkers.'

In Genoa, the police feared an occupation of the dock silos and warehouses generally. The prefect called for 'the immediate despatch of at least one warship which could contribute effectively to defence if necessary'.[4] Meanwhile, in the port, the workers took over three ships.

This extension of the movement did not escape the government, which put its agents on the alert against the danger of seizures in other industrial sectors (which also seriously worried Turati and Treves, for that matter).

'There has been hesitation so far,' wrote one of those agents on 8 September,

> because the Confederation and FIOM do not want to go so far. But those two organizations want to save themselves at all costs

and they know that everything will fall to pieces unless the mass can boast of having won at least a notable success. A general occupation would cause such chaos that one cannot foresee the consequences of such a revolt by the working classes, not least because it would provoke a reaction from the middle sectors and from nationalist and anti-bolshevik elements.[5]

These were not idle speculations. On 9 September, Turin industrialists, three hundred strong, went to the prefecture to protest against government indifference to 'yet more offences against property'. They threatened that 'they would be forced themselves to provide for themselves that protection which the government refused them'.[6] However, there were no reports of serious violence by workers. The blood flowed later.

The atmosphere in the factories was a compound of objective realities and subjective responses. Work and production continued, at levels which varied from place to place, factory to factory. Officially, the orders for obstructionism remained in force, but in many factories the internal commissions dropped them, to step up production. Many working-class families had been without wages since the end of August; their situation was getting desperate. There were many demands to sell the goods produced.[7] FIOM suggested an inventory and in some cities, notably Turin and Milan, *camere del lavoro* did try to sell off some products. But this was insignificant. Urgent needs were met by subsidies from the co-operatives,[8] above all by popular solidarity, in 'communist kitchens' and a thousand gestures of aid and fraternity.

The absence of clerks, and still more of technicians, had painful effects. These varied from place to place, but they were felt most wherever the class struggle was sharpest, in the great cities. This was an important factor. Not only did it severely limit productive efficiency and experiment with new forms of management. It clearly proved that the great majority of white-collar workers chose solidarity with the employers (though passively and often out of personal fear). The latter set out effectively to persuade clerks and technicians to abandon the factories by guaranteeing their salaries. The propaganda of the non-socialist press also weighed on them. Even more decisive was a general climate of 'wait and see'. In these critical days, people in effect waited to see which side was the stronger; they did not want to break with the employers before the match had been decided.

At the same time, it has to be recorded that absenteeism among workers was negligible, discipline effective, combativity widely diffused. No credible global figures of production exist. Those furnished by industrial associations after the struggle are no less partisan (for obvious reasons) than those published by worker management committees in the course of it. But the factories did not remain inactive and many worker cadres tested themselves in new technical, directive and managerial functions, often with striking results. The form of management in most factories was the factory council. This was sometimes formed from members of the old internal commissions, sometimes from workshop commissars nominated to the job by the local FIOM section, or on occasion by workers' assemblies.

This factory council movement, however, was not uniform. It was not an instrument comparable to the workers' 'soviets' of the Russian revolution or analogous movements in Germany, Hungary and England. This kind of experience was nearly everywhere lacking. The movement had no co-ordinating centre. The day-to-day problems which the councils had to face were too pressing. For the base organizations, often politically disunited (particularly in Genoa and Florence but also in Milan) the *camere del lavoro* remained the natural, hierarchical outlet.

Generally speaking then, during this critical week of trial, the movement proved incapable of improvising a structure which had not previously existed. Effective leadership by factory councils was organic and robust only in Turin, essentially because such organizations had been active in the metal factories there for almost a year (the first factory councils date in effect from the autumn of 1919). Elsewhere the factory council emerged but lacked the 'autonomist' criterion of Turin. It was more obviously the product of collusion between internal commission and local FIOM section.[9] This in itself explains why the movement had no national organization, no political platform of its own. The Turin men made some tentative efforts in this direction, but they were too vague and by this time insufficient.[10] The Milan convention of the CGL was to prove this.

The council movement, then, did not offer a revolutionary alternative to the trade unions. Nevertheless, everywhere in the factories, there was a drive towards an extension and an intensification of the struggle. Here and there some symptoms of weariness leaked out. Workers were often moved by exasperation rather than enthusiasm. 'Some of them, poorly educated, too utilitarian perhaps, were already insisting, at the price of everything else, that they had to be given the means to live day by day, if they were to stay in the factories,' recalled A.Baratono at the socialist congress of January 1921.[11] D'Aragona summed up the situation on the eve of the convention in these terms:

> We had plants where the workers gave a real demonstration of maturity and consciousness; other plants where the workers knew how to run their own business as it had run when there was a capitalist to run it. But we had other plants, where, for a multitude of reasons which had nothing to do with the maturity of the mass but everything to do with lack of raw materials, absence of technicians, leading personnel etc, the running of the factory proved impossible. We had plants, too, which were deserted by the workers; we had to transfer workers from one plant to another to get a little nucleus inside which would give the impression that there were still workers there, to rule and run it.[12]

There is other evidence, however, of a quite different character. The secretary-general of USI, for example, Armando Borghi, reporting innumerable cases of extension of the struggle, talks of 'a truly revolutionary situation', of 'order, enthusiasm, exchange of products, fraternization among all the trades, regular labour, a will to action'. He emphasizes the significance of a regional convention of the Ligurian unions held in Sampierdarena on 7 September in which agreement was reached 'on a bold decision: to create a *fait accompli* by the occupation of Genoa, greatest port of Italy, together with all the other ports of Liguria, and to follow it up at once with a general occupation of every branch of production.'[13]

This agreement was not translated into action, asserts Borghi, only because Maurizio Garino, a celebrated Turin libertarian and leader of the local FIOM section, maintained that at Milan, the CGL would itself call for a general occupation. Therefore, 'to make sure of the success of the movement and in order not to prejudice it by a premature regional action, it was necessary to wait. And the convention agreed to this postponement.'

In Turin, the majority of the workers seemed to support an extension and radicalization of the movement. Great anger had been aroused by the discovery among the papers of the Fiat offices of blacklists of rebellious workers to be sacked (and not re-employed by any associated firm) and evidence of an 'espionage' service in labour conflicts.[14] From Fiat-Centro on 9 September went a telegram to the co-ordinating committee in Milan: 'The workers of Fiat-Centro intend to negotiate only in terms of the abolition of the ruling and exploiting class. Otherwise immediate war to total victory.'[15]

The movement, then, was not homogeneous; there were certainly different levels of power and tension within it. But everywhere now there was the conviction that a political solution was essential. 'A merely economic solution is no longer possible,' D'Aragona himself told a meeting of the socialist parliamentary leadership in Milan.[16]

Meetings followed, one after the other. On Thursday, 9 September, the directive council of the CGL met in the presence of some party representatives for a first 'inventory' of the situation. And it was there that the Turin socialists were subjected to direct interrogation. It is possible to reconstruct this crucial episode from multiple testimony.[17]

Present for Turin were Palmiro Togliatti, secretary of the city's socialist section, and Nino Benso of the party's provincial federation. The CGL chiefs put the question to them: are you ready to move to the attack, yourselves in the van, where to attack means precisely to start a movement of armed insurrection?

Togliatti said no:

> If there is an attack on the factories, the defence is ready and should be effective; not so an attack. The city is ringed by a non-socialist zone and to find proletarian forces which could help the city, we would have to go as far as Vercelli and Saluzzo. We want to know if you have decided on a violent, insurrectionary attack. We want to know what your objectives are. You cannot count on an action launched by Turin alone. We will not attack on our own. It demands a simultaneous action in the countryside. Above all, it demands action on a national scale.[18]

Togliatti was for extending the movement, as the Turin delegation was to be, at the convention of 10-11 September.

Benso said the same. He simply added:

> There are some plants which are well armed, others far from it. Fiat-Centro which seems to be one of the best supplied, has only 5,000 rounds of machine-gun ammunition . . . The revolution, if it is to happen, must be Italian. Otherwise the two cities in the

van, Turin and Milan, will be overwhelmed. Nothing is ready . . .[19]

Why did the CGL leaders put the question in those terms to the Turin comrades? Were they now in favour of insurrection? Or did they know that the reply would be a refusal? Or did they mean to send the Turin vanguard to its destruction? With this episode, an era of mutual abuse began.

The suspicion of the *ordinovisti*, their obsessive fear of being left isolated as in April, are obvious in Togliatti's reply. A year later *L'Ordine Nuovo* expressed this suspicion and explained its causes, precisely and with extreme bitterness:

> How was it possible for the Turin men not to see in the offer a skilful trap? Designed to make sure that the Turin movement was finally broken by the police who had concentrated in Turin a powerful military apparatus? . . . In Turin, in the context of a national struggle, we could stand up to the onslaught of government forces, with many chances of success. We could not, however, assume responsibility for an armed struggle without being sure that the rest of Italy, too, would struggle no less. Without being sure that the Confederation, as is its custom, would not have allowed the whole military power of the state to concentrate on Turin, as in April.[20]

D'Aragona replied to this charge. 'We questioned the Turin comrades,' he said to the CGL congress,

> because we thought that Turin was the city best prepared for an action of this type, and we asked them: are you in a condition to launch the struggle if we transfer it to the political terrain? And they replied: if you are talking about defending the factories, yes, we can defend them. If you are talking about a sortie from the factories to fight in the streets, we would be finished in ten minutes. But the struggle we have to launch is indeed a struggle in the streets . . .[21]

An official CGL document carries the significant note: 'An insurrectionary movement in Italy,'

> would have given the bourgeoisie the opportunity to unleash a violent and bloody reaction which would have broken our strength and blocked the future development of socialist politico-syndical action. This, our belief, was enormously strengthened, because the representatives of the section and the provincial

federation of Turin had to state explicitly that, even in that city, which was thought the most ready for revolution, the suppression of the proletariat in the event of an insurrection would have to be deemed certain.[22]

This was the focus of the controversy. That the CGL was opposed to insurrection is obvious. If the continuous and breathless activity of D'Aragona, Bianchi and other leaders, their talks with the prefect of Milan and Corradini himself, their endless quest for compromise were not enough, this document proves it. A political, no longer a merely economic solution? This was the knot to untie. The CGL would under no circumstances cut it with the sword of insurrection. A different reply from the Turin men would certainly not have changed this attitude. The CGL's response the following day, when the party proposed extreme measures to its national council, proves it.

Nevertheless, it remains significant that the Turin leaders themselves thought an offensive battle impossible. One towering, central reality: that total military unpreparedness of the movement. If in Turin, the insurgents could command 'ten minutes of fire', if in the stronghold of Fiat-Centro, there were only 5,000 rounds of machine-gun ammunition, what was there elsewhere? On that 9 September the police, at Lecco, with the agreement of the occupiers, confiscated 60,000 explosive charges in a warehouse of the Metalgraf.[23] And *L'Ordine Nuovo*, which was to cite the incident as a symptom, reported that 'in Milan, headquarters of the movement, not a single attempt has been made to list and collect the arms and ammunition in the factories'.[24]

Perhaps hopes centred on an overwhelming popular uprising? On the morning of the 10th, the party directorate seemed to move in that direction. In an order of the day, it announced its intention to 'assume the responsibility and the leadership of the movement, to extend it to the whole country and the entire proletarian mass'.[25] The expression meant agricultural as well as industrial workers. It proposed to extend the movement to all industries, to make it a movement for permanent expropriation, to make it a movement which, supporting the movements in being, would drive towards the seizure of the land. And enemy reaction?

'We had to expect,' said the PSI leadership to its Seventeenth Congress, and we did expect that the bourgeoisie, in reaction, would not allow itself to be finally expropriated but would resort to extreme defensive measures, while it kept its grip on political power and all the defensive force of the state; that consequently, the government would abandon neutrality. We pressed for rapid and immediate preparation, to sustain momentum, to move to the attack, to seize political power. The expropriation could have become definitive, reconstruction in a communist sense possible, only with a victory of the proletariat in the political field. But at the same time, the security they held in their hands would have been such that the workers would have deployed all their power, all their revolutionary audacity, confident that this was the final and decisive battle which, sparing no one, demanded every sacrifice.[26]

It is impossible not to be shocked by the contrast between the sweep and utterly imperious tone of this position and the shifts which, a few hours later, precipitated its total abandonment.

The party leadership, unanimous on this programme, met first on its own. The leadership of the parliamentary group was present in Milan, but had no say in the matter. The national council of the party was absent; it could not be summoned in time. A situation was in the making here which would seem absurd to anybody unfamiliar with the complicated and byzantine dualism of the movement. For at this meeting began the process which was to erect the national council of the CGL into a kind of court of appeal for the socialist movement, summoned to pass judgment on a revolution proposed by the party. And the national council of the CGL was composed of representatives of the *camere del lavoro* and the craft organizations; an assembly therefore dominated by those union officials and delegates often most marginal to the political meaning of the struggle.

On that same 10 September, the directive council of the CGL, meeting separately, elaborated its own programme which was entirely opposed to that of the socialist leadership. The CGL had no intention of surrendering control of the campaign to the party; it reasserted its leadership. It decided: 'The objective of the struggle shall be the recognition by employers of the principle of union control over industry. This will open the way to those major gains which will inevitably lead to collective management and socialization, and thus organically solve the problem of production.'[27] No revolution, then, but union control. No general occupation of factories and estates, but an increase in financial aid to the metalworkers. It was up to the directive council to take subsequent decisions, to take such steps as were necessary towards the government and the industrialists along this road.

Had they discovered a political alternative to insurrection? Was 'union control' an escape hatch for the movement? Was it an opportunistic device or the product of a general political attitude? On this issue, controversy was to rage long and loud. The idea of union control certainly reflected the ideological inclinations and political convictions, if not of D'Aragona, then of other CGL leaders. It also met one demand of the workers (some link the project directly to the discovery of the 'secret documents' at Fiat). It is no less true, however, and can be proved, that the programme arose from the urgent necessity of what Tasca was to call 'a retreat forward', precisely to escape extreme solutions. When the CGL was attacked on this point by the Russian trade union representative A.Lozovsky, its reply was frank. It ran: 'A revolution which implied a civil war of no brief duration would plunge the proletariat into total and desperate famine.'[28] It evoked the spectre of an immediate 'foreign blockade' as an absolute veto.

What was the party directorate's reply to these arguments? It was in the evening of 10 September that the two organizations, on collision course, held a dramatic joint meeting. Here, D'Aragona, Baldesi, Dugoni presented the party leadership with a stark choice: If you want to make the revolution, we will stand aside, we will hand over to you the leadership of the Confederation.

'You believe,' said D'Aragona, 'that this is the moment for the revolution. Very well, then. You assume the responsibility. We who do not feel able to shoulder this responsibility – the responsibility for throwing the proletariat into suicide – we declare that we withdraw. We submit our resignation. We feel that, at this moment, the sacrifice of our persons is called for. You, *you* take the leadership of the whole movement.'[29]

It is interesting to note that Gennari, secretary of the party, publicly acknowledged the honesty of the declaration and added that D'Aragona and the others had told him that 'they were ready to face every risk, every danger', once it had been made clear that theirs was no longer the responsibility in the struggle.[30]

To this clear statement by the CGL leaders, the party leadership (which included Terracini, representative of the *ordinovisti*, as well as Gennari and others who were to join the communist ranks at Livorno)[31] responded by referring the disagreement to the national council of the CGL. This was, technically, a formal fidelity to the position it had taken. In practice, as all the evidence shows, it was an answer heavy with renunciation and defeat. All the members of the directorate agreed that, without the men of the CGL at the head of the masses, what one of them called 'the great leap' could not be made.[32] Umberto Terracini was the first to admit it, in a speech to the Third Congress of the Communist International in July 1921:

'When the comrades who led the CGL submitted their resignations,' he said, 'the party leadership could neither replace them nor hope to replace them. It was Dugoni, D'Aragona, Buozzi, who led the CGL; they were at all times the representatives of the mass.'[33]

Gennari admitted it, too, in even blunter terms at Livorno:

Gennari: the leadership of the party could never accept the offer ...
Voices: Because you were afraid ...
Gennari: The leadership of the party could not accept such an offer, which implied so grave a responsibility.[34]

Schiavello, representing the left opposition within the CGL, confirmed it, too, in sorrowful tones:

We have all been subjected to a *fait accompli*; perhaps we wanted it; perhaps we did not. We lack organization. We lack a party which can capture the spirit of the people. We lack a party which does not live divided, with two different souls. We lack the iron hand. Maybe we lack a communist party, comrades![35]

The national council of the CGL was thus faced with two motions on the 11th. One was D'Aragona's, already cited. The other, reflecting the party's position, was signed by Schiavello and Bucco of Bologna. It ran:

The national council of the CGL requests the directorate of the party to take over the direction of the movement and to lead it towards the maximum solution of the socialist programme, that is the socialization of the means of production and exchange.

On the first day, a third, intermediate position was outlined, supported by Buozzi in the name of the FIOM leadership, which proposed to extend the movement to all industries with the programme of 'effecting all the political and economic reforms most insistently demanded by the socialist proletariat which are compatible with the condition of the country'. However, confronted with the radicalization of the two opposing currents, Buozzi decided to abstain. In fact he was much more worried by the maximalist motion than the other.

> 'I grew heated above all,' he recalled the next year, 'against Gennari and his resolution, which seemed naïve to me. But how, I said, can you submit such a motion to public debate in a convention? To warn the whole Italian bourgeoisie that tomorrow we are going to extend the campaign to all industries for an immediate overthrow of the bourgeois regime? And I said to Gennari: with this resolution you are inviting the most immediate and ruthless of reactions.'[36]

Even among supporters of the Bucco-Schiavello resolution, we know that scepticism prevailed. One of them, Bensi of Milan, commented in turn: 'We felt the revolution could not be made. Because a revolution is not made by first calling a convention to decide whether there is going to be a revolution or not. This was Mexican stuff they were trying to import.'[37]

At the meeting of 10-11th, Tasca (who voted for the Bucco-Schiavello motion), Giulietti and Donati spoke in favour of an extension of the movement, but the ballot was decided by the secure majority the CGL leadership could command. This majority was guaranteed by the reformist *camere del lavoro* from Genoa to many other smaller centres, and by the leaders of the landworkers' federation, Federterra, under Mazzoni, who rallied to D'Aragona and Dugoni because they were opposed to committing the rural workers to the struggle (while the land occupations in the South rolled on wholly outside their influence).[38] It is enough to recall that nearly half the CGL membership were labourers in the agricultural sector. Representatives of the two autonomous unions, the railwaymen and the maritime workers, of course, had no vote. The men of USI, the revolutionary syndicalists, had not been invited to the convention.

> The voting went:
> D'Aragona motion   591,245.
> Bucco motion   409,569.
> Abstentions (many FIOM sections) 93,623.
> The revolution was rejected by majority vote.
> Immediately after the result was announced, Gennari made

a declaration which became a symbol of the socialist 'great refusal'. Under the Pact of Alliance between the party and the CGL, he said, the party had the power unilaterally to take over the movement; in a sense, to 'annul' the decision taken by majority vote (a substantial but not overwhelming majority: 181,676 votes). However, 'at the moment, the party directorate does not intend to avail itself of these powers accruing to it from the Pact of Alliance'.[39] It might happen, added the PSI secretary, that in the future, in changed circumstances, in a new political situation, the leadership would do so. At all events, it did not do so. It accepted the democratic postponement of the revolution 'sine die'.

With remorseless sarcasm, Angelo Tasca was to write:

> Gennari's vague allusion to the future meant nothing. Reality was quite different. The party directorate had lost months preaching the revolution. It had foreseen nothing, prepared nothing. When the vote in Milan gave a majority to the CGL theses, the party leaders heaved a sigh of relief. Liberated now from all responsibility, they could complain at the tops of their voices about the CGL's betrayal. Thus they had something to offer the masses whom they had abandoned at the decisive moment, happy in an epilogue which allowed them to save their faces.[40]

In more laconic but essentially similar judgment, Nenni wrote that the convention of 10-11 September 'liquidated the political solution with the complicity of the party leadership itself, which wanted to lose'.[41] Luigi Einaudi in turn observed that 'the socialist leaders wanted to attack the regime only with words' and that 'they resigned themselves easily to the victory of the union moderates'.[42]

In all this talk of resignation rather than deliberate will, one point, however, became clear. Given the tension throughout the country, there remained a margin of uncertainty even after the convention. One solution was projected by the 'victors' while the 'vanquished' in the Milan *Avanti* commented: 'Revolutionary action develops in waves, and after one is thought to have failed, look, here's another rising even stronger, perhaps decisively.' Did the ebb and flow of hope and deferment continue? It would seem so. At that moment, no one was sure that the 'revolutionary opportunity' had been definitely lost, neither the left nor the right, not the reformists, not the bourgeoisie, not the masses in occupation.

Even the syndicalists of USI remained ambiguously hopeful over the 'sooner or later'. At the 'interproletarian' convention held on 12 September (in which the Unione Anarchica, the railwaymen's and maritime workers' unions participated) the syndicalist union decided that 'we cannot do it ourselves' without the socialist party and the CGL, protested against the 'counter-revolutionary vote' of Milan, declared it minoritarian, arbitrary and null, and ended by launching new, vague, but ardent calls to action.[43]

Umanità Nova incited peasants to occupy land, sailors to take over ships, railwaymen to stop trains, postal workers to 'suppress the correspondence of the bourgeoisie', soldiers to turn their weapons on the oppressors.[44] Even in these proletarian assizes, however, reality was very different. The very representatives of the revolutionary fractions were the first to admit the isolation of the class movement from the countryside, from intermediary circles in the cities, from the ex-combatants.

It was an isolation which the CGL prophesied on the international plane; and no one contradicted its pessimism. No echo reached these meetings of the opinion of the Third International; no one even knew whether it was going to be expressed. Serrati was on his travels, so was Borghi, so was Bordiga, on a long return journey from Moscow, with many halts. Although some conservative newspapers fantasized during the next few days about Gennari's 'orders from Moscow', there was in truth no connection between the executive of the International and the leadership of the PSI. The latter felt its isolation. News from Italy was in turn slow to reach Moscow. Only on 21 September did the executive of the International discuss Italian affairs and assign to its secretary-general Zinoviev the task of drafting an appeal to the Italian proletariat.

By 21 September, the movement was exhausted and the appeal's exhortations – to the seizure of power, armed insurrection, a purge of the party, the formation of councils of workers, soldiers and sailors – could not fail to sound anachronistic,[45] if militants in fact saw them, for *Avanti* did not publish them.

This failure in communication was not the least of the factors which contributed to the weakness and political difficulty of the PSI, to the mutual incomprehension which grew worse over the months stretching ahead to the Third Congress of the International in July 1921. Then there was the failure of the Red Army's advance in Poland, which was already evident at the end of August 1920. This could only reinforce among the socialist leaders assembled in Milan all the promptings of prudence, their fear that an Italian revolution would be left isolated and 'under blockade' in western Europe.

7.
Giolitti's Masterpiece

Meanwhile, the irritation and panic of the Italian press grew louder and louder. From organs of strict Giolittian observance like *La Stampa* and *La Tribuna*, through Lombard conservatives like *Il Corriere della Sera*, Roman sheets which were the mouthpiece of industrial groups, *Il Messagero*, *L'Idea Nazionale*, *Il Giornale d'Italia*, to the reformist *Il Lavoro* of Genoa, it was by now a unanimous, urgent, noisy chorus, begging Giolitti to intervene. Some in scepticism, some in faith, some evoking the 'strong hand', others an honourable arbitration. Stoking up the campaign were very alarmist reports of workers arming and subversives plotting.

Even louder was the echo of events abroad. French, British, German, American newspapers were full of revolution, chaos, violence. One Buenos Aires paper reported that the Italian government had abandoned Rome and fled to Bardonecchia! The exchanges slumped. From 1 to 10 September the rate against the French franc fell from 148 to 154, against sterling from 76 to 81, against the Swiss franc from 355 to 376, against the dollar from 21.50 to 22.80.

The fall of the lire was the burning question for *bienpensant* journals. *Il Messagero* called for a settlement 'from love of country',[1] *La Tribuna* insisted that 'the moment for government intervention has come'.[2] 'Is there no way out?' cried *Il Lavoro*,[3] evoking the horrors of civil war and repeating the advice so dear to Albertini, to look long on the squalor and hunger which were Soviet Russia. According to *Il Corriere della Sera*, 'the feeling that we have reached the ultimate is general':[4] there were bitter attacks on the ineptitude of the government in its confrontation 'with that socialism which is eroding the bases of the state'.

The tone did not change much after the Milan vote, though an initial sense of relief informed the more sensitive papers. They rejoiced, as *Il Corriere della Sera* put it, that the extremists had been beaten and that there had been 'found among the socialists courageous men capable of appreciating the peril we were running into and of demonstrating it to those most desperate'.[5] At the same time, however, they were scandalized at the sight of a government impotent before an assembly of 500 citizens who, under its benevolent eye, 'in partial and plenary meetings, in full consultation among themselves, coming and going from Casa del Popolo to prefecture, solemnly debated whether they should or should not make a revolution'. *Il Corriere* added, 'The state seemed permanently resigned to surrender to every violence'. *Il Giornale d'Italia* echoed it: 'We lived through the day of Saturday, 11 September, literally on the brink of maximalist ruin.'[6] Moreover what worried the press closest to the industrialists was precisely the formula with which the CGL had triumphed over the maximalists in Milan. What did 'union control' mean? Were the relations of production to change? Was it the beginning of collective or state management? What was in D'Aragona's mind? More important, what was in Giolitti's?

Luigi Einaudi warned of the danger of a solution imposed from above. 'At stake,' he wrote on 8 September, 'is the problem of the factory councils, of interference by workers in industrial management. Can we allow decisions of such importance to be taken by a minister preoccupied with winning a vote of confidence in his arbitration in the Chamber? Can we allow them to be taken without public opinion having been instructed on their merits?'[7]

Less limpid and liberal were the anxieties of other papers controlled by industrialists. Telephone conversations between the secretariats of Milan and Rome (intercepted and transcribed by the Ministry of the Interior) record the turmoil of nervousness, fear, exasperation and uncertainty in industrial circles. Perrone asked Olivetti whether he should 'have his papers attack the government' (*Il Messagero* and *Il Secolo XIX* of Genoa).[8] The secretary-general of Confindustria was too perplexed to reply.

Between 9 and 12 September, government policy towards Confindustria developed along the classic Giolittian lines: a firm reassertion of the refusal to use force; an increase in the pressure on the great banks; the definition of a concrete basis for compromise around the theme of union control. The premier telegraphed the prefect of Milan on 11 September:

> It is necessary to make the industrialists understand that no Italian government will resort to force and provoke a revolution simply to save them some money. The use of force will mean, at

the very least, the ruin of the factories. I place my faith in a peaceful solution.[9]

At the same time – the day of the Milan vote – the Viminale [Ministry of the Interior] received from Bardonecchia another coded telegram giving precise instructions to the police and armed forces in the event of an extension of the workers' movement.[10] Troops of the line were to be confined to barracks and were not to be used in security operations. The royal guards and the *carabinieri* were to be used only to block street outlets. The use of individual firearms was absolutely forbidden. If grave disorder broke out, officers were to withdraw their men from streets and squares, leaving in operation only machine-guns and, where necessary, light artillery. On every occasion, moderation was to be drilled into subordinates, even if crowds started to use weapons. As for the railways, we already know the precautionary measures agreed with Bonomi.

So much for Giolitti, Minister of the Interior. Giolitti, President of the Council, was no less committed to a peaceful solution. The man to bend to the will to conciliate seemed to be the managing director of the Banca di Sconto, Achille Pogliani,[11] and with him, that Ansaldo group which held most of the shares in the bank and exercised great influence. The prefects were set on a veritable manhunt for Pogliani. They found him in Parma. The prefect of that place, ordered Corradini, 'should invite Pogliani, in the name of the government, to work with the utmost speed on those Milanese industrialists who are the most obdurate and are said to be under the influence of the Banca di Sconto'.[12] Corradini stressed that 'the Banca di Sconto could propose policies contrary to the agreements between metalworkers and industrialists'. He added: 'Pogliani's mediation could be decisive in this most critical and delicate moment.'

Pogliani went to Milan and held important meetings. But his activity was rather ambiguous. From a press controversy which broke out later, and from documents we have been able to consult in the archives of the Banca Commerciale Italiana, it would appear that Pogliani tried in effect to manoeuvre between two contradictory pressures – that of the government, seeking to conciliate the workers, and that of his 'own' industrial groups (Ansaldo particularly and also Ilva), who were the most intransigent and the least ready for concessions. Pogliani later tried to unload all responsibility for the 'industrialists' surrender' which followed the ultimate compromise on to the managing director of the Banca Commerciale Italiana, Toeplitz, who according to him, had 'threatened to cut off all credit from employers if they did not immediately submit to the CGL's conditions'.

Toeplitz, however, who was without doubt himself very active as a mediator at the time, forced Pogliani publicly to withdraw his charge and to admit that he acted in concert with the Banca Commerciale Italiana in discussions with industrialists.[13]

In any case, it proved very difficult indeed to convince the intransigents[14] and it finally took an imperious gesture from Giolitti to overcome this extremely tenacious resistance.

The President of the Council had no intention of postponing the meeting with his French colleague Millerand at Aix-les-Bains on 12 September. Worried as he was by foreign reaction, he meant by this gesture to 'prove' that nothing untoward was happening in Italy.[15] In sticking to this line, he had to resist not only the press with its cutting charges of impotence and inconsequence, but the opposition to his departure expressed within his own cabinet, by Fera in particular, according to Frassati, Natale and Soleri.[16]

Giolitti was convinced, however, that matters would not go to extremes. His trust in the CGL chiefs was vindicated when Corradini's despatch reached him at the Hotel Albion, Aix, confirming the victory of the moderates.[17] Corradini referred to the platform of 'control' rather than 'socialization of industry'; was it a platform or an inclined plane to chaos? Giolitti had no doubts: he had a solution in mind which fitted perfectly into his perspective on relations between capital and labour in the new era. He replied immediately to Corradini:

> A final solution of the industrial question lies in the integration of workers, if necessary as shareholders, into the structure of industry, in full practical participation. Above all, workers' representatives must participate in administrative councils, so that they learn the real conditions of industry and the state of profits.[18]

It was the classic reformist attitude which the postwar Giolitti shared with the Popolari,*[19] but charged with a peculiarly

---

* Popolari: Members of the PPI, the Italian Popular Party, a Catholic party founded by Luigi Sturzo, in 1919; congress in June, absorbed many local groups, largely rural, but with support of 'small men' in urban centres. Won over 100 seats, second only to socialists in elections of November 1919, but lacked inner cohesion.

liberal and pedagogic tone. Had he not maintained from the beginning and affirmed in public that this occupation of the factories would itself teach the workers that they could not manage on their own, would involve them in the real problems of production? For that matter, did he not believe, in his sincerely held anti-plutocratic conviction, that super-profits had to be controlled, the speculative and absolutist mentality of employers subjected to efficient surveillance, a corrective by the collectivity?

Corradini, however, wanted to know more about union control and the CGL's interpretation of it. And he demanded explanations from his old friend Turati. The correspondence between the two men, which Gabriele de Rosa has published, is very revealing.[20] In the comments Corradini made and the information he supplied, borrowed from Giolitti and 'a person of very high banking position' (Toeplitz?), the essential distinction was that between 'control' exercised through participation in administrative councils and a 'control' imposed through 'factory councils' which deprived factory management of its powers over factory life and discipline.[21] Furthermore, Corradini did not rule out further stormy days, more dangerous situations, given the CGL's tendency to 'exploit the question to the hilt, to force victory all along the line', which threatened to wreck all 'spirit of moderation' on the other side.

More interesting is Turati's answer, which has understandably struck de Rosa in that it reveals an extraordinary 'inter-penetration, not only political but structural and ideological as well, of Turatian socialism with the Giolittian political system'. Turati in fact understood control exactly as Giolitti understood it: a stimulus to production, an instrument for the economic renaissance of the country. So that there should be no equivocation, he added 'in other words, collaboration of labour with the enterprise (not antagonism and destructive political struggle) and collaboration of labour and the enterprise with the interest of the public and consumers, more or less represented by the state'. Not factory councils, but a full development of trade unions, 'drawing them into a more intense collaboration and a wider vision of the national interest'.[22]

This reformist-productivist interpretation was certainly in total opposition to that of the *ordinovisti* who made workers' control an instrument of class autonomy, a fulcrum for the building of proletarian power, a revolutionary conquest by the labouring masses.[23]

De Rosa cogently argues that the divergence between a Turatian socialism embedded in the Giolittian system and the revolutionary socialism of the *ordinovisti* was already so acute that schism at the socialist congress of Livorno was almost inevitable.

But at this delicate moment, when the prospect of a split first became serious, what chiefly interested the CGL, and a FIOM which had now largely rallied to the reformist line (as was proven by one of the Milan motions),[24] was the search for a way out of the crisis: a solution which would guarantee to the union not only its wage claims, but a right of surveillance over management, discipline and the union rights of workers. They searched, therefore, for an honourable compromise, perhaps as a first step towards that joint participation in industrial management, which both Giolitti and Turati hinted at.

All were agreed on the need to act quickly. Food vouchers on the co-operatives,[25] petty subsidies, minuscule sales, 'communist kitchens', were not enough for workers deprived of wages for two weeks. Exasperation, discontent, suspicion at the ending of the Milan convention were general. They found expression in both the classic forms: extremist slogans and absenteeism, threats of sabotage and widespread weariness.

Symptoms of the malaise multiplied, in Turin, Milan, Genoa. On 13 September, FIOM had to recall its members to discipline and calm. The Turin *camera* urged workers to 'stop the unjustified exodus of goods and raw materials',[26] to cut out individual dealing, to hold back from extending the occupation. That night, there were many bursts of small-arms fire, alarms, incidents. A Turin industrialist killed two workers of the Capamiento, and bitterness deepened.[27] The factory council of Fiat-Centro felt it necessary, 'in view of the large number of absentees',[28] to threaten to dismiss any worker absent for two days; so did the factory council of Ansaldo San Giorgio. The workers were losing direction. They were for ever waiting for something new.

The CGL, on the basis of the Milan decision, called for the creation of a joint commission to work out the application of the principle of control.[29] In the Milan prefecture, representatives of the 'constitutional' party of the financial, industrial, political world met to concert action. Agnelli was there, the senators Conti and Albertini, the bankers Toeplitz and Pogliani. According to the prefect of Milan,

Conti came out for conciliation, but acceptance of the principle of union control was going to be nothing like as easy as the prefect's report suggested.[30] For the great majority of the industrialists, Olivetti, secretary of Confindustria, at their head, rallied against it. They launched a propaganda campaign in their newspapers against so utterly intolerable a prospect.[31]

Against the prison of union control, employers over the next few days, now quietly, now loudly, directly and indirectly, staged repeated demonstrations of intransigence, impatience, rebellion. But a very different tactical line began to emerge among their more sagacious leaders. This was not so much a line of acquiescence in Giolitti's wishes or the CGL's demands as a 'neck-wrung' acceptance under duress of the principle of control (though with substantial reservations) coupled with a determination to postpone its application as long as possible. All with an eye to the looming economic crisis which seemed certain to transform the whole context of the argument.

This group, which included Conti, Falck, the directors of the Banca Commerciale as well as Agnelli, had to fight very hard against a much more rigid position, or rather an explosive anger, which was general among industrialists. The policy of the 'moderates' was grounded in a more realistic assessment of the situation (the need to move towards the hand extended by the CGL, the impossibility of forcing Giolitti to retreat) and in a more skilful co-ordination of ends and means, which was also apparent over the problem of wage concessions.

There were, in consequence, some spectacular somersaults in the industrialists' world. Conti and Olivetti had to put up a whole series of façades to convince sulky associates that they had yielded only to a government *ukase*, while behind the scenes, in tough negotiations, they made the best of a bad job and manoeuvred to save everything that could be saved.

The government, finally, began to dangle compensations before their eyes, tax reductions, customs concessions. Press leaks which hinted at these were not denied. Indeed, on 14 September, the automobile industry was bailed out by a decree which raised the duty on foreign cars to 40 per cent.[32]

This is not to suggest that the whole process was a farce, a game played out between Giolitti and the industrialists or between the latter and the unions. That Giolitti's celebrated programme of union control remained a dead letter was not the fault of its author. From the moment he took his decision, he had to face and overcome a fierce resistance, not least among the 'moderate' industrialists themselves. The final compromise was rather the product of a conciliatory tendency which made slow but steady headway, despite the most rooted mental reservations and sporadic summons to renewed battle from both sides, until it finally imposed itself as the only reasonable solution upon all the contenders.

On 14 September, the *chef de cabinet* of the prefect of Milan went to CGL headquarters to tell D'Aragona and Buozzi that the President of the Council wanted to confer with representatives of the CGL in Turin on his return from Aix-les-Bains. A similar invitation went to Confindustria. Both organizations agreed and the delegates – D'Aragona and Baldesi for the CGL, Buozzi, Colombino and Bertero for FIOM, senator Conti, Olivetti, the civil engineer Meneguzzi as technical consultant, for the industrialists – travelled in the same coach, accompanied by the prefects of Milan and Turin.[33] They met Giolitti, who had just got off his train, late in the afternoon in the Hotel Boulogne. At first both sides simply confronted each other in total opposition. Senator Conti strongly opposed any form of control and rehearsed the set-pieces of Confindustria: immediate evacuation of the factories, punishment of workers guilty of violence, kidnapping etc. D'Aragona promptly answered that discussion in such terms was pointless. And the industrialists did not insist.

At this point Giolitti spoke – and he spoke in favour of control. The president asserted that the historic moment demanded radical changes in the relations between capital and labour. It was no longer tolerable that in a great enterprise, one man should command and thousands obey. 'We must give the workers,' said Giolitti, 'the right to know, to learn, to raise themselves, the right to share in the running of the firm, to assume some of the responsibility.'[34]

When D'Aragona spoke, it became clear once again that the CGL's concept of control was perfectly compatible with Giolitti's. Common to both was a preoccupation with productivity and hostility to financial speculation.[35] As for the CGL's own demands, D'Aragona claimed that workers needed control in order to learn what work-processes, what procurement systems, what financial operations entered into production costs; what profits on sales actually were. Only then could the unions really know whether wage demands were practicable or not. On the other hand, said D'Aragona, reaffirming his hostility to any council interpretation, such control could not be entrusted to individual factories: this would breed craft and work-group egoism.

The debate was lively. Giolitti ended it by confronting the industrialists with a *fait accompli*, which they ultimately accepted: the draft of a decree which appointed a joint commission of six CGL representatives and six from Confindustria 'with the duty of formulating proposals to be submitted to the government for the preparation of legislation on control'.[36]

The next day, the parties returned to Milan, where negotiations were resumed within 48 hours. In Milan, however, where the national council of the industrialists had met in plenary session, news that Giolitti had imposed union control struck like a thunderbolt. When it left for Turin, the industrialists' delegation had been given a mandate for intransigence on that very point. Had Conti and Olivetti sold the pass? The Stefani news agency broadcast the news on the afternoon of 16 September. The announcement, carried into full assembly, was greeted with uproar. According to Mario Missiroli, 'It was a thunderbolt. The assembly was struck by a kind of panic and dissolved, to reconvene some hours later in indescribable tumult, a confusion of words and ideas.'[37]

Later in the evening, when the debate was resumed, Conti and above all Crespi, in a very cogent speech, managed to win them over to a resolution which accepted the principle of control.[38] Twenty-one voted in favour, 14 against, led by Rotigliano. It is clear, from subsequent controversy, that the spokesmen closest to the Banca Commerciale (from its president Crespi to its directors Conti and Volpi) had to overcome resistance not only from the steelmen and the Lombard consortium of engineering industries, but from sectors of AMMA and the metallurgical industries of Liguria.[39] Conti and Olivetti worked to present the Turin decision, to their colleagues and to public opinion, not as an agreed compromise but as a surrender imposed by an authoritarian act of Giolitti.[40] The latter, in turn, complained to his friend Frassati about the leaking of the decree to *La Stampa*, which published it on 17 September.[41]

There was, in short, a truly massive resistance, all the more persistent in that union control affected every sector of industry.

Government had to overcome it by manoeuvre, by promises, by isolating the most 'ultra' groups. The knot, however was now cut. Subsequent events proved that Giolitti's action had been decisive.

The crisis of 15-17 September had grave consequences. It had forced the industrialists to retreat and had shown that those most eager for last-ditch battle (the steel groups Ilva, Ansaldo, the more adventurous and aggressive, those which had mushroomed during the war and now faced serious problems of production and finance) were unable to force such a battle. But the 'surrender' had a double motive: one was an awareness, particularly among the more far-sighted, that they were facing a situation which was by now intolerable; the other was the calculation on an economic crisis which would bury the project of control.

The transcript of a telephone conversation between Albertini and Amendola is perhaps the document which most vividly conveys the exasperation, the fear, the sense of impotence which had gripped conservative circles.[42] On 15 September, even as the delegations set out for Turin, Albertini was convinced that there could be no escape from an intolerable predicament unless power passed to the CGL. The man of order thus preferred socialist order to current disorder! Conti was no less resigned, though more cynically prescient: 'Since it is easy to foresee,' he wrote in his diary, 'that a commission of this kind [the joint CGL-Confindustria commission] will never produce any reasonable plan, the matter will end without victors or vanquished. Unfortunately, a labour crisis is imminent and there'll be no more talk of control.'[43]

Telephone conversations between industrial leaders in Milan and Rome register a strengthening of the opinion, through a welter of recriminations, reservations and 'revanchist impulses', that it would be better to submit than fight to the bitter end.[44] These first, spontaneous reactions in large measure justify the peculiar weight which historians give to psychological explanations for the industrialists' future support of fascist reaction.

On 19 September, Giolitti summoned the parties to Rome, to conclude the dispute formally. D'Aragona, Baldesi and Colombino for the CGL, Marchiaro, Raineri and Missiroli for FIOM, Conti, Crespi, Olivetti, Falck, Ichino and Pirelli for the Confederation of Industry, and the prefects Lusignoli and Taddei met in the hall of the council of ministers in the Viminale. Giolitti had D'Aragona sit next to him.[45] The first issue to be settled, though only after long discussion, was the question of the punishment of workers in individual conflict with employers. It was decided that 'personnel must remain at their posts'; all unresolved cases were referred to a joint commission.

After six hours, a general agreement was reached. It represented a notable success for FIOM in trade union terms. There was a wage increase of four lire a day on effective global earnings, substantial improvements in minimum pay, cost of living bonuses, percentages for overtime; paid holidays (six days) and compensation for dismissal.

Wages were to be paid for the slowdown period, though on the basis of nominal wage rates without cost of living bonuses. There was no firm pledge on payments for the working days of the occupation period. Individual firms were to assess the value of useful work done and pay for it. FIOM was to submit the agreement to a referendum of all workers.

On union control, Giolitti signed a decree at the end of the meeting which set up a joint commission of twelve and charged it with the duty of formulating those proposals which would serve the government in its preparation of legislation. The decree repeated the CGL statement that, 'given such control, the CGL undertakes to secure an improvement in disciplinary relations between the buyers and sellers of labour and an increase in production.'[46]

Though the occupation was to last for another week and sudden upheavals in the factories were not wanting, though disputes continued over controversial issues like the workers' demand to be paid for September, the meeting in Rome in effect put an end to the campaign. Many therefore, demanded an emergency recall of the Chamber which had closed for the summer vacation.

8.
The Response

During the decisive days, 15-17 September, the national council of the Popular Party (PPI) was meeting in Rome. Here, too the general uncertainty registered. A Turin councillor, Attilio Piccioni, asked the council not to concern itself with concrete legislative proposals which could be overtaken by events, but to consider 'the vast phenomenon in its general synthetic outline, as the latest manifestation of the conflict, now time-honoured, between capital and labour'.[1] And not only in Piccioni but in the whole council, there was a general awareness that what they were discussing was their part in 'the destiny of labour' – labour which was pressing its claims on society, moving towards a solution founded on a new order in the factories, grounded in participation and shared power.[2]

The example of the PPI was symptomatic. This kind of thinking, this interpretation of the crisis spanned a very wide arc of the political spectrum. Men and tendencies from Giolitti and the Giolittians to Gramsci and the *ordinovisti*, from Einaudi and Albertini to the extreme socialist left, were all convinced of the necessity for a new order in the relations between capital and wage-labour. Everyone said they were living through a moment of transition, of passage. But towards what, with what means, by what stages? It is against such a scale that the declarations of these days must be measured.

One question, however, must be asked first. Was there at this moment, if there had not been on 12 September, within any political group, any very clear sensation of having missed the great 'revolutionary moment'? This is the key problem, the crux of the controversy which racked the workers' movement when it was all over, after September 1920.

One striking piece of evidence from outside Italy is the testimony of Paul Levi, president of the German Communist Party, in an interview with *Avanti*. It shows what hopes were being cherished in the international communist movement and what criticism was already being directed at the PSI. Paul Levi claimed that a great revolutionary class action was in train, but that the masses lacked 'a clear revolutionary objective' to work for, because nobody gave them the necessary word. Nobody, least of all the party.

'It is my firm belief,' said Levi, 'that the party runs the risk of succumbing to general inertia if, at this moment, it does not seize the reins of the movement, master events and become a motor force.'[3]

Should it then launch the revolution? Paul Levi thought that even 'if the time has not yet come to establish the Italian soviet republic', the time was certainly ripe for the slogan of political councils, the institution of a national workers' power as a rival to the bourgeois state.

This testimony is interesting because, given its date (14-15 September), it seems to be the first public declaration by a representative of the Third International. The International's Executive was to take the same line. It further anticipates the bitter criticism of the PSI which was to be common to that Executive and the communist groups in Italy which promoted the Livorno schism. Within ten days, Lenin himself spoke of events in Italy, given a new twist by the reformist success:

> Events in Italy must open the eyes of even the most obstinate of those who see no danger in *unity* and *peace* with the Crispiens and Dittmanns. *When it comes to the point of actual revolution* (Lenin's emphasis) the Italian Crispiens and Dittmanns (Turati, Prampolini and D'Aragona) at once do their best to *obstruct* the revolution in Italy.[4]

A genuine revolution: absence of the party: reformist sabotage: these were the master-themes of the Third International's analysis, as 1921 was to show. At the time, reactions in Italy were more nuanced and varied. On the party and its 'absence', one independent reformist curiously echoed the German and Russian communists. This was Giovanni Ansaldo in *Il Lavoro*: 'In short,' he wrote, 'this is the situation in Italy: a movement of a political nature, along class lines, begins and ends under the direction of trade union organizations and the socialist party itself does not assume the leadership.'[5]

And the men of the party? The first impression is that the PSI leadership was fairly satisfied with the turn things had taken and relieved by the settlement. As early as 20 September, Giacinto

Menotti Serrati, four days back from Russia, reflected this satisfaction in very measured terms, adding a few reservations useful to his polemic with the *ordinovisti*. Serrati, observing that the economic struggle had ended in a settlement which registered a notable working-class victory from the trade union viewpoint, added:

> The principle of sacred private property has been violated. For twenty days the red flag flew over the factories and armed workers went on working and producing in defiance of the exploiters. Now the bosses surrender. They pay increases. They pay arrears. They pay annual holidays. And they bend before the government's order to re-employ all workers without victimizing those who took part in the movement.[6]

And from the political point of view? It was also a victory for Giolitti, replied the editor of *Avanti*. A limited victory, since the occupation of the factories was only the first blow against the big bourgeoisie. Others would follow. What left Serrati totally dissatisfied was the formula of union control:

'It is evident,' he wrote,

> that the control won over the factories, once it starts to work, can only be either mystification or corruption. Control in itself is collaboration. If it becomes effective, it will inevitably transform workers into interested aides to bourgeois management.

The *ordinovisti* were naturally very sensitive on the point. In the Piedmont *Avanti* (the weekly *L'Ordine Nuovo* suspended publication throughout September) Togliatti wrote on 17 September that class control could not tolerate equivocal forms of collaboration. The creation of councils had value only if it was conceived as the conscious initiation of a revolutionary process. The exercise of control had meaning only if it were an act, a moment, of that process.

As for the Giolittian decree: on the day it was officially promulgated, 19 September, the Turin communists added a note to Serrati's comment:

> The decree on workers' control in the factories is a skilful bourgeois manoeuvre. It has the clear political purpose of preserving the regime. Industrialists who hesitate, for authoritarian or technical reasons, are short-sighted. Giolitti saves their old tub by dumping as much ballast as possible.[7]

Giolitti in short was trying to break the proletarian bloc and establish himself immovably as the saviour of a country trapped between bosses and workers, by nudging them both into a common enterprise of collaboration within the factories. But his manoeuvre, ended the note, would not succeed. Workers' control was a stage, not an end. It was a strategic position to be captured in preparation for the new struggle of the morrow.

As the days passed, the position of the Turin communists was strengthened by reactions from the factories and other critical and polemical responses. It is nevertheless significant that this combination of hostility towards the conservative character of the settlement with a certain satisfaction, an optimistic tone, was common (though with different reservations and from different motives) to the entire socialist movement.[8]

On the extreme left, only the anarchists returned a totally negative verdict. On 20 September, Errico Malatesta wrote in *Umanità Nova*:

> The workers come out of the factories feeling betrayed. They will come out, but with anger in their hearts and revenge in their minds. They will come out this time, but they will profit from the lesson. They will not 'work more and consume less', so the crisis will not be resolved. The revolution remains both imminent and necessary.

Even in this quarter, there was the conviction that the revolutionary process was still at flood tide.[9]

That this feeling was widespread (or spread wide) on the other side is obvious from the conservative press. *Il Corriere della Sera* deserves particular reference, not only because of the polemical presence it asserted throughout the conflict, but because of the personal activity of Albertini, who pushed more prudent men like Luigi Einaudi and Giovanni Amendola, the other two authentic voices of the paper, towards more extreme positions. The line of the Milanese paper was coherent through the week which ended in the Rome agreement and even more so afterwards. On 16 September, Luigi Einaudi had written that 'reason and sentiment counsel the industrialists' to give way on control, to put an end to 'a state of affairs which cannot long continue without the state decomposing and disintegrating'.[10] When Giolitti's imperious act followed the next day, Albertini supported the arguments of his distinguished collaborator: the industrialists had to submit.

But out of this acceptance of the hard necessities of the hour, grew a new and violent attack on the government, on its 'last-minute intervention'[11] which might have thrown the game to the workers' leaders. To Giovanni Amendola fell the duty of expressing, though with a certain indeterminacy of language, the most obvious fear of his director, expressed to him privately as early as 15 September: that the authority of the state had emerged from the conflict so crippled that its total collapse could be averted only by the most courageous act of decision. 'The fall of a regime can be painful,' wrote Amendola, 'but nothing is more wretched than the agony of thoughtlessness and inconsequence in which a society declines.'[12] But what decision? The decision, to be precise, to compel the CGL and the parliamentary socialists to assume the responsibilities of power.

The allusion, quite patent in Amendola's note ('The many, reconciled under the tutelage of all the political powers party to the dispute and ensured of their communal protection tomorrow, seem infinitely preferable to the few who abandon us day by day') became an explicit statement of position on 21 September, when the director of *Il Corriere della Sera* argued: 'Today, would not a government of the best men of socialism and the trade unions be less dangerous, stronger, than a government of these accomplices of our perdition?'

Albertini did not stop at a hope. He went to find Turati and put his proposal to him. The incident, which must have occurred around 21-23 September, was publicly admitted by Albertini three years later[13] and confirmed by Turati who, however, demoted it to a mere 'exchange of ideas'.[14] In whose name and in what capacity could Albertini offer power to the socialists?

More interesting is the strictly conservative explanation he offered for his conduct in 1923. This was a double argument. Certainly, he was to write then, better D'Aragona and Turati in office than anarchy. In the circumstances, 'the shameful agony' of 1920, 'the inevitable consequence of a regime which was no longer functioning, which was corrupted by impotence in all its organs, would have been anarchist communism'. In 1923, however, Albertini stressed the other motive. 'But above all else, I was hoping for a profound reaction from the bourgeoisie; that reaction which has fortunately come and of which the Hon. Mussolini has been the organizer.'[15]

Turati and Treves in September 1920 were deeply reluctant

to move in the direction indicated by Albertini. It is a reluctance which can be called historical, for it reappears in every crisis of the first twenty years of the century. It was the reformists' fear of not being followed by the party and the masses, of forming a government doomed from the start and abandoned as such by the bourgeoisie. It was no accident that in *Il Resto del Carlino*, even before Treves rejected the suggestion, Mario Missiroli judged Albertini's proposal 'too simplist' and said that 'the tragic quality of the situation lies precisely in this, the impossibility of a change of government which could calm the spirit and impose a new order on conscience'.[16]

Some days later, in the same paper, Treves replied to Albertini. The reformists in the socialist party could not assume power as isolated individuals, because they would assume 'an impotent power'. They could not and would not take power as a party. Perhaps, Treves quizzed Albertini, he wanted an 'all-engulfing power'? 'In any case,' he said, 'they would not restore order, the only kind of order the spiteful and malcontent bourgeoisie of *Il Corriere della Sera* understands.' Treves then turned to that theme which was so common (in its many variations) to the whole socialist movement and to much of that Giolittian bourgeois-democratic movement which shared so much ground with it, that it constituted a vital subjective reality: the conviction that this was an historic crisis whose inevitable outcome was a socialist revolution – whether that revolution was envisaged as a gradual mutation of the relations between capital and labour or as a violent rupture of established order.

Albertini asked himself in anguish – 'How do we get out of it?' Treves replied in drastic terms: 'We do not get out of it.' 'This so-called crisis is a revolution. We are in it and we will stay in it, who knows, for quite some time, until the cycle, which may last for years, is closed.'[17] All that Turati's collaborator would concede to his opponent was this: 'We can hope and we can act because the revolution which fulfils itself hour by hour, skirts the rock of civil war, avoids the savage onset of conflict, and in every day, every hour, completes its simultaneous work of destruction and reconstruction, without unnecessary brutality.' It was at this point that Albertini was to cry – as he recalled three years later – If you take power, there will be some hope of a 'salutary reaction' from the bourgeoisie.[18]

In the conservative press there was a widespread sense of defeat. *L'Idea Nazionale* spoke repeatedly of a capitulation by the industrialists. Mussolini in *Il Popolo d'Italia* went further still; he was at once peremptory and lyrical: 'What has happened in Italy in this September which dies, has been a revolution,' he wrote, 'one can say a great revolution. A many-centuried juridical relationship has been broken. The worker as producer breaks into the sanctuary which was denied him and conquers the right to control all economic activity in which he plays a part.'[19]

The public statements of many industrialists struck an apocalyptic note. Harsh protests jostled threats of swift revenge – to which Mussolini in the same article promised his support, if the 'bolsheviks' mastered this 'revolution'. In Milan, an employer told an interviewer from *Il Secolo*: 'What they propose is a disaster. But what can we do except submit to Giolitti's diktat?' And Jarach: 'Very well then! We say what *Avanti* said after the defeat of the Turin metal strike. Beaten but not conquered! If we have lost, that does not mean we were wrong to fight.' In Turin, the president of the industrial league resigned in protest against the settlement.

A quite different note was sounded by that Giolittian-reformist movement which was so close to government policy. Alfredo Frassati in *La Stampa* intoned a hymn to the President of the Council in unwontedly epic terms:

'Commonsense,' he wrote, 'has won a great victory. The accord between industrialists and metalworkers which cowards, preachers of catastrophe, the lividly sectarian, had pronounced impossible, has been achieved . . . The government's liberal and therefore conciliatory policy has built a bridge to reconciliation for the contending interests. Thanks to the accord, the madness of both revolution and reaction simultaneously crumbles. The rhythm of social destiny proceeds uninterrupted.'[20]

Communism had been warded off, added the director of the Turin paper, thanks to the prudence and equanimity of Giolitti:

> Just as Cavour put himself at the head of the revolution, channelled it into liberal institutions and drew from its contradictory politico-moral elements that unifying force which was to create the Kingdom of Italy, so today Giolitti has mastered the incandescent stuff of a vast social conflict and, containing the extremist elements on one side and the other, intervening at the precise moment, has succeeded in channelling this material towards parliament, to extract from it a new norm of law, to give new and fecund peace to labour. An essentially political rev-

olution in those days, a more peculiarly economic revolution now, but then and now, a revolution dominated and controlled by the state, with the force and in the service of, the liberal ideal. The conservatives who opposed Cavour then cannot understand Giolitti now.[21]

No different, if more concrete, were the words of *Il Secolo* of Milan, in whose columns Attilio Cabiati stressed the profound distinction between union control, 'a democratic principle now applicable', and factory councils, a revolutionary institution which the agreement had rejected.[22] But in closest consonance with the Giolittian interpretation of *La Stampa* was *Critica Sociale*, where Claudio Treves wrote:

> The notion of an immediate catastrophe of the whole bourgeois regime and a revolutionary seizure of power by the proletariat dissolves. That revolutionary gradualness which is consonant with reality asserts itself in the brilliant proposition of the Confederation of Labour, to which, with the consent of the party directorate, the socialist group in parliament promptly offers the support of legislative action. From this new, full and radical application of the method which we have constantly recommended, there opens out an immense consensus among the proletariat and those strata which have suffered most from the agonies of this convulsive and tormented aftermath of the war.[23]

Luigi Salvatorelli struck a similar balance. 'This victory of gradualism,' he wrote in *La Stampa* on 29-30 September,

> cannot represent an isolated act, a momentary solution. It acquires maximum value, it signifies a direction, it implies a general programme. It signifies an undertaking by the gradualists to work in continuous coherence and inexhaustible energy so that the crisis of the capitalist regime in Italy works itself out in harmony with the peculiar conditions of our country and its national economy, does not climax in a single violent or destructive shock. So that the transformation of the economic structure of society is accomplished without a dissolution of its wealth.

If the rapprochement between reformist socialists and Giolittian democrats was thus perfect, it is not surprising that an independent observer, reformist but anti-Giolittian *par excellence* like Gaetano Salvemini found himself sharing the opinion of no less anti-Giolittian revolutionaries like Gramsci and his friends. So the *Unità* school cultivated their suspicions of the Giolittian system with its corporative-protectionist economy and its suffocating politics. In both camps, it was the conservative character of the statecraft of the 'man of Dronero' which was spotlit.

L'Unità drew a parallel between workers' control and universal suffrage, two moments of the same Giolittian technique: 'So once again,' said the Florentine journal,

> Giolitti goes far beyond the hopes of the most ardent reformists and manages to appear more socialist than the socialists. But behind the façade, his game is always profoundly conservative. He is trying, at the price of serious disturbance in industrial life, to keep power in the hands of the traditional ruling cliques. By anticipating and universalizing under the rule of law, a conquest for which the working masses are totally unprepared, he has already succeeded in devaluing the conquest in the opinion of the most intransigent, who already dismiss it as one more of so many trivialities. In this way, he robs it of that identity as an unambiguously and powerfully revolutionary weapon which it ought to have. At the same time, he imposes a pattern on it with the aid of bureaucrats of the ministry and bureaucrats of the workers' organizations, and succeeds in turning it into an instrument which will certainly be harmful to industry, but innocuous in terms of that objective of political-administrative conservatism which he has set himself.[24]

Salvemini's words could have been those of the Turin communists.[25] For them, Giolitti the conservative was ever an enemy to the revolution, on a level with the 'union mandarins', while for Salvemini, he was the corrupter of democracy who, dragging with him the social democrats, was preparing 'the decisive triumph of reformist maximalism'.

At all events, Salvemini was perceptive on the effects which Giolitti's manoeuvre would have on the workers' movement:

> It is true that workers' control could repeat the history of universal suffrage. At first it will serve the ends of the man who has unexpectedly and prematurely granted it, but later, little by little, it will regain its power to renew and transform. In the meantime, however, what matters to Giolitti and the groups he defends is to ward off an immediate collision at the moment when it seems most menacing, to create splits and suspicions in the enemy camp, so as to be able to build new defences. And this time, moreover, the game has worked out better for him than he perhaps hoped. The socialist schism which is now certain and which has in part been accelerated by the outcome of the conflict

in the metal industry, can be considered in a certain sense, a victory for Giolitti.

To establish the limits of that victory, one has to look to 1921, when Giolitti's 'new defences', against both fascism and the socialist party itself after the schism, proved insufficient to restore the old equilibrium, which had been finally dislocated by the crisis of 1920.

9.
The Last Week

On 19 September, when the agreement was being signed in Rome, the workers were spending their third Red Sunday in occupation. Their situation was not happy. For most of them it was painful. For three, sometimes four weeks, they had been without wages. Proletarian solidarity was hard pressed to meet their most elementary needs. Euphoria, the hopeful anticipation of revolution, had faded. Bitterness and disillusionment displaced it, above all among those men in whom the flame had burned brightest.

But it is not possible to capture in a single phrase either the condition or the state of mind of the workers. There was too much variation, from place to place, factory to factory, even within the same workshop. Some entries from the diary of a communist worker in Turin during the days of 'the turn', 18-19 September, give the measure of the contradiction:

> 16 September: great agitation among the workers. Lively discussion of yesterday's events and our failure to react. We saw defeat looming. In the factories practically nobody worked. Between us and the sector committee there were many contacts, discussions, meetings of workshop commissars. A sense of weariness everywhere now. On the 16th and 18th, the absence of many workers noted, about 60. The workers' discouragement grew. A hundred lire on account were given to every worker, the exchange of production material continued. The guards had to be increased because the disappearance of tools had been spotted. On the 19th the thieves were caught. Two workers who later turned out to be spies. The making of bombs was stopped. Great struggle between us and the reformists who wanted to withdraw the guards and take away their weapons. During the night, several shots were fired.[1]

It was working-class Turin which at this moment presented the richest and most moving spectacle: in its shocks and alarms, its deeds of blood, the intense political debate kindled among its workers, in its resistance to the settlement. The explanation is essentially structural. In no other city was the occupation so strong, armed, uniform, organized. No other city was so dedicated to workers' control. From the first days of the occupation, the organizing committees went into action at the *camera del lavoro*; committees for purchase and sale, exchange and production, credit, subsidies, kitchens. The purchase-sale committee (directed by the engineer Romita) channelled all proceeds into a single fighting fund; the exchange and production committee mobilized all available means of transport and technical personnel for common use.

The factory councils were the disciplined core of this whole complex of activity in workers' management. They delegated specific and determinate functions to particular sub-sections of their executive committees: provisioning, subsidies, kitchens, internal discipline, defence, propaganda. 'Workshop commissars,' said a technician who took part, 'were in every department representatives of workers' power and executors of the orders of the factory council. Their work was not only valuable; it was essential.'[2]

Largely because of this capacity for organization, absenteeism in Turin was low (on average some 10 per cent of the workforce), production considerable, and not only at Fiat.[3] But for that very reason, it was these people who were hit all the harder by the compromises which took shape at the Turin meeting, to harden with the signing of the Rome agreement. The first responses were confused. The Piedmont *Avanti* itself talked of 'a resounding and indestructible victory'.[4] But very soon, disillusionment and uncertainty set in, as the general committee hurried to call on workers to continue the occupation and wait calmly for decisions from the competent organizations. Restlessness broke out into shooting affrays between red guards and the security forces, particularly at night. On the 19th a workman was killed in front of the Beccio e Grava foundry. On the 22nd, a brigadier of the *carabinieri* was fatally wounded outside Fiat-Centro and at the Gilardini plant there was a full-scale battle in the streets: a royal guard and a passer-by were killed and there were many wounded among both police and workers. The next day, two bodies were discovered – a young nationalist, Mario Sonzini, and a prison warder, Costantino Scimula. The trial two years later unmasked a brutal murder.[5] *Avanti* had to warn workers not to succumb to the disastrous temptations of individualist anarchism, to put them on guard against provocations which could serve only the interest of the employers.

Among the revolutionary vanguard the political reaction was no less sharp. Turin was the only city in which the future split in socialism was anticipated in the factories, to take even the communist leadership by surprise. The workers of the Bordiga abstentionist fraction of Fiat-Centro, led by Giovanni Parodi, took the lead. Meeting on the night of 20 September, the militants of the fraction bitterly denounced the trade union and political leadership of the PSI. They decided 'no longer to share responsibility with those elements, but to separate themselves from the official socialist party and to constitute themselves into a revolutionary communist party. They therefore call on all comrades who share their principles to join the communist party . . .'[6]

The Neapolitan leaders of the fraction[7] as well as the Turin *ordinovisti*[8] reined in this impatience. They all thought the split premature. They did not imagine, however, that it could be avoided. The Turin socialist section now thought the formation of a communist party inevitable: an automatic consequence of the factory occupation and the line taken towards it by the leaders of the PSI.[9]

But the workers' reaction was mixed, even in Turin. On the one hand, there was a massive sense of relief (did not the proletarian press itself talk of victory?); on the other, there was the vexed question of payment for the workdays of the occupation, which had been referred to local arbitration. In Turin, where they had produced so much during the three weeks, workers were peculiarly sensitive on the point.[10]

The situation in Genoa, Milan and Florence was no different, though the contours were less clear-cut: satisfaction, disillusionment, hope and regret, uncertainty and worry. In Genoa, the men of the USI in their Sestri Ponente stronghold played on the discontent. The response of the USI to the Rome agreement, as may be imagined, was totally hostile. They denounced it as a betrayal and did not consider themselves bound by it.[11] In Sestri on 21 September, a meeting presided over by Borghi, Negro and Giovannetti, passed a resolution calling on workers not to abandon the factories under any circumstances. But the majority of the workers in the industrial areas seemed ready enough to quit. There was a striking gesture of solidarity with the metalworkers of Genoa in the last days, from the powerful co-operative movement of the port and maritime workers.[12] The *camera del lavoro* had distributed food credit-vouchers to the workers in occupation, to be presented at the private shops which usually supplied working-class families. Not one shopkeeper refused those vouchers. The council movement in the factories, however, remained sporadic and ill-co-ordinated. After two weeks of occupation, the co-ordinating committee was still begging the workers to prepare lists of factory council members.[13] There was some disorder and violence in Sestri between the 21st and the 24th: a bomb was thrown at the *carabinieri* barracks. But this was essentially a matter of individual exasperation directed especially at the white-collar workers who had refused to rally to the cause.

In Milan, overt opposition to the settlement was even weaker; here there was neither a strong communist current nor an audacious revolutionary-syndicalist alternative. This does not mean there was no reaction. Though he did not dare propose a rejection of the agreement, whose economic gains were widely appreciated, Schiavello submitted a resolution to the internal commissions of the metal trades which expressed a general distrust of the CGL leadership 'which no longer corresponds to the political and union thinking of the masses themselves' and voiced disquiet because 'the movement in the metal trades could have and should have been exploited to the limit by a broad political movement which entirely corresponded to the aspirations of the proletariat'.[14] The resolution was carried.

Milan was typical. Everywhere, the most combative minority, which had led the factory movement, were disillusioned and indeed very hostile to the settlement. The majority, by now weary and confused, yielded to it gladly, and concentrated instead on wringing some payment for the days of occupation out of individual managements.

The FIOM referendum reflected this range of response. No organized force opposed it. The revolutionary syndicalists preached abstention in Sestri and fomented some trouble in Verona and Brescia, but this was a flash in the pan.[15] The anarcho-syndicalists themselves realized that the game was lost. Errico Malatesta, in some bitterness, admitted it two years later:

> Every factory was afraid of being left isolated in the struggle. Because of this fear, and the difficulty of feeding the different garrisons, everyone surrendered, despite the opposition of a handful of individual anarchists. The movement simply could not last unless it were broadened and generalized.[16]

With a compromise already settled, the referendum was a walk-over. There were some uncertainties – trouble in Livorno over payment for occupation workdays,[17] the government eager to finish things off in a hurry[18] – but the result of the referendum was a foregone conclusion. Everywhere prudence prevailed: the prudence of the less committed, of those masses who, in a different situation, had cherished 'extremist' hopes, but now no longer believed in them. Gramsci explained it in theoretical terms: 'The form of a referendum is exquisitely democratic and anti-revolutionary. It gives weight to, and exploits, the amorphous masses; it breaks the vanguards who direct and give a political consciousness to those masses.'[19] A revolutionary movement could be founded only on a proletarian vanguard, and had to operate without 'prior consultation' and an apparatus of representative assemblies.

Gramsci also seemed to respond to the argument of the Milanese militants in the Schiavello resolution, and to respond to it in a self-critical manner:

> The proletarian vanguard, today disillusioned and on the point of disintegration, should ask itself: is the responsibility ours? It is a fact that, within the CGL, there is no single organized opposition, concentrated at the centre and able to exercise control over the bureaucracy; in a position not only to substitute one man for another, but one method for another, one objective for another, one will for another.

This perspective was to become central a few years later, when Gramsci was arguing for a reappraisal of the policies of the *ordinovista* group. For the moment, he simply called on the vanguard to work for 'a tighter, more disciplined, better-organized activity' in future.

Militants and leaders in other cities said the same thing in simpler terms. In Florence, the workers were to remember even thirty years later the comment on the referendum made by the popular Ruggero Chiarini of the Muzzi: 'Boys, we have to have a referendum. If we say yes, we move out of the factory; if we say no, they boot us out.'[20] According to the prefect in Naples, Bordiga, a week after his return from Moscow, was saying to a thousand workers of the Bacini on the 21st, 'For the moment, the proletarian class must strike the red flag and abandon the factories. We must postpone the struggle to overthrow the bourgeois regime to a more opportune moment.'[21]

Before the referendum, an extraordinary congress of FIOM approved the federation's conduct by a large majority.[22] Only the anarchists who led the Turin section, Ferrero and Garino, were critical. Only a minority of the metalworkers took part in the referendum on the 24th. By now, absenteeism was massive and only small groups stood guard within the factories. In some lesser centres, like Udine with its 400-strong steelworks, and some individual plants in the great cities, work restarted after agreement on payment for occupation workdays. Elsewhere, work stopped completely. The defences were dismantled. In many factories, particularly in Turin, the communist workers who had organized armed defence hid the weapons in the countryside or walled them up in warehouses.[23] Some were to be used against fascist expeditions later. Others were rounded up by the police. The booty was sparse.

The first referendum returns, from 133 centres, on the 25th, showed 127,904 'yes' votes, 44,531 'no', with 3,006 abstentions. In all the great cities the 'yes' majority was substantial: in Milan, 23,571 against 6,668 (with 1,455 abstentions), Genoa, 2,944 against 47 (222 abstentions), Voltri, 2,477 against 23. In Sampierdarena, there were 3,692 'yes' against 458 'no'; the Ciampi steelworks refused to vote, thanks to the anarcho-syndicalists. The narrowest majority was in Turin – further proof of the climacteric which the occupation was in that city – 18,740 against 16,909, with 1,204 abstentions (in Fiat-Centro the 'yes' were 6,000 and the 'no' 4,000). Results were similar in lesser centres where the *metalos* were few in number, though there were some rejections because of local circumstances (Livorno and Rome were against, Naples, Alessandria, Pisa, La Spezia, Bologna and Brescia for).

The evacuation, between the 25th and the 30th, passed off quietly, sometimes in bitterness, sometimes in joy, often in solemnity. At the Galileo in Florence, for example, the workers marched out on the 30th, in procession, red flags flying. It was the spectators who took down the flags still flying over the stacks. In Milan, the evacuation took place on the 25th and 26th. Sometimes there was a farewell banquet, as in the Radaelli plant and the Milan foundry. In Turin the big factories were evacuated only on the 30th, generally after favourable settlements on occupation working days. Here the leave-taking was at once more solemn and more caustic. This was particularly true at Fiat-Centro, which had been the pilot-plant for the whole movement. Giovanni Parodi described the scene on 30 September:

> Between 8 and 9, the whole labour force gathered in the great workshops, in two large assemblies. The comrades of the council explained the terms of the agreement; its implications were made clear. They referred once more to the ultimate objective, which had not been achieved, but had not been forgotten. The meetings were supposed to end at 9, but for more than two hours, the workers stayed in the *corso Dante* outside the gates and in the inner courtyards. They were waiting for the bosses who were to come to take over again. Around 11.30, a long, angry whistle like an alarm signal, a howl of pain, announced the arrival of the blacklegs, returning to their posts with an escort of thugs. A great shout greeted them, a cry which was all protest, all promise – *Evviva i Soviet!* The bosses passed, livid, between two ranks of red guards, halting before the council of the factory in full assembly . . .[24]

Parodi handed Agnelli a list of 'blacklegs and thieves', warning him that if he re-employed the former, he would have to re-employ the latter. Naturally, the council did not indicate which was which! This was an armistice, not a peace treaty. Agnelli himself recognized this a few days later. He formally proposed, if the workers' organizations agreed, to transform Fiat into a co-operative. In an interview with *La Gazzetta del Popolo*, Agnelli said:

> Under the present system, relations between management and workers are simply impossible. The masses today no longer have a mind to work. They are moved only by political notions. Their recent gains are nothing to them. Their leaders make no mystery of the fact. The workers themselves do not hide it. How can one build anything with the help of 25,000 enemies?[25]

Agnelli's proposal was rejected by the workers' leaders and the socialists of Turin. They rejected it on principle and for trade union reasons.[26] It was, however, symptomatic of the defeatism to which some employers succumbed and which, in a sense, justified the optimism which flooded the workers' movement, straining at the leash for new victories, even if divided over stages, methods and means. From the trade union point of view, in any case, Bruno

Buozzi was not mistaken when he said, several years later, that 'the victory of the metalworkers has no parallel in the whole history of the international workers' movement'.[27] And other workers, within a few days, followed the *metalos*.

The occupation ended, moreover, without struggle, without violence, without pillage. During a movement which for nearly a month, throughout the country, involved over half a million workers, barricaded in factories with arms at their disposal, only a few instances of violence were recorded. There can be no more telling testimony to the maturity and human generosity of the movement.

Gaetano Salvemini, in some heavily documented pages written in exile and loaded with unchallengeable statistics, unmasks the myth of 'bolshevik violence'.[28] Throughout the *biennio*, according to fascist sources, 'subversives' were responsible for thirty homicides. In Turin during the occupation, five members of the security forces and one young nationalist perished; so did three workers. In one single day, 18 December 1922, the Turin fascists killed 21 people. Press reports during 1919-20, as Salvemini stresses, list 65 victims of workers' violence against 109 'bolsheviks' killed by the police in street battles and 22 killed by other persons.

Police sources for September 1920 confirm the bloodless character of the occupation, the minimal relevance of disorder and violence and attacks on property to the vast majority of arrests. Here and there, workers broke open the safes in company offices. They sometimes found documents, hardly ever any money and then only in derisory quantity. The employers had decided on the lockout in their own good time; their money was safely put away.

During the debates in the Senate on 25-27 September, the Ministers of Labour and Justice, Labriola and Fera, and Giolitti himself were subjected to a barrage of questions and interjections. No one mentioned theft or homicide. The real indictment of the government was its failure to use state power against the violation of the principle of private property. To everything, Giolitti replied with one of his rare ironies. Confronted with a movement of 500,000 workers, what was one to do – summon them all to the nearest police court?

As the occupation of the factories was ending, news came in from the South of the occupation of estates and uncultivated land: from Palermo, Cosenza, Caltanissetta, Caserta.[29] In essence, they were similar to those which had been going on, sporadically but frequently, for months; they affected a total of some 30,000 hectares occupied without consent of the owners and about 60,000 occupied by agreement.[30] In the context of the total area of cultivable land (27 million hectares) this was a modest movement. It had no direct connexion with the occupation of the factories. Its promoters, almost everywhere, were local sections of the Popular Party or of the ex-combatants' associations. In the autumn of 1920, the movement was linked to the local elections which were imminent.

A long essay could be written on the socialist and working-class organizations' indifference to this movement, on what might have happened had the peasants' movement been fused with that of the metalworkers. The PSI projected such a union in purely propagandist terms at the start of the agitation, but the game was lost, even as an opportunity for agitation, in the course of the struggle. Federterra was opposed. The notion, then, of an historic moment which could have seen the simultaneous and massive invasion of both industrial factories and agrarian estates is a myth. The movements, on the contrary, were quite separate, each with its own absolutely independent dynamic. Even the agitation of the farm workers of the Po Valley, which became intense in the autumn of 1920, was completely distinct from the land occupations in the South.

Leaders of the international communist movement were to indict the PSI and its irresolution, in strongly polemical terms, precisely over this issue. The passion of controversy, however, and perhaps a simple lack of information, led the spokesmen of the communist International to talk of a common movement in town and countryside in terms which bore no relation whatever to reality. It is enough to quote Karl Radek at the Third Congress of the International:

> As the workers in metal, in textiles and in chemicals occupy the factories and show yesterday's bosses the door, so masses of proletarians without a roof to their heads, move into action, occupy the villas and the palaces of the rich and install their wives and children. The movement extends to the countryside. Beginning in Sicily and moving on to southern and central Italy, the peasants march, red flags at their head, to seize the great estates and form the red guard.[31]

10.
Was it really
the Revolutionary Moment?

'After the occupation of the factories, the union rank and file *felt*, in a confused way, that they had been defeated, but did not see clearly how or by whom.'[1] Armando Borghi's comment serves to open discussion on the extraordinary experience of September 1920. All observers, when they reflect on the 'turn' of the autumn, stress contradiction. Giovanni Agnelli's bitter comments at the end of the occupation have been noted. A few days before the proprietor of Fiat offered to turn the firm into a co-operative, Albertini urged Turati to enter the government. 'His action was a surrender to despair,' say Salvatorelli and Mira; but they add, 'Albertini was reduced to this state just at the point when his colleagues of the high bourgeoisie had already emerged from it or were beginning to emerge'.[2] Within a few weeks the big landowners unleashed squadrism in Emilia; anti-socialist reaction began to gather strength in the cities. The first hints of a plan, as yet vague, to resist working-class 'violence' in arms, were picked up by the government as the occupation of the factories was ending.[3]

That plan swiftly became reality. Gabriele de Rosa writes of the transition:

> The workers' movement emerged from this struggle enervated and disillusioned. The factory owners swore never to forgive the workers for the offence done to their rights as proprietors. They also cherished a blind rancour against Giolitti who had forced them to a settlement and who had categorically refused to allow the security forces to expel the workers from the plants. From this situation, fascism soon 'took courage'. It exploited the weariness of the workers and the thirst for vengeance of the proprietory bourgeoisie. It became more aggressive just at the point when Giolitti thought he had imposed the authority of the state on both industrialists and unions.[4]

Many commentators agree on the point. Angelo Tasca, for example, follows de Rosa.[5] He in turn insists on both the psychological shock suffered by the bourgeoisie, which explains its subsequent 'subversive' fury and on the disillusionment of the workers who 'had drunk from the intoxicating springs of free production only to find themselves at the end in the atmosphere of a wake -- and, more seriously, without perspective on the future'. Pietro Nenni and Federico Chabod offer a similar interpretation.[6] Their writings bring into focus the crux of the debate: the occupation was the climax of the postwar social and political crisis. From that point, the work of 'bourgeois restoration' began; to be more exact, the fascist reaction gathered momentum – that reaction which was to destroy the old liberal state along with the socialist movement.

Had the 'vanquished' then triumphed, while the 'victors', whether workers or government, lost? Was the 'great fear' of the bourgeoisie transformed into an extraordinary reflex thrust for revenge? Only serious analysis, free from myth, can answer these questions – an analysis of that shock which brought the 'machine' of bourgeois power shuddering to its foundations but did not bring it to collapse. Indeed the paradox is that the shock was sufficient to provoke a reactionary movement, which proved the more successful the less a collapse seemed imminent.

The crisis of constitutional power taught the ruling classes, entrepreneurs and political establishment alike, a bitter lesson. They were all now obsessed with the need not only to create an anti-socialist bloc, but to erect new defences for the system, to elaborate new methods, a new apparatus for defensive and counter-offensive action. The prostration of the workers' movement facilitated this design, but its residual power made it all the more necessary.

Giolitti's conduct from the autumn of 1920 to June 1921 was symptomatic in that it reflected both aspects of the new situation: a renewed reactionary offensive and the persistence of a massive socialist movement.

Before the congress of Livorno, Giolitti was hoping to win the collaboration of the PSI or at least a section of it. After the congress, he was trying to manipulate the squadrist movement to preserve the existing balance of power, as he had manipulated the reformists in September 1920. His handling of the occupation had indeed been successful: he had reined in the extremism of both parties, saved the established order and thrown the socialist party into crisis. But this very success broke the equilibrium he thought he had maintained. It created the very conditions which made a subversive convulsion from the right possible; this he found he could not 'manage' as he had 'managed' the left.

Vilfredo Pareto had praised Giolitti's skill in giving his opponents enough rope to hang themselves – 'the Giolittian art of giving its head to the party he wanted to weaken, by allowing its errors free play': the danger, he added, was that the party so unbridled might plunge ahead too far.[7] So it was to prove with fascism. At the same time, Giolitti succeeded in breaking off reformists from communists, but the way the split happened made it impossible for the former openly to collaborate with the government without precipitating a further schism in the PSI. Neither Turati nor Treves could openly become government men.

Is it then correct to see the grave crisis of September 1920 as the direct and principal cause of the fascist reaction? Was there something fortuitous, disproportionate, fatally 'accidental' about the advent of so illiberal a class dictatorship at the very point when the old liberal regime had already defeated the revolution with *its own,* classic methods? Must we accept the theory of 'a preventive counter-revolution', so popular in anti-fascist circles after an Italian anarchist first suggested it?[8]

The first sign of a reactionary reflex in response to September was the bourgeois coalition which formed for the local elections of November 1920. This certainly was a first fruit of the 'fear' (but had not this kind of thing happened on so many other occasions, since 1904?). It did not, however, imply any general ('strategic' in today's jargon) re-alignment of forces on a national scale. The groups clustered around the socialists were not yet defeated (it is enough to note their success in the November elections)[9] nor was there any fascist predominance within the anti-socialist bloc. The occupation of the factories precipitated not so much a preventive counter-revolution as an active response, which remained a 'necessity' to the bourgeoisie throughout 1921. It is true, however, that this response found the proletarian bloc more divided and weaker than the bourgeoisie expected. This in itself set in motion the reactionary mechanism which was ultimately to overthrow even those liberal groups which still thought fascist support indispensable to curb the workers' movement.

This disaster was without doubt rooted in the events of September 1920. But two other factors need to be fully understood: the split in the socialist party, and the economic crisis which in 1921 robbed the working class of its bargaining power and hit it hard with mass dismissals in the metal and engineering sector. It was at that point that men began to perceive that the occupation of the factories had ended in defeat, that the working class at that moment had mobilized its full power to overthrow the old order and replace it with a new one, and was no longer capable of mobilizing again in short order. The 'political solution' devised by the CGL had been built on sand. Deceiving itself that it had anchored the ruling class in compromise, it was unable to avoid the worst.

The fate of the union control scheme was all too symptomatic. Now that the real relations of force had changed, the joint commission created by Giolitti did not manage to produce a single proposal; negotiations dragged on interminably. Giolitti himself presented his own plan in February 1921, but the Chamber never debated it. All the plans (those of the CGL, Confindustria, the CIL, the PPI and Giolitti's own) remained a dead letter.[10] No one talked about union control any more. As soon as the working class was no longer in a position to impose any real control at all over production and management, the whole monstrous paper debate sparked off in September – all the complex argument over class control, union control, state control, participation, the share-holding worker – crumpled.

The schism in the PSI gravely weakened the proletarian front. The events of September, which proved that the co-existence within the same organization of totally opposed groups and ideologies was no longer possible, lacerated party ranks. It was no accident that the debate over Moscow's '21 points' became so violent at the end of September. In immediate response, anger at the decisively anti-revolutionary role of the CGL and its reformist friends drove a majority of the PSI directorate in its meeting of 28 September-1 October to accept the 21 points, and by implication, the expulsion of Turati's followers.[11] Between October and December, however, the real incompatibility emerged: between the party in its traditional dichotomy of maximalist and reformist tendencies on the one hand, and on the other, the extreme wing of communists, now united in an authentic fraction. Not only was it impossible for *ordinovisti* and *turattiani* to co-exist within the same party; the distance which separated the 'unitarian' maximalists from the communists was now greater than that between the former and the reformists.

'The party,' said Nenni, 'was nothing but a great electoral

machine, equipped only for the struggle which, in theory, it repudiated.'[12] To Serrati, Lazzari, Bacci, it was utterly inconceivable that they should deprive themselves of those political and administrative forces and tendencies and those trade union organizations which were an essential historical ingredient of the party's identity. This was probably the root cause of the maximalist leadership's surrender to the either-or of D'Aragona: the prospect of having to go forward without the CGL, without the parliamentary group, without the men most closely associated with the Giolittian decade, was simply too bleak.

The communists, for their part, were unable then or earlier to win over the rank and file of the party, the worker and peasant masses, to a different programme of action on a national scale. At the Seventeenth Congress of the PSI, they suffered the consequences. They believed that a rupture with the reformists was inevitable; they shared Lenin's thesis that they could no longer remain prisoners of a party which had hesitated at the decisive moment.[13] In that choice – a vital element of contradiction which must not be forgotten – lay one lesson of September 1920: the lesson that the movement was charged with an offensive potential which the leadership had failed to mobilize. The demand for a new party was born of this perception.

Events, however, were to prove that this struggle, and its ending, strengthened the centrifugal rather than the centripetal forces of the socialist movement; demonstrated its insufficiencies, its vices, its inadequacy more than its strength, its energy, its *élan*. In this light, Gramsci's comment on the split of 1921 assumes its full, truly tragic meaning: 'The schism at Livorno, which detached a majority of the proletariat from the communist international, was without doubt reaction's greatest victory.'[14]

Gramsci expressed this opinion in 1923. But the full meaning of what has been called the tragedy of Italian socialism and its spectacular defeat – whose effects were to endure through a whole historical epoch – cannot be grasped unless another factor is borne in mind: the 'state of anticipation' which gripped the movement on the very morrow of the occupation, precisely in that arc of time, from the autumn of 1920 into 1921, in which the situation was transformed. That anticipation was to be brutally contradicted by reality. Widely diffused throughout the movement, nevertheless, was the conviction that the occupation of the factories had been a kind of dress rehearsal for revolution, one of its stages, its moments. This conviction was common to the men of *L'Ordine Nuovo*,[15] who were preparing, with their allies, to split the PSI in order to make it communist, to the Third International, even to the maximalists and reformists. Gramsci, like Lenin himself more acutely alert to the revolution-reaction dialectic, was still sure that the revolution was imminent in the autumn of 1920 and said so openly.[16] So were Lenin, Zinoviev and Bukharin, who addressed an appeal to the Italian working class at the end of October, in the name of the Third International.[17]

Not even Serrati's statements leave any doubt on the question, even if they introduce a different calculus of opportunity. He asserted that he was no less convinced than the communists of the revolutionary character of the crisis of autumn 1920 and of the need to profit from it; it was on tactics he differed.[18] Even reformists (recollect Treves's remarks to Albertini) not only in October 1920 but at the beginning of 1921, while pushing to the limit the distinction between 'revolutionary situation' and 'opportunity to make the revolution', contested neither the one nor the other; they simply suggested a more circumspect approach (and chronology). D'Aragona himself said to the CGL congress in Livorno in February 1921: 'I am among those who have always believed we are in a revolutionary period, and I am among those who have always said that they did not believe it would be easy when revolution broke out in Italy.'[19]

It was partly for this reason that the Third International's polemic against the PSI carried power. During the crucial period of the occupation itself, Moscow's opinion came very late, as we have seen. Comintern's comments of 1921 were nearly all couched in that accusing tone, which in Germany and Hungary no less than Italy, reflected its 'general line': seize every opportunity, inflame every revolutionary conflict, break with the opportunists – anything, even defeat, is preferable to inaction. This was the line throughout 1920.

Radek's criticism of the Italian socialists at the Third Congress of the Communist International in July 1921 was typical:

> We did not know whether, in these circumstances, the conquest of power was possible. But much could have been won, above all, real control over production. This would have been a way to concentrate and to arm the workers, spontaneously, in great proletarian organizations in confrontation with the capitalist state. If it was not possible to conquer power in this struggle, the

Italian working class would at least have fought a great battle against capitalism under the leadership of the communist party. Even if it had been defeated, it would have emerged from the struggle rich in experience and in lessons for the future.[20]

The attitude of the International's executive at the Third Congress generally reflects this line – but here, too, we run up against the general contradiction: the situation was now beginning to evolve in a totally opposite direction.

In this respect there is perhaps no document more eloquent – and more dramatically eloquent – than Serrati's letter to Jacques Mesnil of April 1921. 'Our old movement,' he said,

> is falling to pieces in a storm of violence without equal in any other country . . . Giolitti is irrelevant. Giolitti counts for nothing. That old hack of the old parliamentary routine called up the fascist devil to win an election and now he himself is its victim.

And he commented bitterly on the occupation of the factories:

> While everyone talked about revolution, no one prepared for it . . . The famous occupation of the factories, which was in fact a trade union action fully in harmony with the interests of the Giolittian bourgeoisie, was interpreted as a decisive revolutionary action; this was just a façade . . . Now, the bourgeoisie, frightened by our barking, bites back and bites blind. It defends itself ruthlessly by attacking first.[21]

Serrati's outburst certainly stimulates historians! It rehearses his immediate comments on the compromise of 'control' and on the 'victory' of Giolitti and his clientele. Yet even after the disastrous experience of the civil war of 1921-22, the debate circles back endlessly to the crucial point: was it possible, in the conditions of September 1920, to 'make the revolution'?

Between 1924 and 1930, some on the other side affirmed just that. Arturo Labriola, for example, writing in 1924, said that 'the socialists would have been able to take power without meeting appreciable resistance'.[22] Gaetano Salvemini, with the passage of time, tended to emphasize his scepticism, but in 1928, he could still write: 'If the leaders of the CGL and the PSI had wanted to strike a decisive blow, they had the opportunity. The bankers, the big industrialists, the big landowners, were waiting for the socialist revolution like a ram waits to be led to the slaughterhouse.'[23] Foreign observers like Pronteau and Palme Dutt also thought so: the revolution was possible, the classic conditions for a revolution were present.[24] Luigi Einaudi's general assessment is no less interesting: 'The situation would really have become revolutionary if the leaders of the socialist movement had exploited the revolt of the factory workers and moved to an assault on the regime.' He adds, however, that in an armed conflict, the rebels would have found it hard to win.[25]

The opinion of Giolitti, however, probably carries most weight. Not only because he was then at the helm and never lost confidence at any time in his ability to contain the workers' movement, but because his later views in no sense contradict the statements he made at the time.

> For me, this episode was a repetition, in different circumstances and different forms, of the famous experiment with a general strike in 1904, which created such fear only to demonstrate its own inanity. I was firmly convinced that the government should behave as it had behaved then: to let the experiment run its course to a certain point. The workers would then be convinced that their proposals were impracticable and the ringleaders would be deprived of the chance to throw responsibility for failure on to others.[26]

Ivanoe Bonomi's judgment is similar. He talks of neurosis, discounts the credibility of revolution and stresses one consequence: 'The occupation ended in the defeat of the extremist tendency in Italian socialism. The dead weight of failure irremediably burdened the socialist movement.'[27]

For Luigi Sturzo, who awarded the palm to Giolitti for his performance as the Old Fox of the crisis, 'the typical compromise all'italiana surmounted a dangerous phase in the development of the proletariat'.[28]

Among Italian communists, in the period 1921-24, during the emigration and after the Liberation, the verdict was uncompromising. Yes, the revolution could have been made and should have been made.[29] The men of L'Ordine Nuovo, however, were more judicious on the promise of September. Gramsci, in the heat of polemic against the socialists during the 1920s, never failed to use the occupation of the factories to lash them for their failure to give revolutionary leadership to the movement, but his more candid opinion can be found in a private letter to Zino Zini in 1924, where he wrote that, if power had been taken, 'with a party such as the socialist party then was, with a working class which mostly saw everything rosy and loved bands and ballads better than sacrifice, a counter-revolution would have inexorably swept us away'.[30]

As for Togliatti, he was to claim in 1951 'that the high peak of the movement was reached in the spring of 1920, when there was a general strike in Turin, in Piedmont, which threatened to engulf the whole of Italy'. 'When the occupation of the factories began,' he added, 'not only were there already signs of weariness; the socialist and militant groups were already well aware that the whole movement lacked a leadership capable of taking it to victory on either the economic or the political terrain.'[31]

Thirty years earlier and a year after the experience, Togliatti stressed another aspect which does not in fact contradict his later interpretation: the power which the Italian working class displayed in 1920, even in September, a power which, for the first time in Italian history, dominated the national political scene as an autonomous force, 'capable, in its turn, of creating new social relations'.[32]

Particularly interesting is the opinion of Luigi Fabbri of the libertarian movement, which approaches Togliatti's.

> That occasion (the occupation) revealed a power in the proletariat of which it had been unaware hitherto; the aspirations which exploded as a result were so sweeping that everyone sensed himself on the brink of victory. Looking back in cold blood, I think today that the moment for revolution had already passed, two or three months earlier. During July and August, the revolutionary temperature was already cooling. The police were becoming more hostile, the industrialists more surly.[33]

Leo Valiani of the Giustizia e Libertà movement, in his historical assessment, stressed above all the profound difference between the revolutionary crisis in Russia and that in Italy, where in contrast, there was no possibility of mobilizing a united front of workers, peasants and soldiers. But even here, the main emphasis is on the contradictions and uncertainties of the political leadership:

> The occupation of every factory in the country, if it had taken place under the aegis of the socialist party, would have given it the authority necessary to demand, and perhaps obtain, the resignation of the ministry and the formation of a socialist

government. But it was precisely this which the maximalist leadership was afraid of.[34]

Besides, even the reformists rejected this prospect, for the reasons Treves gave Albertini. And through twenty years of exile, their spokesmen never deviated from the arguments in favour of renunciation which they adduced at the moment of decision; to them, responsibility lay with the left wing of the movement, from the communists to the maximalists.

Outstanding, however, in its awareness that the whole movement bore the responsibility, was the bitter testimony of Bruno Buozzi, in which the doubts and perplexities which induced him to abstain during the convention of 10-11 September still echo:

The ex-secretary of FIOM wrote from his Parisian exile in 1935,

> To raise the question today of whether the occupation of the factories could have resulted in political action which would have prevented the rise of fascism and led Italy towards socialism is perhaps a waste of time. One thing, however, we must say if we want the experience of the past to serve as a lesson for the future: what the Italian socialist movement really lacked was decision . . . The party could make up its mind neither on revolution nor on participation in government. It did not understand that there are times when the worst road is the road of inaction . . . At a distance of fifteen years, we can state objectively that the main cause of the defeat of the Italian socialist movement was lack of decisiveness in the leading organizations of the party.[35]

Even at forty years' distance, the historical reconstruction of daily events tends to lend support to Buozzi's view. The basic contradiction was between the opportunity presented by some objective conditions and the failure of the principal subjective factor 'from the revolutionary point of view' – the proletarian party, which faded away at the moment of truth. As early as 1922, in the heat of controversy after the Livorno schism, Lenin had made the point, in a cutting rhetorical question: 'During the occupation of the factories, did even one single communist reveal himself?'[36]

In this at least, as his letter to Mesnil shows, Serrati was at one with Lenin.

None of the different groups which comprised the PSI strove for a share in government, even if many reformists wanted it; none of them dared take a revolutionary initiative, even if many communists and maximalists invoked it. They were all prisoners of each other. Agreement on common tactics, on 'transitional objectives' to show the masses how the revolution could in practice begin, was virtually unthinkable. A party so constructed could not fail to be taken by surprise by a moment which, as Togliatti justly says, saw the factory proletariat perhaps for the first time in the history of Italy since unification, emerge in full socialist momentum as a major protagonist in the political struggle. In this sense, there can be no doubt that in the September of 1920, the essential core of the Italian working class was to the left of its leaders.

To rest content with this answer, however, is not to explore the problem but to evade it. No less striking than the power of the class movement of the urban proletariat in the September of 1920 was its isolation (for ideological or structural reasons) from the middling strata of the population and from the peasant movement. From this point of view, the situation had been better in 1919.[37] And such factors did much to aggravate defeatism and hesitancy among the leading socialist groups.

But was there no profound crisis in the liberal state, in the power and coercive apparatus of the bourgeoisie? Certainly. No less certain, however, is the fact that there was no single day on which the government felt that it had lost all control over the situation. That the neutralist and 'wait-and-see' tactics of both Giolitti and the CGL entailed ceaseless labour to avert insurrection does not alter the fact. And in a sense it makes pointless any conjectures on the government's capacity to repress a revolutionary movement which never even got off the ground. This basic reality tends to diminish the revolutionary potential of the crisis; it suggests that their lack of military preparation influenced revolutionaries the more strongly in that the 'bourgeois' repressive apparatus, in its weakness, might not have been able to contain the forces of reaction.

There are stronger reasons for scepticism. At the critical moment, the crucial days of 10-11 September, when the struggle moved towards compromise, it became obvious that the masses, in the nation as a whole, lacked the power to resist. The differences between Turin, the most advanced sector, and the other cities, sharpened. The parochial, localized, character of the movement intensified. Those working-class groups which still wanted to extend the struggle, to carry it into insurrection, had no contact with each other. Reformist groups in the factories at once assumed much greater weight. So, one of the classic conditions for revolution, the decision of the masses to make it, was critically subject to dislocations, to uneven development in organization, maturity, homogeneity and ideology, which were to prove no less significant in the struggle against squadrism during 1921-22. As early as 1921, a German communist in strong opposition to the leaders of the Communist International put the question openly: were the Italian masses as a whole really animated by a revolutionary will? [38]

In fascist propaganda, the occupation of the factories conjured up a vision of chaos and violence and was used to justify the Mussolinian reaction. This negative myth ultimately called forth a positive counter-myth which inflated the idea of a revolutionary moment to heroic proportions and drenched it in romantic nostalgia. To restore the problem to its real dimensions and to subject it to minute examination is not to rob the movement of any of its grandeur and originality, or to stifle in us all sense of the 'great fear' of the bourgeoisie or the courage of the worker occupiers. On the contrary, it restores to them those multiple, complex features and that sense of anguished crisis which were properly theirs.

References

Chapter 1 The Protagonists

1. The sub-division by category was: 200,000 building workers, 160,000 metalworkers, 155,000 textile workers, 68,000 in the gas industry, 60,000 state employees, 50,000 in chemicals, 50,000 private employees, 30,000 wood workers, 25,000 railway workers, 23,000 leather workers, 22,400 workers in the building crafts, 22,000 tramway men, 21,000 paper workers. 890,000 land workers were organized by the CGL.
2. IV Congresso nazionale dell'USI, Roma, 10-12 marzo 1922, *Programma, relazione e statuto* (ed. *Guerra di classe*, Milan 1922); see also Ugo Fedeli, *Corso di storia del movimento operaio* (Centro di sociologia della cooperazione, 1957), pp200-225.
3. Riccardo Bachi, *L'Italia economica nel 1920* (Città di Castello, 1921), p338.
4. For this controversy and also for an analysis of the theory of factory councils developed by Gramsci and the *ordinovista* group, see my introduction to the anthology *L'Ordine Nuovo 1919-20* (Einaudi, Turin 1963), pp42-46.
5. Report of the President of the Council to the Senate, session of 26 September; *Atti parlamentari*, Senato del Regno, legislatura XXII, 1st session, pp1709-13.
6. Speech of Ludovico D'Aragona, session of 27 February 1921, in *Resoconto stenografico del X Congresso della Resistenza, V della CGL* (Cooperativa grafica, Milan 1921), pp38-48.
7. On 25-28 November 1918, the directive committee of the CGL voted a motion calling for the Constituent. On 8 March 1919, the national council specified: 'Convocation of the Constituent in elections by professional categories, based on a distribution among all social grades to be decided by appropriate census, without discriminating between the sexes.' 'This Constituent,' asserted the directive committee on 1 May 1919, 'of all professional categories will prepare and accelerate the political transition from capitalism to socialism.'
8. The mission included political and trade union leaders. Its members were Serrati and Vacirca for the PSI directorate, Graziadei and Bombacci for the parliamentary group, D'Aragona, Bianchi, and Colombino for the CGL, Dugoni for the National League of Co-

operatives, Fernando Pozzani, director of the communal trust, Nofri and others. The delegation left Milan for Moscow on 25 May and returned to Italy in July. D'Aragona and Dugoni remained in Moscow to the beginning of August; Serrati and Bombacci stayed longer to be joined by other Italian delegates to the Second Congress of the Communist International.

9. Luigi Salvatorelli and Giovanni Mira in their *Storia d'Italia nel periodo fascista* (Einaudi, Turin 1956), p144, justly attribute great importance to the 'confidential information' leaked by the delegation on its return from Russia.

10. The document was unanimously approved by the directive council of the CGL at its meeting of 19 August 1920. See the text in *La Confederazione generale del lavoro*, ed. Luciana Marchetti (*Avanti*, Milan 1962), p295. Franco Catalano makes some interesting comments on the uncertain and contradictory conduct of the CGL in the preface to the volume (xliii).

11. The formation of soviets had been decided on by the congress of Bologna in 1919. The Bombacci project won majority approval in the national council at Florence, 8-10 January 1920.

12. The speech was delivered in person in the Chamber on 26 June 1920 and had enormous impact. It was later published as a pamphlet under that title and may now be consulted in Filippo Turati, *Discorsi parlamentari* iii (Rome 1950), 1736-76, under the title *Un programma d'azione socialista.* On the direct connexion between Turati's problematic and the plan for union control elaborated during the occupation of the factories, see Chapter 7.

13. The Baldesi project was presented to the directive council of the CGL in Rome on 20 May 1920. To the scepticism of D'Aragona, Baldesi retorted 'that the functions of company councils, at present minor only because the forms of capitalist economy predominate, will become increasingly important as soon as all the members of an industry are united in single purpose.' *La CGL, cit.*, p284. The text of the Baldesi scheme is published in Francesco Magri, *La crisi industriale e il controllo operaio* (Unitas, Milan 1922), pp273-75.

14. On this episode, which has essentially been treated in terms of government requisitioning of factories, see Luigi Einaudi, 'Il caso Mazzonis,' *Corriere della Sera*, 3, 20 March 1920, reprinted in *Cronache economiche e politiche di un trentennio* (1893-1925), v (1910-20) (Einaudi, Turin 1961), pp672-82; also Pietro Borghi, 'Un esperimento di gestione diretta,' *L'Ordine Nuovo*, 13 March 1920.

15. Angelo Faggi, 'L'esperimento dimostrativo di Sestri Ponente,' *Comunismo*, 15-29 February 1920; Palmiro Togliatti and Andrea Viglongo, 'Rapporto sui fatti di Sestri,' *L'Ordine Nuovo*, 13 March 1920. See also, for a chronicle of the occupation, *La Lotta Operaia*, 28 February 1920. Gaetano Perillo has an essay on the

subject, 'I consigli di fabbrica a Sestri,' *Movimento Operaio e Contadino in Liguria,* anno iii (1957) nos 2-3 (March-June).

16. Raffaele Colapietra, *Napoli tra dopoguerra e fascismo* (Istituto G. Feltrinelli, Milan 1962), pp103-105.

17. On 29 September 1918, a convention was agreed between the PSI and the CGL, which, rehearsing the provisions of the Florence convention of 1907, reaffirmed 'the independence and autonomy of the Confederation and the Party, each in its own field', and established that strikes and agitations of a national political character should be called and led by the leadership of the party, the CGL having been consulted, and those of an economic character by the CGL, the party having been consulted; the latter pledging itself not to obstruct the carrying out of CGL decisions.

18. Antonio Gramsci, 'Party and union', now in the volume *L'Ordine Nuovo 1919-20* (Einaudi, Turin 1954), pp404-408.

19. *Corriere della Sera,* 9 March 1920.

20. The expression is that of Gino Olivetti, secretary-general of Confindustria, who used it in his report to the Milan meeting. The text of the report was published under the title 'The opinion of the industrialists on factory councils', in *L'Ordine Nuovo,* 15 May 1920.

21. References to this episode are innumerable. Note, for its relevance to our researches, the letter sent by Crespi, president of the Banca Commerciale Italiana, to Giolitti on 6 April 1921 which talks of this 'violent attempt to establish a monopoly', in *Quarant'anni di politica italiana, documenti inediti tratti dalle carte giolittiane,* iii (1910-20) ed. Claudio Pavone (Istituto G.Feltrinelli, Milan 1962), pp331-32.

22. Rodolfo Morandi, in his *Storia della grande industria in Italia* (Einaudi, Turin 1959), p151, writes that the Banca Commerciale Italiana 'could be considered a direct product of German finance, operating as the *long arm* of German industry', adding, however, that after the war the question of foreign finance ceased to be important.

23. Typical is a letter from Giuseppe Toeplitz, director of the Banca Commerciale Italiana to Giolitti on 26 June 1920, in which he 'places at the disposal' of the latter, 'all the capacities and faculties of himself and the Bank he directs in the service of that programme of national reconstruction which the government has undertaken'. The letter is published in *Dalle carte di Giovanni Giolitti. Quarant'anni di politica italiana,* iii, *cit.,* p278.

24. Giampiero Carocci, *Giolitti e l'età giolittiana* (Einaudi, Turin 1961), p182.

Chapter 2   The First Phase of the Dispute

1. Francesco Magri, *La crisi industriale e il controllo operaio, cit.*, p45.
2. Calculation made by Riccardo Bachi, in *L'Italia economica nel 1920, cit.*
   [Trans: In this paragraph I have supplemented P.Spriano's material with data from the ILO report on the factory occupations. International Labour Office (Geneva), *The Dispute in the Metal Industry in Italy, Studies and Reports*, series A, no. 2, 11, B, no. 7, 9 (September 1920-April 1921). I owe this reference to Nina Stead of the British and Irish Communist Organization.]
3. The weekly costs of this type-family: June 1919, 120.05 lire; July, 109.24; August, 108.07; November, 118.53; January 1920, 124.67; August 1920, 176.25; December 1920, 189.76.
4. According to FIOM's figures, minimum daily wages in Milan were 27.20 lire for typographers, 18.96 for wood workers, 24 for tramway men, 23 for coach-builders, 19 for electricians. Minima for metalworkers, in contrast, were 13.30 lire. The figures were considered valid by Arturo Labriola in his speech to the Senate on 25 September 1920. See the text in the appendix to Arturo Labriola, *Le due politiche* (Morando, Naples 1924), pp293-311.
5. See the document prepared by FIOM at the beginning of August 1920, included in *Relazione del Comitato centrale della FIOM sull'agitazione dei metallurgici italiani* (Tip. Alleanza, Turin 1921), p20.
6. At the anarchist congress in Bologna, however, Malatesta opposed the formation of workers' councils in a bourgeois period.
7. Magri (*La crisi industriale e il controllo operaio, cit.*) maintains that for metalworkers, the cost of living oscillated between 600 per cent and 605 per cent above the 1914 level and was virtually covered by increases in wages which reached 575 per cent. L'Unione Industriale di Torino (see interview in *La Stampa*, 2-3 September 1920) asserted that car workers earned an average of 22.50 lire (an increase over 1914 of 515 per cent) while the cost of living had gone up by only 358 per cent. *Avanti* (article by E.Ugolini on 14 September, Piedmont edition) on the contrary claimed that metalworkers' real wages were lower than in 1914.
8. Rodolfo Morandi, *Storia della grande industria in Italia, cit.*, p228.
9. If 1909 = 100, the index for these reached 385 in 1913; 480 in 1919; 637 in January 1920, 774 in June and 832 in September.
10. According to the data furnished by Rosario Romeo, *Breve storia della grande industria in Italia* (Cappelli, Bologna 1961), p88, in Piedmont, 203 companies declared a profit for the war period of 61,634,000 lire on a nominal capital of 445,800,000 lire; in Lombardy, 596 companies a profit of 148,622,000 lire on capital of 1,845,100,000 lire; in Liguria, 183 companies a profit of 78,365,000 lire on capital of 662,700,000 lire.

11. Rodolfo Morandi, *Storia della grande industria in Italia, cit.*, p257, calls Ansaldo 'a monster with a thousand gullets' and adds: 'Governed by a bold and adventurous hand . . . it had all the critical characteristics of a vertical trust in its highest form.'

12. Rosario Romeo, *Breve storia della grande industria in Italia, cit.*, p89.

13. From newspapers for 14 August 1920. The industrialists' commission included Monacelli, Benni, Meneguzzi for Lombardy-Emilia; Rotigliano for Tuscany; Ricci and Jachini for Liguria; Pellicciotti and Boella for Piedmont; Casalini for Venezia Giulia; Parisini for Campania; FIOM was represented by Buozzi, Guarnieri, Uberti, Falchero; SNOM by Salvadori; Cucini and Bachi took part for the Unione Sindacale of Milan and Giovannetti for USI.

14. Bruno Buozzi, 'L'occupazione delle fabbriche,' in *Almanacco Socialista Italiana* (PSI ed., Paris 1935), p79.

15. The union issued no official list of rules for obstructionism. They can be learned, however, from a confidential circular which came into the possession of Taddei, prefect of Turin, and which he summarized in a telegram to the minister (ACS, *Ministero degli Interni* (1920) *Direzione generale di PS, Affari generali e riservati*, D.13 busta 75). 1. Reduce production to the minimum. 2. No one to move from his workplace. 3. No one to use tools unsuitable to the work in hand. 4. Take as long as possible over the repair of every machine. 5. Do not work at jobs you are not trained for. 6. Clean and lubricate no machinery until it is stopped. 7. If the company sacks anyone for this behaviour, make him come to work notwithstanding. 8. If the company proclaims a lockout, occupy the factory and work there for your own account.

16. From the *Relazione della FIOM, cit.*, p32.

17. This decision was taken at a meeting of metalworker members of USI held in La Spezia on 17 August 1920. The text of the resolution is in *Guerra di Classe*, 25 August 1920.

18. *ibid.*

19. The vice-prefect of Milan, Flores, reported in this sense to the Ministry of the Interior: ACS, *Ministero degli Interni* (1920) *Ufficio cifra*, telegram of 17 August, 15.15 hours.

20. See the *Relazione della FIOM, cit.*, p33.

21. On all these aspects, see Paolo Spriano, *Storia del partito comunista italiana*, i, *Da Bordiga a Gramsci* (Einaudi, Turin 1967), pp64-108.

22. *Critica Sociale*, 1-15 August 1920, p229; the article is signed *Noi*.

23. For the discussions in the national council of the PSI (Milan, 19-21 April 1920) see Pietro Nenni, *Storia di quattro anni (1919-22)* (Einaudi, Rome 1946), pp79-82.

24. In Moscow were Serrati, Bombacci, Bordiga, Graziadei, Polano, A.Balabanoff.

25. Angelo Tasca, *Nascita e avvento del fascismo* (La Nuova Italia, Florence 1951), p117.
26. The manifesto signed by Buozzi, Turati, Prampolini, Treves, Baldesi, Zanardi, Tiraboschi, G.Pieraccini refers to a fraction meeting in Reggio Emilia on 19-20 September. Its concepts were precisely the same as those which informed the articles of *Critica Sociale* in polemic against maximalism.
27. The Piedmont edition of *Avanti*, 20 July, gives an account of a meeting of members of the internal commissions at the headquarters of FIOM, chaired by the secretary Ferrero, which in a final resolution, asked the national organization to undertake the struggle in alliance with USI, 'the masses in Turin being ready for anything'.
28. See the text of Bruno Buozzi's speech on p168 of the report of the congress, *op. cit.*

Chapter 3   From Go-Slow to Lockout

1. Apart from USI, already mentioned, note that both CIL and UIL had doubts about the efficacity and practicality of obstructionism, but they fell in line to maintain solidarity with FIOM wherever the majority of the workers were 'confederal'.
2. *Gazzetta del Popolo*, 19 August 1920.
3. *Avanti* (Piedmont), 20 August 1920.
4. Particularly interesting is the testimony of Arturo Labriola. In a note to Giolitti, which Gaetano Natale published in his *Giolitti e gli italiani* (Garzanti, 1949), p745, the Minister of Labour wrote: 'Resistance has come from the industrialists, who appear to be more worried by the condition of their industry vis-a-vis customs duties than by the action of the workers. One suspects that the industrialists wanted to saddle the government with the necessity to resort to force, as if to compel it to take up a position against the workers.' The note is undated.
5. ACS, *Ministero degli Interni* (1920) *Ufficio cifra*, despatch, 18 August, 17.40 hours.
6. *ibid.*, despatch, 19 August, 20.00 hours.
7. *ibid*, telegram, 25 August, 12.00 hours; see the text of the document and the reply of the prefect of Milan, Lusignoli, in Appendix.
8. Minister of Labour's report to the Senate, *cit.*, p300.
9. See note 4 above.
10. Luigi Einaudi, *La condotta economica e gli effetti sociali della guerra* (Laterza, Bari 1933), p336.
11. *Corriere della Sera*, 27 August 1920.
12. ACS, *Ministero degli Interni* (1920) *Direzione generale di PS, Affari*

References / 143

    generali e riservati, D.13, busta 75, telegram, coded, 24 August, 19.00 hours.

13. The prefect of Florence, Crivellaro, reported that at Pistoia, 'the workers who run USI have so reduced production that industrialists have said that as long as this state of affairs continues, they will be forced to reduce basic wage rates'. (Telegram, 25 August, 19.40 hours.) The prefect of Genoa reported, 'Where the extremist element predominates, the go-slow has degenerated into a sit-down strike. The syndicalist leaders agitate to intensify the struggle.' (Telegram, 25 August, 23.15 hours.) ACS, *Ministero degli Interni* (1920) *Ufficio cifra.*

14. *ibid.*, telegram, 26 August, 22.00 hours.

15. *ibid.*, telegram, 27 August, 23.00 hours.

16. ACS, *Ministero degli Interni* (1920) *Direzione generale di PS, Affari generali e riservati*, D.13, busta 74, telegram, 30 August, 23.30 hours.

17. See *Atti parlamentari*, Senato del Regno, legislatura XXV, 1 Sezione (1919-20); session 25 September 1920, pp1700ff.

18. Giovanni Giolitti, *Memorie della mia vita* (Treves, Milan 1922) ii, p596.

19. *Relazione del Comitato centrale della FIOM sull'agitazione dei metallurgici italiani, cit.*

20. *ibid.*

21. H.Massoul, *La leçon de Mussolini* (*Mercure de France*, Paris 1934) quoted in Henri Pronteau, *cit.*

22. Telegram, coded, 1 September, 2.45 hours; ACS, *Ministero degli Interni* (1920) *Direzione generale di PS, Affari generali e riservati,* D.13, busta 74.

23. Giovanni Agnelli, in a letter to the press, published 7 September, stated that Giolitti refused government intervention. Ugo Camurri, director of the Ferrieri di Avigliana, reported that Agnelli returned from Cavour, where he had gone on 31 August to ask the President of the Council to take a stand, with a negative reply from Giolitti: *Nuova Antologia*, 16 March 1934, pp260-67.

24. Alfredo Frassati, *Giolitti* (Parenti, Florence 1959), p30.

25. *Atti parlamentari, vol. cit.*, pp1711-12.

26. In a leading article in *Il Popolo d'Italia*, 28 September, entitled 'L'epilogo', Mussolini wrote: 'Could the invasion of the factories have been prevented? Perhaps, but once the invasion had happened, within 24 hours such a conflict already seemed much more difficult. Every day of occupation made the task of expelling the workers from the factories by military force all the heavier. The miseries which government policy has caused have certainly been very serious, but who could be sure that a "strong hand" would not have ignited an infinitely more dangerous conflagration?'

27. ACS, *Ministero degli Interni* (1920) *Ufficio cifra*, 1 September. See full text in Appendix.

28. In particular by Arturo Labriola in his speech to the Senate, cited above several times; see also Gaetano Natale's biography of Giolitti.

29. Gabriele de Rosa in his *Storia del partito popolare* (Laterza, Bari 1958), p134, quotes the despatch from Giolitti to Corradini dated 2 September. He took it, with others, from the Camillo Corradini archives, *Occupazione delle fabbriche* portfolio. A copy of the despatch is in ACS, *Ministero degli Interni* (1920) *Ufficio cifra;* see text in Appendix.

30. The communiqué of FIOM, 1 September, is reproduced in the *Relazione, cit.*, p29.

31. Angelo Tasca, *Nascita e avvento del fascismo, cit.*, p119.

32. Antonio Gramsci, 'Domenica rossa,' *Avanti* (Piedmont), 5 September 1920, now in the volume of his collected works, *L'Ordine Nuovo, cit.*, p164.

33. Recollect how Gramsci was to talk, with reference to this 'lack of interest', of serious errors committed at this time by the *ordinovista* group. He identified them in a failure to create a communist fraction within the PSI and a failure to create an autonomous directive centre out of the council movement as an alternative to the reformism of the CGL. See his letter to Alfonso Leonetti from Vienna, 28 January 1924, in Palmiro Togliatti, *La formazione del gruppo dirigente del PCI* (Annali Feltrinelli, Milan 1960), p461.

Chapter 4   The Occupation of the Factories

1. ACS, *Ministero degli Interni* (1920) *Direzione generale di PS, Affari generali e riservati*, D.13, busta 74, telegram, 2 September.

2. On the occupation of the Galileo, see G.Procacci and G.Rindi, *Storia di una fabbrica. Le officine Galileo di Firenze*, in *Movimento Operaio*, vi (1954) no. 1 (January-February), pp32-37.

3. ACS, *Ministero degli Interni* (1920) *Ufficio cifra*, telegram from prefect Pesce, 3 September, 11.25 hours. On the occupation in Naples, see also Raffaele Colapietra, *Napoli tra dopoguerra e fascismo, cit.*, pp126-27.

4. *Avanti* (Rome), 6 September 1920.

5. *ibid*, 7 September 1920.

6. The telegram of the prefect Taddei, ACS, *Ministero degli Interni* (1920) *Direzione generale di PS, Affari generali e riservati*, D.13, busta 75, 1 September, 16.30 hours, coded, states: 'Workers who have

turned up for the most part enter the factories without violence and occupy the plants.'

7. *La Stampa*, 1-2 September 1920, in 'Ultime di cronaca'.

8. *Avanti* (Piedmont), 2 September 1920. The communiqué was reproduced (but with the following variation after the word 'work-places': 'carrying on calmly and peacefully with the work of production as in the past') in the chronicle which Giovanni Parodi wrote, under the title *La Fiat Centro in mano agli operai*, in *Lo Stato Operaio, rassegna di politica proletaria*, iv (1930) no 10 (October) (Bureau d'Éditions, Paris), p638.

9. The notice which the factory council of Diatto Frejus issued on 3 September was typical: 'The factory council gives notice to all technicians, office personnel and workers that from tomorrow 4 September, anyone absent without good cause will be considered dismissed. Great new events are preparing for the proletarian future. In expectation of victory, solidarity, solidarity, solidarity!' *Avanti* (Piedmont), 4 September 1920.

10. The prefect Taddei reported: 'The technical personnel has been allowed out to eat; it may not return, but the companies want some faithful men to stay in so that they can know what is going on.' ACS, *Ministero degli Interni* (1920) *Direzione generale di PS, Affari generali e riservati*, D.13, busta 75, telegram 2 September, 10.00 hours.

11. The text of the letter, published by all the Turin newspapers the next day, was sent by the prefect Taddei to the Ministry (the same archive source) in a coded telegram, 2 September, 11.30 hours.

12. *Avanti* (Piedmont), 3 September 1920.

13. Telephone message of prefect, 2 September, 20.50 hours. ACS, *Ministero degli Interni* (1920) *Direzione generale di PS, Affari generali e riservati*, D.13, busta 75.

14. See below, Chapter 9.

15. At Fiat-Centro, according to Giovanni Parodi, they produced 37 machines a day, compared to a normal production of 67-68 (though during the slowdown in the last days of August, production had fallen to 27 a day).

16. The railwaymen's union in Turin had given instructions to this effect on 3 September; see *Avanti* (Piedmont), 4 September 1920.

17. *Avanti* (Piedmont), 5 September 1920.

18. See Giovanni Parodi, *La Fiat Centro in mano agli operai, cit.*, p638.

19. G.Parodi, 'L'occupazione delle fabbriche' in *Fascismo e antifascismo (1918-36) Lezioni e testimonianze* (Feltrinelli, Milan 1962), p91.

20. *Avanti* (Piedmont), 4 September 1920.

21. *ibid*, 5 September 1920.

22. Unsigned article, *ibid*; now in the volume *L'Ordine Nuovo, cit.*, pp163-66.

23. See Gino Bianco, 'L'attività degli anarchici nel biennio rosso,' *Movi-*

mento *Operaio e Socialista in Liguria,* vii (1961) no. 2 (February), pp134-55; and Arrigo Cervetto, 'Dopoguerra rosso e avvento del fascismo a Savona,' *Rivista Storica del Socialismo,* i (1958) no. 4 (October-December), pp511-62.

24. *Il Giornale d'Italia,* 5 September 1920.
25. From a telegram of the prefect of Milan, 2 September, 22.15 hours. ACS, *Ministero degli Interni* (1920) *Ufficio cifra.*
26. *Il Giornale d'Italia,* 4 September.
27. ACS, *Ministero degli Interni* (1920) *Ufficio cifra,* telegram, signed Lusignoli, 4 September, 22.00 hours.
28. Bruno Buozzi, *L'occupazione delle fabbriche, cit.,* p82.
29. Gaetano Salvemini, *La dittatura fascista in Italia,* now in *Scritti sul fascismo* (Feltrinelli, Milan 1962), p22. The episode was also reported in *Giustizia,* 13 December 1922 and *Il Corriere della Sera,* 11 May 1923.

Chapter 5   The Government's 'Non-Intervention'

1. Gaetano Natale, 'L'artiglieria di Giolitti,' *Il Mondo,* 12 July 1955, p13.
2. The Minister of Labour immediately made vain efforts to call the two parties to Rome; the industrialists were the more reluctant. That this initiative was not cleared with Giolitti is proven by his correspondence with the Treasury minister Meda, quoted in Gabriele de Rosa, *Storia del partito popolare, cit.,* p145.
3. The reports of Lusignoli to Corradini and Porzio are full of this matter, which was a serious attempt at mediation. On 1 September, the prefect of Milan reported that his proposals had definitely interested Jarach for the industrialists and Buozzi for FIOM (ACS, *Ministero degli Interni* (1920) *Ufficio cifra,* telegram, 22.45 hours). On 2 September, he claimed that a settlement was possible, if the intransigence of the immovable Milanese industrialists could be overcome, while 'according to information received from the prefect of Turin, the industrialists of that city begin to grasp the seriousness of the crisis': ACS, *Ministero degli Interni* (1920) *Direzione generale di PS, Affari generali e riservati,* D.13, busta 74. On 4 September, he expounded his own proposals in the above-mentioned terms: ACS, *Ministero degli Interni* (1920) *Ufficio cifra,* telegram, 21.00 hours. (See the text in Appendix.) Action intensified on the 5th, while Labriola was still hopeful about getting the parties to Rome.
4. See the telegram which the prefect of Milan sent to Porzio and Corradini at 11.00 hours on 5 September (text in Appendix): ACS, *Ministero degli Interni* (1920) *Ufficio cifra.*
5. Telegram, 7 September, 14.00 hours. ACS, *Ministero degli Interni* (1920)

> *Direzione generale di PS, Affari generali e riservati*, D.13, busta
> 74.

6. In a telegram to Corradini on 6 September, Giolitti asserted: 'If the government had been maintaining neutrality from the beginning, I think I would have been called on to arbitrate by both parties' (G. de Rosa, *Storia del partito popolare, cit.*, p136). This does not mean that Giolitti disavowed all the approaches made. He wanted them established on a more solid basis, however, in future.

7. 'Buozzi said again what he has repeatedly said, that the workers' side was always ready to reopen discussions the moment the industrialists got out of their rigid and preconceived refusal to make any concession whatever. And he hoped that the conflict could usefully return to the path of negotiation.' *Corriere della Sera,* 3 September.

8. From a telegram, 4 September, 21.00 hours, it appears that Buozzi shared the opinion of the prefect of Milan who thought it 'absolutely necessary to settle the dispute promptly, before the movement spreads to other industries'. ACS, *Ministero degli Interni* (1920) *Ufficio cifra.*

9. In a despatch of 5 September, 16.00 hours, Lusignoli informed Giolitti that 'Turati is very worried, not so much by the metalworkers' movement as by the probability, if the settlement of the dispute is not accelerated, of an extension of the agitation to other industries, which he thinks would be extremely dangerous'. ACS, *Ministero degli Interni* (1920) *Ufficio cifra.*

10. ACS, *Ministero degli Interni* (1920) *Direzione generale di PS, Affari generali e riservati*, 4 September. The document is entitled *Intorno alla vertenza metallurgica*: text in Appendix.

11. *Umanità Nova*, 4 September, wrote: 'For us anarchists the movement is very serious and we must do everything we can to channel it towards a massive extension. We must lay down a precise programme which can be realized, completed, perfected in radical action every day; we must foresee today the difficulties and the obstacles of tomorrow, so that the movement does not run aground and break up on the rocks of reformism.' See Armando Borghi, *L'Italia tra due Crispi* (Libreria Internazionale, Paris 1924), p259.

12. *Avanti* (Piedmont), 2 September 1920. The editorial, anonymous and entitled *L'Occupazione*, warned that a factory occupation pure and simple could not in itself create any new and definitive positions because 'power stays in capital's fist'. For the attribution of this article to Gramsci, see Antonio Gramsci, *Scritti 1915-21,* ed. Sergio Caprioglio (Milan 1968), pp130-31 and 186.

13. *Avanti* (Piedmont), 3 September; the editorial, anonymous, is entitled 'Il simbole e la realta'.

14. From the editorial 'Domenica Rossa', several times cited.
15. Present at the meeting were, for the CGL leadership: Altobelli, Bellelli, Buozzi, Del Buono, Dugoni, Quaglino, Zirardini, D'Aragona, Baldesi, Bianchi; for the PSI leadership: Gennari, Baratono, Regent; the *camere del lavoro* of Turin, Milan, Genoa, Bologna, Naples, Florence, Savona, Sampierdarena were represented. See the report in *Avanti* (Rome), 7 September 1920.
16. See *Relazione del Comitato centrale della FIOM sull'agitazione dei metallurgici italiani, cit.*, p32.
17. Luigi Einaudi had already intervened in the controversy during the go-slow ('Obstructionism and Strike', article of 25 August, now in his *Cronache economiche e politiche di un trentennio*, v, *cit.*, pp289-833) and had warned the workers' leaders not to use so risky a weapon, which could ignite the conflagration, 'that is to say, invasion of factories, smashing of machinery, battles with the security forces'. On 2 September ('The two principles: cost of living and condition of industry,' now in *op. cit.*, pp833-38) Einaudi examined the economic aspects of the dispute. Without contesting the validity of the workers' wage claims, he put prior emphasis on factory discipline and a spirit of collaboration in the labour force.
18. See below, Chapter 8.
19. Benito Mussolini wrote an editorial on 5 September under the title 'Alla moda russa?' Asserting that the situation was rapidly changing and passing from the control of the workers' leaders, he said: 'At this moment – we repeat it at the top of our voice – we will resist a bolshevik experiment with all the means at our disposal.' Evidently the article was written after Buozzi's refusal of Mussolini's offer of support.
20. Lusignoli's letter, from the Corradini archives, is quoted by G. de Rosa, *Storia del partito popolare, cit.*, pp134-35, note 7. It was sent to the commandants of the *carabinieri* and royal guards in Milan and dated 5 September. It stated, among other things: 'The situation created by the occupation of the factories is one of exceptional delicacy. The slightest incident provoked by the rashness or impulsiveness of an agent could have the most serious repercussions and compromise the peace of the Realm. No one must resort to arms except on the orders of superiors in cases of extreme necessity, to protect the lives of himself or others. There must be no bloodshed; and if any tragedies should occur, not only will the actual authors be held to account, but also those who may be charged with any indirect or moral responsibility.'
21. Giolitti's despatch is quoted by G. de Rosa, *Storia del partito popolare, cit.*, p134, note 7.

22. Ettore Conti, *Dal taccuino di un borghese* (Garzanti, Milan 1946), p233.

23. Labriola and Meda were busy between 4 and 6 September, bringing pressure to bear on the industrialists through the banks, with the good offices of the Banca d'Italia. But their efforts failed to overcome in good time the resistance of the employers. Meda wrote to Giolitti on 6 September, 'confirming their uncompromising stance' (see G. de Rosa, *op. cit.*, p145).

24. The police records are full of detail. The prefect of Palermo (telegram, 5 September, 13.00 hours) reported that 300 peasants of San Giuseppe had invaded the former Bommario and Quastella estates and said that the movement, apparently economic, was led by spokesmen of the Partito Popolare. The prefect of Potenza (telegram, 5 September, 18.30 hours) reported that at Matera, a march of 600 ex-combatant peasants 'demand the promised grants of land formerly the property of some charitable fraternity; they threaten to invade'. ACS, *Ministero degli Interni* (1920) *Ufficio cifra.*

25. The manifesto was published in a full blaze of publicity on the front page of *Avanti* on 6 September, in all its editions.

26. See Armando Borghi, *L'Italia tra due Crispi, cit.*, p260.

27. *Il Giornale d'Italia*, 7 September 1920.

28. ACS, *Ministero degli Interni* (1920) *Ufficio cifra*, telephone message, 5 September, 19.10 hours. Text in Appendix.

29. A letter, dated Vienna, 6 March 1924, to Giulia Schucht, published in *Rinascita*, xix (1962) no. 1 in the new weekly series (5 May).

30. *Il Giornale d'Italia*, 7 September 1920.

31. Vincenzo Bianco, 'La organizzazione militare rivoluzionaria durante l'occupazione', *Lo Stato Operaio*, pp733-38. Bianco says in particular: 'Far from emulating each other and co-ordinating everyone in a common action, each thought only of himself and sometimes even felt a little jealous of the others.'

32. Angelo Tasca, *Nascita e avvento del fascismo, cit.*, p121.

33. *Avanti* (Piedmont), 7 September; the Turin section of the railway union SFI decided on the 6th that railwaymen should refuse to return the goods wagons in Turin stations to their stations of origin; they were, on the contrary, to be directed to the factory rail junctions.

34. These telephone conversations, which yield the information given above, were transcribed by monitors of the Ministry of the Interior. The text of the conversation between the departmental manager of the state railways in Turin and Tondelli, of the general management of the railways in Rome, is in the Appendix. Further information may be obtained from a letter which the Turin manager sent to the director-general of the State railways at Rome on 9 September. ACS, *Ministero degli Interni* (1920)

Direzione generale di PS, Affari generali e riservati, D.13, busta 75.

35. *Corriere della Sera*, 7 September 1920.
36. ACS, *Ministero degli Interni* (1920) *Ufficio cifra*, telegram, 7 September, 2.35 hours. Text in Appendix.
37. The prefect of Milan, in despatch no. 1164, 6 September, reported: 'The anarchist Malatesta continues to give lectures and yesterday in Sesto S. Giovanni, he recommended discipline . . . He urges them to respect the machinery.' ACS, *Ministero degli Interni* (1920) *Direzione generale di PS, Affari generali e riservati*, D.13, busta 74.
38. Telegram, 8 September, 12.50 hours. ACS, *Ministero degli Interni* (1920) *Ufficio cifra*.
39. Telegram, 7 September, 23.15 hours; *ibid.*
40. G. de Rosa, *Storia del partito popolare, cit.*, p146 quotes a letter from Labriola to Giolitti, in which the Minister of Labour complains to the President of the Council that he had been superseded by Corradini.
41. Giolitti's despatch is quoted in G. de Rosa, *Storia del partito popolare, cit.*, p136.
42. Milanese newspapers of 8 September reported that on the previous day, Lusignoli had met Bianchi of the CGL, Buozzi, senator Conti, Olivetti, Treves, Turati and Agnelli.
43. Bruno Buozzi, *L'occupazione delle fabbriche, cit.*, p81.
44. On the night of 6 September, Corradini told Lusignoli that D'Aragona wanted Bianchi to try to get an agreement between the industrialists and the CGL by any means possible (text in Appendix). Lusignoli replied that he had passed on the request, but stressed that neither Bianchi nor D'Aragona could act as leaders of the Confederation of Labour, but only as individuals. ACS, *Ministero degli Interni* (1920) *Ufficio cifra*, telegram, 6 September, 24.00 hours and *Direzione general di PS, Affari generali e riservati*, D.13.
45. The council of the national syndical federation of the engineering industry, meeting in Rome on 6 September, issued a communiqué which referred the matter to the council of the syndical section within *Confindustria*. The latter, meeting in Milan on 7 September, took the position outlined above.
46. The under-secretary at the Ministry of the Interior, on 7 September, sent a telegram to all prefects instructing them to prepare measures for the maintenance of public order in the event of riots and insurrections and to revise earlier defence plans in consultation with the military. ACS, *Ministero degli Interni* (1920) *Ufficio cifra*, telegram, 6 September, 7.00 hours.
47. Ivanoe Bonomi, *La politica italiana dopo Vittorio Veneto* (Einaudi, Turin 1953), p158.

48. Vincenzo Nitti, *L'opera di Nitti* (Gobetti, Turin 1924), p163.
49. Leo Valiani makes some interesting comments on the point: 'In Italy, a victor not a vanquished country, only the ex-combatants could win the army to revolution. These had certainly led land occupations in recent months but there was no link between them and the factory councils; indeed they suspected and often disliked the councils as they disliked anything which smacked of either that pacifism which scorned war service or a marxist dictatorship of the proletariat.' Federico (Leo Valiani), *Esperienze internazionali del movimento operaio tra le due guerre* ('Quaderni dell'Italia Libera', Partito d'azione, 1944).

Chapter 6   Revolution by Ballot

1. See on this point the testimony of an industrialist, from a fascist source: Mario Finzi, *L'occupazione delle fabbriche* (Bologna 1935), p23.
2. Ettore Conti, *Dal taccuino di un borghese, cit.*, pp236-37.
3. For a fuller analysis, see Pietro Borghi, 'La gestione operaia delle officine occupate a Torino,' *L'Ordine Nuovo*, 2 September 1921.
4. ACS, *Ministero degli Interni* (1920) *Ufficio cifra*, telegram, 9 September, 20.45 hours.
5. Anonymous typescript, dated Rome, 8 September 1920, among the *Informazioni fiduciarie* in ACS, *Ministero degli Interni* (1920) *Direzione generale di PS, Affari generali e riservati*, D.13, busta 74 (text in Appendix).
6. The Turin newspapers for 10 September published the communiqué which the industrialists issued after their visit to the prefect.
7. *Avanti* (Piedmont), 10 September, reported: 'By order of FIOM, the slow-down remains in force in all the factories. But the workers would prefer to abandon it, to step up production and sell the products.'
8. FIOM arranged for a loan with the credit organization of the co-operatives. According to the indiscretions of I.Minunni, 'Storia della capitolazione industriale,' in *L'Idea Nazionale*, 19 September 1920, the loan was for 25 million and was guaranteed by the Banca Commerciale Italiana. Angelo Tasca also refers to it: 'The directors of the Banca Commerciale assured FIOM of their benevolent neutrality, offered and asked for pledges in case the movement ended in revolution.' We have found no trace in the archives of the Bank of any letter or warrant to that effect. The Istituto Nazionale di Credito of the co-operatives was founded, with a capital of 8 million, in 1914, by royal decree, with the assistance of various savings banks, the *Banca d'Italia*

and the social security fund. In 1925 its assets totalled over 300 million. (B.Riguzzi and R.Porcari, *La cooperazione operaia* (Gobetti, Turin 1925) pp136-47.)

9. The Florentine section of FIOM ordered the formation of factory councils in this manner: 1. Elect one commissar per workshop. 2. Disciplinary power to be exercised jointly by the internal commission and the workshop commissars. 3. The factory council to consist of equal numbers of representatives from the workshop commissars and the white-collar workers (*La Nazione*, 7 September 1920). Obviously this was very far from the spirit of the Turin councils which were to abolish the old internal commissions and create new ones under their control.

10. The Study Committee for Factory Councils of Turin launched an appeal on 7 September which was published by the Piedmont *Avanti* on the 8th and the Milan edition on the 11th. It was very vague: 'Be alert to the possibilities of the present dispute, which may reach a climax from one moment to the next, and get ready to support the struggle in any way you can. Let every workshop elect its representative, every work-unit its own commissar; create factory councils everywhere and stand ready for any eventuality.'

11. See *Resoconto stenografico del XVII Congresso nazionale del PSI* (PSI, Rome, 1921), p81.

12. *Resoconto stenografico del X Congresso della Resistenza, V della CGL, cit.*, pp253-54.

13. Armando Borghi, *L'Italia tra due Crispi, cit.*, pp260-61, 271. Note, however, that Borghi was absent during the crucial days; he did not return from a journey to Russia until 20 September.

14. *Avanti* (Piedmont), 6 September, made it a sensation. The workers found in the Fiat managers' office the draft of an agreement proposed to AMMA by the industrial league of Turin, which suggested a whole series of measures designed to enforce solidarity among employers and to prevent the re-employment by any associated firm of workers who had been dismissed by another for political reasons. AMMA had a full list of named workers classified as 'subversives'. Gramsci devoted an article to the subject, stressing 'the overpowering might of a handful of individuals' within the legal and against the just state – 'L'organizzazione capitalistica', *Avanti* (Piedmont), 7 September 1920.

15. *Avanti* (Piedmont), 10 September 1920.

16. *Avanti* (Rome), 11 September 1920.

17. Apart from official documents and writings from the period 1920-21, see Massimo Masetti in *L'Umanità*, 11-12 August 1949, and M. and M.Ferrara, *Conversando con Togliatti* (Edizioni di Cultura Sociale, Rome 1953), pp80-82.

18. *La CGL nel sessennio 1914-20, cit.*, p87. Togliatti personally verified

the CGL report and found it substantially accurate so far as he was concerned.

19. *ibid*, p88.

20. 'Aprile e settembre 1920,' unsigned article, *L'Ordine Nuovo*, 7 September 1921.

21. *Resoconto stenografico del X Congresso della Resistenza, V della CGL, cit.*, p253.

22. *Battaglie Sindacali*, 20 November 1920. At this meeting the CGL executive discussed the charges of reformism and the stifling of mass action levelled at the CGL by the Russian trade union spokesman A.Lozovsky. See *La CGL nel sessennio 1914-20, cit.*, p309.

23. *Corriere della Sera*, 10 September. Twelve military trucks took away the 60,000 charges after talks between the sub-prefect and the internal commission.

24. *L'Ordine Nuovo*, 7 September 1920.

25. *La CGL nel sessennio 1914-20, cit.*, p30.

26. *Relazione politica della direzione del partito*, XVII congress of the PSI, Livorno 15-20 January 1921 (Tip. Luigi Morara, Rome 1921).

27. *La CGL nel sessennio 1914-20, cit.*, p90.

28. *Battaglie Sindacali*, 20 November 1920: reply of the directive council of the CGL to the letter of A.Lozovsky, member of the presidium of the Russian central soviet of trade unions.

29. *La CGL nel sessennio 1914-20, cit.*, p32.

30. *Resoconto stenografico del XVII Congresso nazionale del PSI, cit.*, p262. Egidio Gennari's speech, afternoon session, 19 January 1921.

31. The PSI directorate elected at the Bologna congress of 1919 included Giovanni Bacci, Ambrogio Belloni, Nicola Bombacci, Arduino Fora, Egidio Gennari, Gino Giacomini, Anselmo Marabini, Vincenzo Pagella, Giovanni Regent, Luigi Repossi, Edoardo Sangiorgio, Giacinto Menotti Serrati, Giuseppe Tuntar, Arturo Vella. After their election as deputies, Bacci, Belloni, Bombacci, Fora, Marabini, Pagella, Repossi and Vella resigned from the directorate and were replaced by A.Baratono, Terracini, G.Bellone, Casimiro Casucci, Emilio Lamerini, Tito Marziale, Cesare Sessa and G.Gimino.

32. Adelchi Baratono, speech at the XVII congress of the PSI, *op. cit.*, p82.

33. Terracini's speech was published in *La questione italiana al III Congresso dell'Internazionale comunista* (Libreria Editrice del PCI, Rome 1921), pp51-58. There were references to the occupation of the factories and the Italian communists' attitude to the emergency in the speeches of Clara Zetkin, Rakovsky, Lenin, Lazzari and Gennari reprinted in the same volume.

34. Speech of Gennari at the XVII congress of the PSI, *op. cit.*, p264.
35. Speech of Ernesto Schiavello at XVII Congress of PSI, afternoon session, 18 January 1921, *op. cit.*, p179.
36. See Buozzi's speech at the V congress of the CGL, February-March 1921, *op. cit.*, p163 and his essay *L'occupazione delle fabbriche, cit.*, p81.
37. Bensi's speech at V Congress of CGL, *op. cit.*, p67.
38. There is an exhaustive analysis of the politics and ideology of the Federterra in Renato Zangheri's introduction to his *Lotte agrarie in Italia* (Feltrinelli, Milan 1960). On this precise moment, Zangheri writes: 'Isolated from the other sectors of the peasant movement, the Federterra had no contact either with the struggles of the industrial workers. In September 1920 when the decisive battle of the postwar years was being fought out in the occupied factories, Federterra within the Confederation openly demonstrated its hostility to any extension of the agitation into the countryside.' Mazzoni himself in an essay in *L'Umanità*, 30 August 1949, admitted that he had openly fought to prevent any irrevocable acts which 'would have recoiled upon the most impoverished and weakest proletariat – the field workers.'
39. See the text of Serrati statement in *La CGL nel sessennio 1914-20, cit.*, p96.
40. Angelo Tasca, *Nascita e avvento del fascismo, cit.*, p122.
41. Pietro Nenni, *Storia di quattro anni, cit.*, p103.
42. Luigi Einaudi, *La condotta economica della guerra, cit.*, p332.
43. Armando Borghi, *op. cit.*, pp283-90 gives a detailed account. In practice, after the convention, textile mills were occupied in Verona and uncultivated lands in Apulia.
44. *Umanità Nova*, 11 September 1920.
45. Zinoviev's appeal to the Italian proletariat was dated 22 September 1920. *L'Internationale Communiste*, i (1920) no. 14 (November) col. 2917-22: *compte-rendu des séances du CE de l'IC, séance du 21 Septembre*. It was fully reproduced in the German edition: *Das Kommunistische Internationale*, ii (1921) no. 14, pp230-31.

Chapter 7 Giolitti's Masterpiece

1. *Il Messagero*, 7 September; anonymous editorial, *Soluzione urgente*.
2. *La Tribuna*, 9 September.
3. *Il Lavoro*, 8 September.
4. *Corriere della Sera*, 10 September, anonymous editorial.
5. *Corriere della Sera*, 11 September, anonymous comment.
6. *Il Giornale d'Italia*, 14 September.

7. *Corriere della Sera*, 8 September, article 'Le condizioni per l'arbitrato'; now in *Cronache economiche e politiche di un trentennio, op. cit.*, p847.

8. Telephone conversation monitored and transcribed as no. 2920, dated Rome, 11 September, 20.00 hours, between professor Vettori (*Confederazione industriale Roma*) and the *Consorzio industriale di Milano*: ACS, *Ministero degli Interni* (1920) *Direzione generale di PS, Affari generali e riservati*, D.13, busta 74.

9. Telegram from Bardonecchia, 11 September, 11.40 hours, no. 20,424, ACS, *Ministero degli Interni* (1920) *Ufficio cifra.*

10. A text of the telegram came to the hands of the *Agenzia Informatore della Stampa* and was published in the newspapers on 12 September. The government did not disown it.

11. G. de Rosa, *Storia del partito popolare, cit.*, p137, note 8, publishes a telegram from Giolitti: 'In Turin there is the feeling that everything will work out. In Milan there is resistance, but the industrialists will give way if they get the word from the Banks on which they depend for their very existence. It is necessary to act energetically, particularly on Pogliani.'

12. Telegram from Corradini to the prefect of Parma, 11 September, 12.50 hours. ACS, *Ministero degli Interni* (1920) *Ufficio cifra.*

13. Pogliani gave an interview to Maxime Baze, Rome correspondent of the Paris *Excelsior*, which published it on 30 September. In the interview, the director of the Banca di Sconto confirmed that 'at a certain point, the BCI and us, anxious to avoid any violent insurrection in Italy, thought it necessary to intervene.' He added that 'his role was difficult' and his counsels of moderation did not have much luck among the industrialists on whom he could exercise 'a certain influence'. As for his colleague Toeplitz, Pogliani said he went in for the grand gesture, threatened to cut credit off from the industrialists, and he insinuated that Toeplitz was the cat's paw of German industry which might be using the Banca Commerciale Italiana to damage Italian industry. In the exchange of letters which followed (preserved in the archives of the Banca Commerciale Italiana in the *Occupazione delle fabbriche* portfolio) Toeplitz protested vigorously at Pogliani's insinuations. The latter promised to disavow the interview, and his withdrawal was published in *Excelsior* on 6 October 1920. The French paper asserted however, that its Rome correspondent had taken Pogliani's statements by dictation. Indeed she had softened the attack on the director of the Banca Commerciale Italiana. The latter then prepared an interview for *Le Matin* of Paris in which he stressed that his bank had threatened no one, but had worked in harmony with the Banca di Sconto and poured ridicule on the suggestion of German pressure and intervention in the affair. This 'interview', which *Le Matin* did not

publish, we publish in the Appendix, together with an interesting letter from a Genoese industrialist which severely criticizes the conduct of Confindustria's leaders.

14. Among whom Giolitti included even senator Albertini; see G. de Rosa, *Storia del partito popolare, cit.*, p137, note 9.

15. As he himself said to Corradini in a despatch of 11 September, 'I am leaving now. I shall stay at Aix for at least two days. If I postpone my departure it will look like a disaster abroad.' G. de Rosa, *op. cit.*, p137, note 8.

16. In his *Giolitti* (*op. cit.*, pp30-31), Alfredo Frassati tells one story: 'At that time, Fera who was Keeper of the Seals, if I am not mistaken, in a coded telephone conversation with the secretary of the President of the Council, told him that he and his colleagues were convinced that the situation was desperate. 'If Giolitti leaves Italy, I and other ministerial colleagues will resign.' Giolitti replied verbatim: 'Tomorrow, precisely at the time scheduled, I shall leave for Aix. I should be very unhappy, on my return, to have to accept the resignation of yourself and perhaps your colleagues.' See also G.Natale, *Giolitti e gli italiani, cit.*, pp744-46; Marcello Soleri, *Memorie* (Einaudi, Turin 1949), p108.

17. Telegram no. 20,552, in code, 11 September (text in Appendix).

18. G. de Rosa, *op. cit.*, p139.

19. On the attitude of the white unions towards control, see Gerolamo Meda, *Dal controllo operaio al partecipazionismo* (Vita e Pensiero, 1922). The PPI, in a manifesto issued at the end of their national council of 15-17 September, proposed a system of participation and profit-sharing; see G. de Rosa, *op. cit.*, pp147-49.

20. *ibid*, pp140-43.

21. This was the problem of 'dual power' in the factory which Olivetti had raised in April and which he was to stress again on this occasion.

22. G. de Rosa, *op. cit.*, p143, note. Turati expressed the same ideas in an article first published by *Il Lavoro* of Genoa on 25 September 1920, 'Il controllo operaio sulla fabbrica': here the author called explicitly for councils of industry representing employers, workers and technicians 'to awaken once more in the worker the lost zest for intensely and joyfully productive labour'.

23. See Avanti (Piedmont), 14 September 1920, 'Cinque mesi dopo', unsigned editorial.

24. 'Unions must be given the opportunity to learn the real condition of industries, their technical and financial operation and must be able, through their factory representation, to participate in the application of regulations, to control the employment and dismissal of personnel, and so support a normal development of

factory life with the necessary discipline.' *La CGL nel sessennio 1914-20, cit.*, pp97-98.

25. In Turin, vouchers on the ACT co-operative were distributed at the rate of 50 lire for young workers under 17, 70 lire for women, 100 for manual workers and 150 for skilled workers with families.

26. *Avanti* (Piedmont), 14 September.

27. According to the prefect's report, Pietro de Benedetti, owner of a family firm 'opened fire on some workers of a nearby factory and they fired back. De Benedetti killed two workers with two shots: Raffaele Vandich and Tommaso Gatti, of the Capamiento.' ACS, *Ministero degli Interni* (1920) *Direzione generale di PS, Affari generali e riservati*, D.1, busta 75, despatch, 13 September, 23.30 hours.

28. *Avanti* (Piedmont), 15 September; see also G.Parodi in his essay in *Lo Stato Operaio, cit.*, p647 who claims that the threat was effective.

29. At the request of the prefect of Milan, the CGL agitation committee presented a memorandum which rehearsed the principles discussed at the convention.

30. Telegram of Lusignoli, 13 September, 18.30 hours, ACS, *Ministero degli Interni* (1920) *Ufficio cifra*. (Text in Appendix.)

31. See the telephone conversation between the Lombard consortium in Milan and Confindustria in Rome, transcribed on 15 September (ACS, *Ministero degli Interni* (1920) *Ufficio cifra*) and published in the Appendix.

32. On this measure, see the interesting article by Gino Luzzatto, 'Le consequenze dell'accordo,' *Il Resto del Carlino*, 22 September 1920. He calculated it would yield Fiat an extra 120 million a year against costs of 40 million in wage increases: all, naturally, at the consumers' expense, as he noted.

33. According to Ghezzi, *op. cit.*, p25, during the journey Lusignoli pointed out D'Aragona to the industrialist Pietro de Benedetti and said, 'See him there? That's the saviour of Italy!'

34. See *Relazione della FIOM, cit.*, p41.

35. G.Natale, *L'artiglieria di Giolitti, cit.*, has some interesting and plausible detail on D'Aragona's speech. He is reported as saying: 'Control was really necessary to find out how capital was built up in financial operations and how subsequent operations worked. He cited the example of big firms which ended up with heavy liabilities which were then cleared by the state with taxpayers' money, because the industries were essential to the armed forces; Ilva was a case in point; its directors, through their own personal subsidiaries in the supply of raw material, in transport, the banks, such as the private companies of Max Bondi, reaped huge profits.'

36. Telegram of the prefect of Turin, 15 September, 23.00 hours. ACS,

  Ministero degli Interni (1920) *Direzione generale di PS, Affari generali e riservati*, D.13, busta 75.

37. Mario Missiroli, *Una battaglia perduta* (Corbaccio, Milan 1924), p172.
38. After deploring workers' violence and government tolerance, the resolution ran: 'The general confederation of Italian industrialists agrees, if the other side is sincerely of the same opinion, to accept a control over industry based on legislative provision, provided that this does not establish a trade union monopoly or predominance and that it means genuine collaboration and co-responsibility between the different factors of production.' *Il Secolo* (Milan), 17 September.
39. In *L'Idea Nazionale*, 19 September, Italo Minunni in his article 'Storia della capitolazione industriale', *cit.*, bitterly attacked the Banca Commerciale Italiana as being responsible for the surrender 'in the interests of German industry' and pointed to the resistance of the majority of the industrialists which had been frustrated by Crespi, Conti and Volpi. Crespi, in an interview with *Il Giornale d'Italia*, 20 September, discounted any undue influence by the Banca Commerciale but pointed to Ilva (Rotigliano) as the group most stubbornly opposed to an agreement on control. Minunni repeated his accusations in a reply in *L'Idea Nazionale* for 23 September. On this point, see also Toeplitz' statement cited above and published in the Appendix. See further the telephone conversation, also in the Appendix, between Rotigliano and one of his Ilva colleagues in Rome on 21 September.
40. See the telephone conversation, 17 September, between professor Vettori and Olivetti (Appendix): ACS, *Ministero degli Interni* (1920) *Ufficio cifra.*
41. *La Stampa* had in effect published a draft of the Giolittian decree as the product of an agreement accepted by the industrialists (as the *Gazzetta del Popolo* did, on the same day.) It was this version which provoked the complaint referred to. Giolitti in a telegram to the prefect of Turin said: 'Pray inform senator Frassati that the premature publication of details of the decree on control has caused the liveliest agitation in Milan, has upset the atmosphere and has also occasioned me some trouble. It would have been helpful not to have published it' (ACS, *Ministero degli Interni* (1920) *Ufficio cifra*, telegram, 17 September, 14.30 hours). Senator Frassati replied: 'As you will see when *La Stampa* reaches you, I have not published the decree as such, but as I agreed with you, in the form of a news item. It pains me infinitely that I have caused you trouble. I am extremely sorry for it' (ACS, *ibid.* telegram, 17 September, 19.20 hours).
42. The conversation, on 15 September, is reprinted in the Appendix. ACS, *Ministero degli Interni* (1920) *Ufficio cifra.*
43. Ettore Conti, *Dal taccuino di un borghese, cit.*, p239.

44. See, in particular, the conversation between Olivetti and senator Crespi on 18 September, 15.30 hours. ACS, *Ministero degli Interni* (1920) *Ufficio cifra.*
45. For a precise and detailed account of the meeting, see G.Natale, *L'artiglieria di Giolitti, cit.*, p14.
46. See the text of the decree, with variant annotations in Giolitti's hand, in *Quarant'anni di politica italiana, cit.*, iii, pp284-85.

Chapter 8   The Response

1. G.de Rosa, *Storia del partito popolare, cit.*, p148.
2. During the next few days, the Popolari strongly pressed their claim for representation on the commission which was to elaborate the control project.
3. *Avanti* (Piedmont), 15 September 1920. The interview was later published in the paper's other editions.
4. From Lenin's *Letter to the French and German workers*, written on 24 September 1920. See Lenin, *Sul movimento operaio italiano* (2nd ed. 1962, reprinted, Editori Reuniti, Rome 1970), p201.
5. Giovanni Ansaldo, 'Un po' di teoria', *Il Lavoro* (Genoa), 23 September 1920.
6. G.Menotti Serrati, 'Ca Ira!' in all editions of *Avanti*, 20 September 1920.
7. The article, anonymous and bearing the title, 'Una nuova posizione di conquista,' was republished in the Rome *Avanti*, 21 September 1920.
8. In *Avanti* (Piedmont), 22 September, Ottavio Pastore stressed the optimism: 'The battle for the factory council, for workers' control is today won . . . Control is today an accepted principle: it can be used to penetrate the most intimate and jealously-guarded sanctuaries of capitalist society.'
9. The official periodical of the anarcho-syndicalists, *Guerra di Classe* was even more bitter (see the editorial of 'Aligio' entitled 'La vittoria politica del governo', 25 September 1920) in that it thought union control a delusion and the settlement a defeat for the working class. Even here, however, was the thought – 'But the game is not yet over . . .'
10. Luigi Einaudi, 'Il significato del controllo operaio', *Corriere della Sera*, 16 September; reprinted in *Cronache cit.*, v, pp848-53.
11. Title of the director's comment, *Corriere della Sera*, 17 September 1920.
12. The note, signed G.A., appears as a leader in *Corriere della Sera*, 17 September, under the title 'Il governo e la situazione'. On its significance in the political development of its author, see Giampero

Carocci, *Giovanni Amendola nella crisi dello stato italiano* (Feltrinelli, Milan 1956), p60.

13. In a letter to *Il Popolo d'Italia*, 10 May 1923.
14. Letter to Anna Kuliscioff, 9 May 1923, published in *Carteggio*, vi (*Il delitto Matteotti e l'Aventino (1923-25)* ed. Alessandro Schiavi (Einaudi, Turin 1959), p17.)
15. Letter of 1923 cited above.
16. From the essay cited above, 21 September 1920.
17. Claudio Treves, 'Un po'di storicismo', *Il Resto del Carlino*, 26 September 1920.
18. See *Corriere della Sera*, 29 September 1920.
19. Benito Mussolini, 'L'epilogo,' *Popolo d'Italia*, 28 September 1920.
20. *La Stampa*, 21-22 September, unsigned leader, 'Dalla piazza al Parlamento.'
21. *ibid.*
22. Attilio Cabiati, 'Il controllo operaio e i consigli di fabbrica,' *Il Secolo*, 22 September 1920.
23. Claudio Treves, 'I metallurgici e il metodo,' *Critica Sociale*, xxx (1920) no. 18 (16-30 September).
24. *L'Unità*, ix (1920) no. 41 (7 October), p167; article 'Il metodo giolittiano' signed 'L'Unità'; republished in the anthology *L'Unità: La Voce politica* (1915), ed. Francesco Golzio and Augusto Guerra (Einaudi, Turin 1962), p708.
25. Gramsci wrote in *L'Ordine Nuovo*, scarcely a week after it resumed publication, 'Union control is a swindle of the collaborationists and reformists . . . Revolutionaries want control to be exercised by the workers themselves, by organizations elected by all the labouring masses. They want control as a weapon of war, not a means of conciliation.' From 'Le cronache dell'Ordine Nuovo', ii (1920) no. 16 (2 October) now in *L'Ordine Nuovo, cit.*, p488.

Chapter 9 The Last Week

1. Battista Santhià, 'La lotta contro i riformisti in una fabbrica occupata,' *Lo Stato Operaio*, iv (1930) no. 1 (1-12 November-December), pp730-31.
2. Pietro Borghi, *La gestione operaia delle officine occupate a Torino, cit.*
3. The suspect evidence of Camurri, director of the Piedmont *Ferrieri* (*Nuova Antologia, cit.*) is an interesting index. Production of steel at the *Ferrieri* was 3,978 tons in July, 3,093 in August and 1,895 in September, a substantial total, given the exceptional situation and the absence of engineers and technicians.
4. *Avanti* (Piedmont), 18 September 1920.
5. The trial, in March 1922 at the Turin Assizes, condemned 11 accused

to terms of imprisonment which ranged from one to thirty years.

6. The document was published by Giovanni Parodi, *L'occupazione delle fabbriche, cit.*, p652.

7. The central committee of the fraction expressed its dissent. It was necessary to go to the congress of the PSI and not immediately to create an abstentionist communist party, retorted the leadership to the Turin comrades. They were also rebuked for adopting 'tactics we do not agree with' – i.e. those of *L'Ordine Nuovo* and the factory councils. *Il Soviet*, 3 October 1920.

8. The executive commission of the Turin section of the PSI, led by Togliatti, deplored the fact that anyone should want to break away from the common organization immediately. 'It is not a matter of playing the game of who can go further; it is a question of making sure that the communist party shall be, from the start, the only major organization in which the proletariat can have faith.' *Avanti* (Piedmont), 22 September 1920.

9. On 17 September, after the Turin meetings, the executive commission noted in an order of the day that 'Events have confirmed the belief that the destiny of the socialist revolution depends above all on the existence of a party which is truly a communist party,' and it called on militants to start work immediately on its formation. *Avanti* (Piedmont), 18 September 1920.

10. According to *Avanti* (Piedmont), 21 September (which blazoned over the whole of its front page: 'The Turin metalworkers want the fullest guarantees against victimization and full payment for the work they have done'), the problem was serious: 'In Turin, in all the factories, men have worked. A little in the first days, a lot in the days which followed. In some factories, they surpassed the average level of production. For whom have they worked? The workers would rather destroy everything that they have produced than work twenty days for the bosses.'

11. USI, invited by the prefect of Milan to recognize the agreement, replied with a declaration that not only did the syndicalist organization hold itself free to take any action it liked; it did not intend to subscribe to any settlement, but proclaimed its intention 'of sabotaging in every way possible the application of control over the factories'. See A.Borghi, *L'Italia tra due Crispi, cit.*, pp295-96.

12. On 16 September, the Co-operative Society (miscellaneous goods) paid out 127,000 lire, the coal-heavers' co-operative 10,000, the metalworkers' co-operative 40,000, while a subscription opened by *Il Lavoro* raised 100,000 lire in a few days.

13. See the committee's communiqué in *Il Lavoro*, 15 September 1920.

14. *Avanti* (Milan), 23 September 1920: report of the assembly.

15. Armando Borghi, who returned from Russia on the 20th, was in Verona on 22 September. The secretary of USI encouraged the

occupation which had extended into non-metallurgical plants. In Brescia, where there were about 2,000 metalworkers, Maestri organized the resistance. Corradini sent an inspector of public security to the city who reported that the situation was not alarming. ACS, *Ministero degli Interni* (1920) *Ufficio cifra*, telegram from prefect of Milan, 22 September, 22.00 hours.

16. *Umanità Nova*, 28 June 1922.

17. In Livorno, where a destroyer was launched in the Orlando yard at a saving of 100,000 lire, the workers called for an application of the agreement which would sanction equitable back payment for work done. Modigliani was said to have taken a hand in the matter with Giolitti, but without appreciable result. See ACS, *Ministero degli Interni* (1920) *Ufficio cifra*, telegram, 25 September, 18.55 hours and Giolitti's reply, 26 September, 12.30 hours.

18. See the telegram of Corradini and D'Aragona, 23 September, 22.00 hours, in the Appendix.

19. *Avanti* (Piedmont), 24 September 1920; unsigned leader 'Capacità politica', now in *L'Ordine Nuovo, cit.*, pp169-72. Albertini replied promptly in the *Corriere della Sera*, 26 September, praising the democratic and indicative value of the referendum.

20. See G.Procacci and G.Rindi, *Storia di una fabbrica, cit.*, p36.

21. Telegram, 21 September 1920. ACS, *Ministero degli Interni* (1920) *Direzione generale di PS, Affari generali e riservati*, D.13, busta 74.

22. There were 148,740 votes in favour and 42,140 against. On the congress, see P.Emiliani (Nenni), 'L'occupazione delle fabbriche in Italia,' *Il Nuovo Avanti* (Paris), 13 June 1936.

23. Apart from the direct testimony of workers, there was a report on the subject by the command of the *carabinieri* of Turin, a copy of which was sent to the director-general of public security on 28 June 1921 (ACS, *Ministero degli Interni* (1921) *Direzione generale di PS, Affari generali e riservati*, D.13, busta 61). It runs, in part: 'At the end of the workers' occupation, that is from 20 September onwards, in expeditions, particularly at night, using motor vehicles and with the complicity of political comrades and people at the receiving end, most of the said material was taken out of the city and hidden in the countryside, at the disposal of the communist party.'

24. From his *La Fiat Centro in mano agli operai, cit.*, p655.

25. *Gazzetta del Popolo*, 3 October 1920.

26. Gramsci took up a position, to open the discussion among comrades. He warned that the risk was great: the risk of a decline in revolutionary energy among workers and the rise of a corporatist spirit; *Avanti* (Piedmont), 1 October 1920, 'La Fiat diventera una cooperativa?', now in the volume *L'Ordine Nuovo, cit.,*

pp172-76. Riccardo Roberto in *Comunismo*, 1-15 October 1920, was more decidedly negative, calling for 'a decisive and absolute No!'

27. In his *L'occupazione delle fabbriche*, 1935, *cit.*, p82.

28. Gaetano Salvemini, *La dittatura fascista, cit.*, pp17-31.

29. Telegrams from the prefect of Palermo, 26 September, 13.30 hours; of Cosenza, 30 September, 9.35 hours; of Caltanissetta, 28 September, 21.30 hours; of Caserta, 30 September, 13.20 hours. ACS, *Ministero degli Interni* (1920) *Ufficio cifra*.

30. See the interview with the Minister of Agriculture, Micheli, in *La Tribuna*, 22 October 1920. See also G.Rocca, 'L'occupazione delle terre incolte,' *La Riforma Sociale*, May-June 1920 and Bachi's reviews, already cited, for 1919 and 1920.

31. Karl Radek, report on tactics to the Third Congress of the Communist International, Moscow, July 1921, 'Le vie dell'Internazionale comunista' (Libreria Editrice del PCI, Rome 1921), p26.

Chapter 10   Was it really the Revolutionary Moment?

1. A.Borghi, *Mezzo-secolo di anarchia* (ESI, Naples 1954), p253.

2. Luigi Salvatorelli and Giovanni Mira, *Storia d'Italia nel periodo fascista, cit.*, p150.

3. The director-general of public security, following a warning from the prefect of Pisa (see Appendix) on 27 September 1920, sent telegrams to the prefects of Turin, Milan, Genoa, Florence, Bologna, asking them whether they had caught any hint of preparations for a coup d'etat: 'Nationalist and conservative elements, perhaps inspired and supported by industrialists and large banks, are preparing soon to launch a movement headed by D'Annunzio to seize the government and use it against the maximalist socialist party to destroy its organized power. D'Annunzio may be counting on solidarity from the army, and may believe he can find support among the *carabinieri* and *royal guards* sick of the vilification and aggression of extremist forces.' ACS, *Ministero degli Interni* (1920) *Ufficio cifra*, telegram 27 September, 12.15 hours. The prefects replied in the negative; none of them found any evidence of this order.

4. G.de Rosa, *Storia del partito popolare, cit.*, p144.

5. A.Tasca, *op. cit.*, p123. Tasca added that the occupation of the factories signalled the inglorious end of maximalism 'whose corpse continued to encumber the battlefield until the fascist gravediggers got rid of it.'

6. Pietro Nenni, *Sei anni di guerra civile* (Rizzoli, Milan 1945), p89, insists particularly on 'the political collapse of the PSI' whose weak

spot was exposed by the agitation. Federico Chabod, *L'Italia contemporanea* (Einaudi, Turin 1961), pp52-53 states firmly 'that between the end of the summer and the beginning of the autumn of 1920, Italy reached the culmination of the crisis.'

7. V.Pareto, 'Due uomini di Stato,' *La Ronda*, July 1921.

8. Luigi Fabbri developed the argument in a book which carried the title *La contro-rivoluzione preventiva* (Cappelli, Bologna 1922). It is interesting to note that Fabbri includes the anarchist and syndicalist groups in his general condemnation of the ineptitude and unreadiness of the socialist movement during the occupation crisis.

9. The socialists won a majority in 2,162 communes and 26 provinces out of 69.

10. See the different plans in Francesco Magri, *La crisi industriale e il controllo operaio, cit.*, pp281-327.

11. The voting on two opposing resolutions ran: for the 'communist' resolution, 7 votes (Terracini, Gennari, Regent, Tuntar, Casucci, Marziale and Bellone); for the 'unitarian', 5 (Baratono, Serrati, Bacci, Giacomini and Zannerini). A very full account of the discussions was published in *Avanti* (Milan), 1-2 October 1920.

12. Pietro Nenni, *Storia di quattro anni, cit.*, p34.

13. See the article, 'Falsi discorsi sulla libertà,' written between 4 November and 1 December 1920, reprinted in *Sul movimento operaio italiana, cit.*, p202 (1970 edition).

14. Letter from A.Gramsci to P.Togliatti, 16 July 1923, published in *La formazione del gruppo dirigente del PCI, cit.*, p433.

15. The Milanese collaborator of the journal, Cesare Seassaro, wrote, 'Those memorable days, which will remain, written in letters of fire, in the memory of the proletariat and in the history of human civilization, have been, as it were, the *grand manoeuvres* of the proletarian army.' *L'Ordine Nuovo*, 6 October 1920, now in the volume of that title, *cit.*, p597.

16. In *L'Ordine Nuovo*, 16-23 October 1920, Gramsci asserted: 'The Italian proletariat can be the determinant of the world revolution.' (See the volume *L'Ordine Nuovo, cit.*, p355.) Lenin wrote (in 'Falsi discorsi') that Italy was passing through 'a moment in which, it is generally agreed, the decisive battles of the proletariat against the bourgeoisie for the conquest of power are approaching.'

17. The appeal ran: 'Italy today experiences all the essential conditions which guarantee the victory of a great proletarian revolution, a truly popular revolution.' See the text in *L'Ordine Nuovo*, 30 October 1920.

18. See his essay 'Il dovere dell'ora presente', in *Comunismo*, ii (1920), no. 1 (October) in which Serrati asserted 'The present situation is without doubt revolutionary. The Italian bourgeoisie can no

longer hold on to power. The state is in financial, political, moral dissolution.' Hence the necessity to maintain unity, 'to prepare ourselves, mobilize all our forces to take over the inheritance of a crumbling regime,' without undue haste, so as not to be burdened with the responsibility for economic collapse, which was the bourgeoisie's, and to keep hold of those reformist groups whose authority and competence were indispensable for 'the necessities of reconstruction'.

19. From the volume on the Fifth congress of the CGL, *cit.*, p254.
20. Karl Radek, *Le vie dell'Internazionale Comunista, cit.*, p30.
21. This letter we found in the Tasca archives, *L'occupazione delle fabbriche* portfolio, in the Istituto Feltrinelli in Milan.
22. Arturo Labriola, *Le due politiche, cit.*, p164.
23. G.Salvemini, *La dittatura fascista, cit.*, p22.
24. H.Pronteau, *Les occupations d'usine en Italie et en France, cit.*, p50; R.Palme Dutt, *Fascism and social revolution* (International Publishers, New York 1934) quoted by Pronteau.
25. From his *La condotta economica e gli effetti sociali della guerra italiana, cit.*, p332.
26. Giovanni Giolitti, *Memorie, cit.*, ii, 598.
27. I.Bonomi, *La politica italiana dopo Vittorio Veneto, cit.*, p158.
28. L.Sturzo, 'La libertà in Italia', (1925) republished in *Il Fascismo,* anthology ed. by Costanzo Casucci (Il Mulino, 1961), p97.
29. See, as an example, Arturo Colombi's pamphlet *L'occupazione delle fabbriche* (PCI, Rome 1950). Colombi claims that the material conditions for a revolution existed. What was missing was the revolutionary party.
30. The letter was published in *Rinascita*, xxi, no. 17 (25 April 1964).
31. In 'Trenta anni di vita e di lotta del PCI', Quaderno of *Rinascita* (January 1961), pp26-27.
32. P.Togliatti, 'La situazione politica a un anno dall'occupazione,' *L'Ordine Nuovo*, September, 1921.
33. Luigi Fabbri, 'L'occupazione delle fabbriche,' *Almanacco Socialista* (Paris 1931) p40.
34. Federico (Leo Valiani), *Esperienze del movimento operaio tra le due guerre, cit.*, p13.
35. From his *L'occupazione delle fabbriche, cit.*, p83.
36. From his speech on the Italian question at the Third Congress of the Communist International, 28 June 1921, reproduced in Lenin *Sul movimento operaio italiana, cit.*, p218 (1970 edition).
37. Among historians, Lelio Basso has most strongly emphasized this point. 'The climax of revolutionary tension in Italy was reached during the riots against the cost of living. The occupation of the factories was a moment in a battle which, from the working class point of view, was essentially defensive.' See his essay, 'Le origini del fascismo,' a paper read in Milan, 30 January 1961

reprinted in the anthology *Fascismo e antifascismo, cit.*, p28.

38. Clara Zetkin, speaking at the Third Congress of the Communist International, asserted 'that it was not simply a matter of putting the PSI on trial . . . I see something else, namely, that the masses who were then in ferment in Italy had made no greater progress than their leaders. Otherwise, comrades, if the masses had really been animated by a revolutionary will, if they had been conscious, they would that day (the famous convention of 10 September) have booed offstage their trembling union and political leaders and taken up the fight themselves.' From *La questione italiana al Terzo Congresso, cit.*, p40.

Appendix

I.
The Action of the Giolitti Government

Corradini (under-secretary, Ministry of Interior)
to *Lusignoli* (prefect of Milan)

Rome, 25 August 1920, 12.00 hours

Meeting industrialists to decide attitude to obstructionism in metallurgical factories to be held your city today, stop. Information reaching me from Turin suggests industrialists will consider necessity for lockout in factories, stop. This could have unpredictable consequences as in such eventuality workers would be prone to greater violence, stop. Essential establish contact most influential industrialists to persuade them not to make hasty decisions which could have serious consequences for further development of agitation, stop. Negotiations on intervention started by government which could, one hopes, reach swift conclusion and agreement. To this end, however, necessary that there be no impulsive acts or rash decisions, stop. Prefect Turin has conferred with *ingegner* Agnelli who has left for Milan meeting, stop. I am assured that Agnelli will firmly recommend calm, stop. Essential to work on other industrialists assembled there with aim of eventual invitation to Rome for negotiations, stop. What matters at moment is that no rash decisions be taken, stop. You must, with maximum courtesy, establish contact with leaders of workers' organizations, stop. I have asked Buozzi to come to Rome, stop. Essential to sound out opinions other organizations on contacts in manner which will not prejudice attempted approach, stop. Keep me informed by telegraph.

Corradini

(*ACS, Ministero degli Interni, Ufficio cifra*, n.18,941)

Lusignoli to *Corradini*

Milan, 25 August 1920, 16.40 hours

Yesterday and today had repeated talks with representatives of industrialists to whom I conveyed gist of His Excellency's telegram. Their meeting is beginning at this moment; have been assured a lockout will not be decided on. I will send another telegram later. President of Council alerted Turin. Industrialists who refused to consult minister Labriola yesterday leave for Rome tonight. Was waiting for Buozzi to make contact other party. Representatives of USI Milan and USI national summoned but did not appear. Will await information from Genoa already requested. I propose to initiate talks.

Lusignoli

(ibid, n.11,156)

Lusignoli to *Corradini*

Coded. Milan, 1 September 1920, 2.45 (arrived 9.00)

Meeting of industrialists metallurgical industry has carried following resolution, stop. 'The federal council of the National Federation of Mechanical and Metallurgical Industry declares that obstructionism, which has degenerated into a condition of complete anarchy in the factories, which in becoming a surreptitious sitdown strike has led to a virtually complete stoppage of production, with a useless waste of raw materials and fuel, which has given rise to repeated outbreaks of violence against persons and sabotage of plant, has already caused so grave a crisis in the metallurgical and mechanical industry that only their desire to demonstrate in every way possible their spirit of conciliation, averse to any unfriendly act, has restrained the industrialists from closing the factories. They cannot maintain this attitude in the face of the latest acts of violence committed by the workers who have not only occupied factories in Milan, but have kidnapped people, among them the president of the negotiating commission, and, before the public, they denounce the behaviour of the workers' organizations which, having failed to answer the arguments of the industrialists, were responsible for the breakdown of negotiations and have advised and authorized the present acts of violence. The council therefore RESOLVES that the firms affiliated to the federation proceed to a closure of the factories in a manner to be decided by individual consortia; reaffirms that only after the definitive ending of the present abnormal and illegal state of affairs will the industrialists' organization, though still reasserting the arguments expounded in the first phase of negotiations, be prepared to re-examine the demands of the workers' organizations, stop.'

The representatives of the industrialists, among them *avvocato* Rotigliano who will be in Rome tomorrow morning and who was present only in the initial stages of my discussions with them, have in the first instance asked me to communicate the resolution only to the government and not to the workers: the resolution will be published this afternoon, stop. I have repeatedly demonstrated, in the most vigorous manner, that the industrialists' decision is not the one demanded by so serious a crisis; I have given them to understand that the government cannot command enough force to protect all the factories simultaneously; and that, since workers continue to hold factory managers hostage, only the gloomiest forebodings can be entertained in case those workers, inflamed by the prolongation of the crisis, still more by the absence of wages on Saturday, commit violent excesses within the factories, stop.

I have also pointed out that the resistance of the industrialists could provoke workers in other industries to imitate the metal-workers, stop. I have suggested the probability of a general strike and convulsions throughout the country, for which the industrialists would be responsible, stop. They were impressed but then when I asked them what I was to say to Buozzi who is seeing me tomorrow morning, they replied that workers must first return to legality and then one could negotiate; but they then ruled out any possibility of a wage increase offering only to take measures to reduce the cost of living through consumers' co-operatives and other means, stop. I said these incentives were inadequate and begged them to concede some increase on condition of an assessment of the financial state of the industry by a mixed commission; but they do not agree to any wage increase, not even the smallest, well below a half, stop.

To my protests against the resolution and the voting, they replied that the Honourable Agnelli talked to His Excellency the President this morning in Turin, whence they inferred that the President was not far from their way of thinking, stop. I challenged this inference, calling it arbitrary, stop. I dismissed them, saying that their decisions were not reasonable or even patriotic, stop. Tomorrow morning I will tell Buozzi that the industrialists are ready to resume negotiations provided that workers return to legality, stop. I will do my best to convince him of this but have little faith in the outcome, stop. Buozzi's answers will determine my action when I resume talks with the industrialists, stop.

Today there have been no incidents except that the deputy manager *sig.* Breda has been detained in the Monacelli plant and other minor ones. During the day I conferred with Albertini, Turati, Treves, D'Aragona to secure their co-operation in a settlement, stop. I have also spoken with senators Conti and Olivetti, who share the views of the industrialists, stop. Tomorrow, in every way, directly and indirectly, I shall keep on trying and will take every opportunity to predispose minds to possible agreements, stop. The movement of security forces, already reported, continues, stop. Tomorrow morning, in implementation of the resolution, there will be a general lockout in Turin, stop.

Prefect Lusignoli

(*ibid*, n.15,464)

Corradini to *Giolitti*

Rome, 1 September 1920

Dear President, I report on the current situation in the conflict in the metal industry which you already know about, from information to hand. Industrialists persist in their intransigent attitude: refusal of negotiations, public denunciation of obstructionism which they say has degenerated into a sitdown strike, acts of sabotage, violence against directors; they proclaim a lockout. Workers, in reaction to lockout, occupy factories. Declarations made to me personally by industrialists reveal a will to go to extremes. I reaffirm that government does not intend to interfere in conflict, responsibility for which is almost exclusively theirs. Industrialists' resolution shows their intentions. Approaches attempted through prefect Milan fruitless. Labriola is here and assures me he is in contact with representatives of both parties: finds industrialists still recalcitrant while workers' representatives would not be averse to discussions to find a way out. Best to wait in my view.

Meanwhile I am checking on the disposition of our forces in the provinces involved. Making arrangements with the Minister of War for convenient deployment. Railway administration asks me whether they should effect delivery of material arriving for particular firms whose plants are occupied. I reply that, especially after public warning by owners against dispatch or delivery of goods or valuables, it does not seem that such deliveries should be made without explicit consent of owners. In any case they are to take legal advice on juridical responsibility and abide by it. If violence threatens at railway sidings we will give orders to defend the said stations.

I discussed with Olivetti the possibility that if events become complicated it might be convenient to call in the Confederation of Industrialists on the one hand, the CGL on the other, as an unprejudiced reserve for further negotiations. Olivetti now sends telegram suggesting moment for such action has come. If you think this opportune cable me and I will invite here representatives local elections. According to information received, electoral preparations proceed without serious incident.

Yours   Corradini

(ibid, n.15,593)

Giolitti to Corradini

Coded. Bardonecchia, 2 September 1920, 11.00 (arrived 13.30)

With regard to dispute in metal industry I believe it would be best for government action to be as little overt as possible. Government, in principle, must not intervene unless summoned by both parties. Any initiative by government will embitter the conflict. In Turin I explained to the industrialists that they cannot count on the use of the security forces. Workers occupying factories have no interest in damaging machinery knowing that this would mean prolonged unemployment. In short, it is necessary to be very calm and to avoid any unnecessary initiatives.

Warmest regards

Giolitti

(ibid, n.15,625)

Corradini to Giolitti

Coded, very urgent, Rome, 2 September 1920

Dear President, stop. Telegram received, stop. Agreed, stop. Action limited to keeping contact and watching situation, stop. Information Milan indicates attempt to extend action to other industries, stop. Treves, Turati, D'Aragona, questioned by Lusignoli, think extension of agitation would make negotiations more difficult, stop. Rotigliano now repeats to me that they are ready to resume negotiations on basis of collateral concessions assistance institutions etc: standing firm on attitude, no wage increases. Prefects Genoa and Alessandria on own initiative prevented invasion of factories giving rise to today's incident. I am working to diminish incident to avoid repercussions, stop. Received Sforza's note about *Tempo* campaign. Will see to it.

Affectionately   Corradini

(*ibid*, n.15,644)

Lusignoli to *Giolitti*

Milan, 2 September 1920, 16.40 (arrived 18.00)

According to government's instructions, have not ceased to maintain contact with contending parties in order to be able to bring them together at opportune moment. Obliged to inform Your Excellency however that there is a disposition to common action among workers of other industries to extend movement with object of creating situation even more serious than present one: extension of obstructionism to other industries with occupation of factories in preparation. In which case negotiations with metalworkers would take place in very difficult conditions. Men of widely different parties agree in this opinion, from senator Albertini to Treves, Turati. D'Aragona also thinks movement could assume very much larger dimensions. While workers' leaders are alive to this, industrialists are not, which makes the desired accommodation of the parties yet more difficult. While Milan industrialists cannot themselves assume responsibility for decision, Buozzi on other hand thinks that solution to conflict must be achieved in Milan, centre of the movement. I have thought it my duty to explain the situation to Your Excellency. I for my part will maintain contact seeking to avoid friction to keep alive possibility of agreement.

Prefect Lusignoli

(*ibid*, n.15,684)

Lusignoli to *Corradini*

Milan, 2 September 1920, 14.30 (arrived 21.00)

Informed by prefect Turin that industrialists begin to understand gravity of situation. Point confirmed by private telegram from director of Radaelli plant to his deputy director. I think moment has come to act especially on Agnelli Turin to reach solution. May be necessary to exert strong pressure because possibly decisive meeting of their federation to be held very soon. Tomorrow, will try to influence Jarach in this sense.

Prefect Lusignoli

(*ibid*, n.15,701)

Lusignoli to *Porzio* (under-secretary, President's office)
Milan, 4 September, 21.00 (arrived 24.00)

Following telephone conversation, it may perhaps be possible to find basis for agreement on these lines: measures by industrialists designed to reduce workers' cost of living through large co-operatives, consumer stores etc. They recognize implicitly the disproportion between wages and the cost of living; and since these organizations cannot function immediately, until they are in action and yield tangible results, industrialists should give workers daily sum to be determined, this sum to diminish in proportion to gains actually accruing to workers through action of said organizations. On the other hand, still controversy over some points financial side; these should be resolved by a joint commission. Such a scheme not ruled out by deputies Buozzi and D'Aragona; not even ruled out by president of the industrialists, of whom . . . is the most resistant. Deputy Turati thinks this the basis for a good agreement. So does senator Della Torre whom I have persuaded to support it among industrialists before they leave for Rome this evening, where they have been summoned by His Excellency Labriola. I add and repeat that it is the unanimous opinion of the most representative people that it is imperative to settle this dispute at once, before serious movements spread to other industries. Deputy Buozzi is of the same opinion.

Prefect Lusignoli

(*ibid*, n.16,059)

Confidential information: on the dispute in the metallurgical industry

Rome, 4 September 1920

I spent part of the morning with the Honourable Treves who is in Rome. He is very pessimistic about the situation because it seems that the other classes of workers, incited by the maximalists, are preparing to imitate the metalworkers on the pretext of demonstrating solidarity with them. The government, according to Treves, cannot remain passive in the face of acts which violate the fundamental laws of the 'bourgeois state'. The intransigence of the parties to the dispute is driving the government into the terrible necessity of asserting itself by force – a return to reaction – or of abdicating to the proletarian dictatorship. Treves, supported by Turati, Storchi and other colleagues and co-religionists, will try to settle the conflict peacefully and legally; but he has little confidence that the voice of reason and of experience will be spontaneously listened to by the masses in ferment.

It is no longer the heads of the socialist party who lead the masses; it is the masses whose mentality has been transformed by a five-year war and its political and economic consequences who, in their violent ignorance, sweep along and sweep away their alleged leaders. According to Treves, the government, which was without doubt aware of the intentions of the metalworkers, should have prevented the workers' action by forcibly occupying the factories; the Honourable Labriola should not have fostered the hope that the government would look sympathetically on the metalworkers' plan to manage the factories themselves, paying the industrialists a rent for the plant, machinery etc which they owned. The speeches of the Minister of Labour, according to Treves, are a powerful stimulus, inciting the metalworkers to resist.

In response to my query, Treves said that he does not rule out the possibility that in the present crisis there is the hand of the foreigner, working for either political or commercial ends.

Finally, he thinks the government is in a very difficult situation; after having angered the industrialists by making them feel abandoned and defenceless before the metalworkers, it will be compelled by the force of circumstances to guarantee its own existence and will anger the proletariat by re-establishing the rule of law.

F.P.

P.S. Note that the writer is an intimate friend of the Honourable Labriola and if ever this note were communicated to the same, he would immediately raise it with Treves who would at once disclose the name of the informant.

(*ACS, Ministero degli Interni, Direzione generale di PS, Affari generali e riservati*, D.13, busta 74)

Lusignoli to *Porzio* and *Corradini*

Coded. Milan, 5 September 1920, 11.00 (arrived 12.30)

For your information, I send to Your Excellencies the following telegram sent by me this moment to His Excellency Labriola, stop.

Conferred with deputy Buozzi who tells me that the federal committee and the co-ordinating committee have reconsidered proposals on basis of pay increases to diminish in proportion to gains accruing as result of functioning of consumer co-operatives and stores together with creation of joint commission to solve other questions, stop. Those present believe that the mass of workers would accept such a solution provided it were prompt, I would say almost immediate, stop. It seems an increase of 5 lire for men, lesser increases for women and boys, would be accepted, stop. I think that, given that this increase would be subject to diminution parallel to the activation of co-operatives, the industrialists would have no sound reason to oppose it, stop. In strict confidence I inform Your Excellency that this telegram has been composed in the presence of deputy Buozzi who has raised no objection, stop.

Prefect Lusignoli

(*ACS, Ministero degli Interni, Ufficio cifra*, n.16,114)

Taddei (prefect of Turin) to *Corradini*

Bardonecchia, 5 September 1920, 19.10 (arrived 19.40)

I send phonogram Prefect Turin arrived 19.00 hours.

Day passed quietly. Many occupied factories continue to prepare measures of defence, making weapons of all kinds from material available. It is said that the occupiers have machine-guns, they are also said to have armed a tank built by Fiat for the state. If such a state of affairs continues, the situation will become extremely serious. In the factories the conviction is growing among the most exalted elements that the moment of triumph for their ideals approaches, and fears that masses of armed workers could plan to invade the city in strong groups with even more criminal intentions begin to be worrying. The security forces and troops available here to oppose them are limited, all the more so since in such an eventuality service would have to be continuous. Given this fact and in the belief that, because of the numbers of the workers and their revolutionary spirit, extreme measures of the kind mentioned above would begin here rather than in other centres, I request Your Excellency to issue urgent orders for the concentration here of at least 400 *carabinieri* or royal guards to be quartered in barracks here by arrangement with the military authorities. I ask you also to fill the quota of 10 officers of the Public Security on detachment, only three of them have so far arrived.

Respectfully

Prefect Taddei

(*ibid*, n.16,158)

Corradini to *Lusignoli*

Coded. Rome, 6 September 1920, 24.00

Please call the Honourable Bianchi immediately and show him this message, stop. D'Aragona is coming tomorrow evening, he wants me to tell him (Bianchi) that it is necessary to support by every means the attempt to reach an agreement between the industrialists and the CGL to put an end to the metalworkers' conflict, stop. Negotiations will be conducted by the General Confederation of Industry with members of the CGL, stop. D'Aragona wants me to alert him (Bianchi), stop. Regards to Bianchi from me.

Corradini

(*ibid*, n.16,257)

Lusignoli to *Giolitti*

Milan, 7 September 1920, 2.35 (arrived 8.00)

Subsequent to my telegram in reply to telegram no. 94,581 signed His Excellency Corradini, I report that from my meeting with the military authorities it appears that the disposition of armed forces within the area makes 3,000 troops available in case of extreme emergency as well as 1,200 *carabinieri* and royal guards. With such numbers it is possible to defend only the line of the Naviglio and a few other important localities, retaining a reserve to be deployed at points where the need is greatest. The Naviglio line encloses only a fifth of the city; vital points like warehouses, wharves, many public offices including the Public Security commissariat, would remain uncovered. In order to be able to defend the greater part of the city and to prevent an influx from the countryside and the factories now in occupation, it would be necessary to hold the line of the city railway, which would require another 5,000 men, troops, *carabinieri* and royal guards. It is also necessary to increase the number of armoured cars, at present only six, and to supply hand grenades; it would be extremely useful to have tanks. Please send a squadron of royal guards, a cavalry barracks is available. In view of the capital importance of Milan, especially at this moment, I think 5,000 men indispensable, otherwise a part of the city could fall, even if only temporarily, into the hands of rebels and suffer inevitable devastation. I repeat yet again that the situation worsens continuously, hence the absolute necessity to implement the measures requested above with the utmost urgency.

Prefect Lusignoli

(*ibid*, n.16,325)

II.
The Participation of the Railwaymen

Telephone conversation between directors of the state railways

Recorded conversation between commendatore *Ehrenfreund, divisional director of the railways at Turin, and* commendatore *Tondelli of the general management of the railways at Rome.*

Rome, 7 September, 12.00

Turin: Look, in this place the delivery of transports to the yards particularly the marshalling yards, is cheerfully going on. Yesterday they delivered another seven trucks to Fiat-Lingotto, which makes 21 trucks in all regularly delivered to Fiat-Lingotto so far, without taking account of what they might have perpetrated during the night.

Rome: What stuff was in those trucks?

Turin: Fourteen carried diesel, which they seem to need most, and 7 had various goods. Then, during the night in the marshalling yards they coupled 10 trucks to train no.5402 which left at six this morning for the Avigliana sidings.

Rome: Those trucks, what was in them?

Turin: A bit of everything. Naturally we'll do everything possible to stop them getting there, but I tell you now, we won't stand a chance.

Rome: Tell me, are they sending trucks for repair into the workshops?

Turin: No, no, not those for the moment. I'm telling you the lot now, we've had information on this. After we arranged things so that, as a rule, the trucks of one plant are held in depot at other stations, the Avigliana station has just learned that 12 trucks directed to the Ferriere are in depot at Sant'Antonio to pick up goods. We already know that the *carabinieri*, though aware of it, can do nothing, and the workers will go there and send them on for sure because there is no one who feels strong enough to stop it.

Rome: Anything else?

Turin: It seems to me that someone's trying to force the hands of the railwaymen to deliver material for repair.

Rome: But those they have, have they serviced them?

Turin: It seems so, and they want more trucks. In effect, what's taking shape here, and there are various signs of it, is a takeover of the railways, understand?

Rome: Ah! A takeover of the railways?

Turin: For sure! They say they are the bosses these days.

Rome: Eh! . . . right! Anything else?

Turin: I think that if there were another stationmaster at the marshalling yards, things would go better, a stationmaster with spirit.

Rome: We've already arranged it.

Turin: The presence of Schiavo at Dora has already improved the situation. I don't say we'll be able to stop all this because by now we're on the slide and it will be hard to stop it.

Rome: Right.

Turin: *Commendatore* Crova told me to lodge a complaint about this with the legal department. The department told me that they don't see any serious criminal offence in this.

Rome: But it's larceny!

Turin: No, they say that for larceny, there must be personal interest; there's none of that; the larceny element is completely absent, the railwaymen gain nothing from it. There could be some administrative offence of irregular delivery, but that's doubtful because even irregular delivery would not stick because the plant exists and in it there are people who go to pick up the goods.

Rome: Anyway, we can always report the fact to the public prosecutor and then he'll decide on the issue.

Turin: Oh yes! . . . In two years he'll decide . . . Anyway, I will report it. At any rate we can plead *force majeure* in our defence, I'll write now to the administration as well to tell them we are in no position to stop it if they want to come and pick up the material themselves and warehouse it. That would be the best thing, it seems to me. I must say, though, that in everything that's going on, I see more than the commercial business, we're fully covered over that, it's the other thing, the question of indiscipline.

Rome: Yes indeed.

Turin: Then there's the other matter, decided by the Bologna committee. You know about that?

Rome: Yes, we know.

Turin: The order was to come into effect on the 9th or 10th.

Rome: Yes, yes, that's known.

Turin: You watch, it'll be no surprise if they do the same in some other places . . . We're walking on hot coals, remember that . . Maybe things will sort themselves out . . . I'm ready for anything . . Anyway, it's good that we're all on the alert.

Rome: It'll be all right, don't worry.

Turin: Last night I had a long talk with the minister and he'll talk it over with Crova.

Rome: All right.

Turin: Goodbye Tondelli, all the best.

Rome: Goodbye.

> (*ACS, Ministero degli Interni, Direzione generale di PS Affari generali e riservati*, D.13, busta 74, n.2957)

III.
The Climax

Confidential information

Rome, 8 September 1920

The metalworkers' movement exhibits unknown qualitie about which it is not possible to be sure at the moment, since whil the movement is controlled by FIOM and the CGL, organizations o reformist character, it is also supported by anarchist and anarchoid maximalist elements.

To judge only from the intentions of the movement's organizers, the expropriation is neither complete nor definitive, because it is not wanted.

But the more time passes, the sharper will be the conflict and the greater the difficulties.

This thing is different from an ordinary strike in which workers can get tired and give in. In this case, the occupiers, as well as standing together day and night, a factor which in itself strengthens resistance and mutual influence, hold a security in the plants, i.e. the machinery and raw materials, which include material of an essentially warlike character. The controversy over payment for work actually done, or to be more exact, for the working days of the occupation, grows more acute because every day the total of money owed increases. The threat of sabotage is discounted by the leaders, but who will listen to them the moment the defeat of the movement becomes obvious? Exasperation at having lost, at having worked in vain, the possibility of a violent expulsion of the workers from the factories will make them angry and violent.

On the other hand, they are fanning the flames everywhere, calling for an extension of the expropriation to other industries. So far there has been indecision, because the CGL and FIOM do not want to go so far; but at the same time, these two organizations want to save themselves at all costs and they know that everything will fall to pieces if the mass cannot boast of having won at least a significant victory.

A general expropriation would cause such chaos that there would be some kind of revolt of the working classes which could provoke a reaction from the middle classes and nationalist and anti-bolshevik elements.

It is not possible to indicate a way out at the moment. It would be prudent to concede some partial improvement of an economic nature to the workers, but the industrialists have risked too much to be able to choose this way out which, however disguised, would signify their defeat. To wait for the workers to wear themselves out is not wise, because they will try anything before quitting the factories, they will sabotage the machinery and inflict enormous damage on Italian industry.

This is not to say it would damage the metalworkers' class, since the action has been foreseen and workers, in the event, would emigrate to countries where metalworkers' skills are in demand, especially Germany and Russia.

The government is neutral and does well to be so, but in the long run, this neutrality could look like complicity with one side or the other, depending on the attitude which its forces would take towards further occupations, and then the movement would cease to be economic and become political and naturally revolutionary.

These are the characteristics of the present conflict which, to judge from today's events, has not entered a decisive phase yet, since the method of occupation is still going through its first trial.

It remains to be seen what will happen this week. At present, no precise or active repercussion in political circles.

(ibid, D.13, busta 74)

Corradini to *Giolitti* (at Aix-les-Bains)
Coded. Rome, 11 September 1920

Discussion in socialist mini-parliament continues Milan. It will go on late. Spoke on telephone Treves. He says conflict between those who want to achieve different order capital-labour relations and those who would accept solution of present conflict on economic terrain is very bitter. Former tendency wants to solve question on parliamentary terrain, or for extreme faction, by revolution. Second tendency would approve economic settlement provided settlement resolved question of factory control and discipline. Treves hopes this more temperate tendency will prevail. General impression rather more pessimistic than this morning's on feasibility of swift solution. Preparation for militarization of railways set in train. Anticipated that railwaymen's movement will take form of occupation not strike. Technical study this possibility. Have notified Bank director your telegram refuting charges made against him Milan. Government asks him to act effectively, giving no credence to charges, asks him to act effectively in support of a settlement. This communication made orally. Effective action taken on all other similar elements. Will communicate other information later. Journalists ask if some statement possible on this convention. If you think it opportune, send me a communiqué which I will circulate.

Affectionately

Corradini

(ACS, Ministero degli Interni, Ufficio cifra)

Lusignoli to *Corradini*

Milan, 13 September 1920, 18.30 (arrived 19.00)

This morning important meeting prefecture senators Conti, Albertini, *commendatore* Toeplitz, Pogliani, Agnelli to decide on line to be taken by senator Conti in industrialists' assembly. Conti declared himself in favour of conciliation. Then CGL presented proposals on issue of recognition of control in a form which does not seem to me unacceptable except for some modifications. This afternoon meeting of deputies and senators Milan called by senator Conti carried resolution for conciliation and acceptance of union control. Other meetings of industrialists of contrary tendency have been held. Now the directive council of industrialists' confederation meets for definitive decision. If this is in favour of conciliation there will be a meeting of the parties to open negotiations tonight or tomorrow morning.

Prefect Lusignoli

(*ibid*, n.17,489)

IV.
The Resistance of the Employers

Telephone conversation between industrialists' leaders

Conversation between the Lombard consortium of the metallurgical industrialists (Minunni) and the General Confederation of Industry at Rome (Vettori)

Rome, 15 September, 12.00

Milan: Listen, I'm telephoning you with some ideas which might be useful as guidelines for statements to the press. This is the point: as you know, the idea of trade union control cannot be accepted because, apart from technical considerations which make it impracticable, it would hand over the factories to the workers, it would be a form of monopoly control, that is, control by one single sector of the collectivity. Union control would be a favour granted to one single category in preference to those which in the country at large might share common interests with the industrialists. There are the consumers, the suppliers of raw material, the state, the whole collectivity which, if control is to be established over the industrialists, ought to have as much right to exercise control as the workers.

Rome: Right.

Milan: Union control, then, is absolutely unacceptable: if it is a question only of a form of union control over the functioning of establishments, a kind of commission of enquiry into conditions in industry, this can be accepted, up to a point. Look, what's important here is the need to make it clear to the Catholics that union control would deliver control of the whole of industry into the hands of FIOM, whereas there has to be a form in which workers of all kinds must finally be involved. Therefore union control: nothing doing, because that would be a trade union trust; instead create commissions in which everyone is represented by proportional representation and talk all the time not of control over firms but of a state commission of supervision etc. This idea can be presented in tentative form as the only one which might eventually be accepted by those who have the interests of production at heart.

Rome: Right. Listen Minunni: it's necessary to keep an eye on Rosati, because yesterday's *La Tribuna* carried an article and correspondence which were all more or less tuned to excessive appeasement of the CGL.

Milan: It's not correspondence from Milan, it's editorial stuff.

Rome: But we must keep our eyes open, with the attitude which Crespi took, about the newspapers tied to the Banca Commerciale, they are obviously taking up an attitude and I don't know what should be done to curb it.

Milan: I know, we agree on this, so I'll throw a bomb in *L'Idea Nazionale* on this business. I will openly accuse the Banca Commerciale of working with the socialists, having daily contacts with subversives, as well as having taken money etc.

Rome: This is in *L'Idea*?

Milan: No, I'll send it to them today.

Rome: Good, are there any details on yesterday's discussions?

Milan: There was no real discussion, that's to say there was first of all a report on the situation, then the introduction of the resolutions by someone from Turin, then the one from the mechanical and metallurgical industrialists, then the idea of state control to which I've referred was aired, then two motions were read, one by Olivetti and one by Crespi.

Rome: Couldn't the terms of the Olivetti and Crespi motions be made known?

Milan: Since they were withdrawn, it would be necessary to know whether the movers want them known.

Rome: But I wanted to know them for my personal information.

Milan: Olivetti's is a very long motion on the subject of control, rather uncertain, confused, not helpful to the adoption of a much stronger directive line in protest against the attitude of the government, against violence and in favour of a return to legality.

Rome: Did Olivetti deny the principle of control?

Milan: It is so vague I couldn't say.

Rome: All right, fetch the secretary, so that I can dictate something.

Milan: Right, here's the secretary.

Rome: Rome, 14th: Here is some information gathered in parliamentary and ministerial circles. A day of little activity in the dispute with the industrialists. At the Ministries of Labour and the Interior they were waiting till a late hour for news from Milan where the discussions were continuing. This morning the Honourable Labriola reached Rome, Giolitti wanted to talk to him first as soon as he returned to the capital and gave instructions to his cabinet to this effect. It seems that the Honourable Labriola will call representatives of the industrialists and the workers' organizations to Rome, to sound out their views on the new legislation which is to regulate the relations between capital and labour. At the Ministry of Labour it is denied that the Honourable Labriola has been set aside during the current economic dispute; on the contrary, when he left Rome, the Honourable Giolitti charged Meda and Labriola with the duty of following and solving the dispute. Then the dispute ceased to be economic, became political and Giolitti assumed responsibility. Now that the issue is being pushed back towards economics, Giolitti has already advised Labriola that he has to reassume responsibility for its resolution. Contrary to rumours current for some time, the Senate, which reopens the day after tomorrow, will hold a limited number of debates, perhaps six or seven. The Honourable Dugoni, questioned by some journalists yesterday on the conduct which the CGL would follow if the industrialists accepted its demands, declared that the CGL would immediately order the clearance of the factories. Questioned further on what action the CGL would take if nuclei of workers refused to evacuate the factories, the Honourable Dugoni declared that the CGL could do nothing but disown them publicly. There's nothing else.

Milan: Good.

(*ACS, Ministero degli Interni, Direzione generale di PS, Affari generali e riservati*, D.13, busta 74, n.2939)

V.
Power to the CGL?

Telephone conversation between Albertini and Amendola
Rome, 15 September 1920, 9.00

Rome (Amendola): Good morning, director.

Milan (Albertini): How disastrous the situation is!

Rome: What? No agreement?

Milan: In my view, we're going to the dogs.

Rome: That's terrible.

Milan: In Milan, the most elementary functions of government no longer exist.

Rome: I see.

Milan: There is nothing, nothing, absolutely nothing remotely resembling a government.

Rome: But what can be done in this situation?

Milan: Give power to the CGL.

Rome: But that's the end!

Milan: No, no, it's much better than what's happening now. It's not possible to go on like this, my dear fellow.

Rome: But what you're saying is – let's make the revolution and goodbye! And it's finished! But isn't there anything we can do not to make the revolution?

Milan: Precisely, the only way to avoid the revolution is to give power to the CGL.

Rome: To do what?

Milan: The factory council, anything they want . . . But at least there'd then be some order . . . There'll be someone to impose his will on industrialists . . . on workers . . . There'll be something which today simply does not exist, today no one imposes his will on industrialists or workers.

Rome: But if the industrialists are coming round to the idea of control over the factories, why don't they come to an agreement?

Milan: They're not all of that opinion, some yes, others no. Then they say that there are so many workers' associations that if there is no government order, no state order, we'll have factories controlled by syndicalists, by priests, by all sorts . . . as many factory councils as pop into their heads . . . It is not possible. The state has to intervene.

Rome: All this is quite true. Everything being discussed in Milan is so serious that it can't be settled as the simple result of a conflict between the CGL and the industrialists. The thing has to be considered from a general point of view.

Milan: But here the industrialists say: let the government take over our factories, turn them into co-operatives, anything in fact, but let's have a government that governs, a socialist government if you like, but the present state of affairs is so outrageous that nothing like it has ever been seen in the world before.

Rome: Quite, quite!

Milan: They say: we cannot accept this unless someone imposes it with authority, because our technicians and clerks will not go back into the factories . . . so you enforce it. But the state seems incapable even of this.

Rome: That's dreadful, that's very serious indeed.

Milan: That's how it is.

Rome: And in the negotiations, where are we?

Milan: Yesterday evening they broke off and they have been adjourned to Thursday because senator Conti has not got a vote of confidence. That's how things really stand.

Rome: But if there's a majority among the industrialists ready to accept . . .

Milan: There isn't, there isn't, if there were . . .

Rome: If there were, it could always lay down this condition, namely that all this should not be sanctioned by the two organizations, but by the government in parliament. This must be the responsibility of the state as a whole.

Milan: But there is no such majority.

Rome: And the others who are not the majority, where do they want to go?

Milan: A substantial number is in favour of a deal, but the others want to resist. Let the state take over . . . let it dismiss us . . . do what it likes, but we cannot finish it like this of our own free will. Therefore the government must intervene and impose a solution. When the government has abandoned any attempt to defend the laws which regulate present society it must at least say: Do this!

Rome: That's right.

Milan: You see, I'm not of your opinion . . . I am unhappy that Rossini last night issued that note against summoning the Chamber . . . On the contrary, we must support it.

Rome: But you see, if there was a government plan to settle the dispute, and if summoning parliament were part of that plan, you'd be right. But in this state of anarchy, to call parliament would do nothing but give the thing still greater publicity.

Milan: And there'll be a Constituent Assembly!

Rome: But then we'll be heading no one knows where.

Milan: And if we go on like this in this anarchy, in a few days there'll be a revolt in the streets! In Rome you don't have the right feel of the situation in Milan and Turin.

Rome: I see.

Milan: There's never been anything like it.

Rome: But do you think the government could have prevented the occupation of the factories?

Milan: Eh! Of course it could!

Rome: It could?

Milan: Not everywhere, but by creating divergences it could have done something in Turin, obviously it might have caused conflict in the streets. Above all this selling of stolen goods would be easy to resist . . . It would be enough to treat this stuff being sold so improperly as stolen goods . . . instead: nothing, nothing! Kidnappings, robberies, killings, everything, anything goes!

Rome: My God! That's really appalling, that!

Milan: Dreadful! Now I think the only thing left is to resign and to give power to the CGL. They must be told: you are the masters now, so take power legally!

Rome: And they'd at once proclaim the Republic . . . and then soviets everywhere.

Milan: Ah no . . . no . . .

Rome: But you should not look to the leaders, if they had enough control over the masses they would not have reached this point!

Milan: Then you tell me what we should do.

Rome: I don't know what to say, it's the result of a beastly policy we've been following for some time.

Milan: And which is now at its climax.

Rome: It's beastly. Contact with the socialists they didn't want, a policy of peace they didn't want . . . and now what is to be done? It's difficult to say. Certainly I take your point, but it means throwing ourselves into the abyss.

Milan: I don't think so.

Rome: If I were in the government, I'd make contact with these people, I'd ask them what they want to do . . . I wouldn't keep it restricted like Giolitti. He has a tendency to limit the conflict to the economic issue.

Milan: But he has understood nothing.

Rome: But this is not just an economic thing, it's a fundamental question which affects the life of the state, given this, it is necessary to solve it with political leaders, ask them where they want to go, and if they answer in an acceptable manner, agree, change the situation in parliament, and move ahead.

Milan: That is why I say parliament must be summoned.

Rome: But to call parliament, given this conception of the situation which the government has, means to throw ourselves on the mercy of chance. The government's idea is the one Giolitti had ten years ago. For example, I've heard it said that if Giolitti had ordered the occupation of the factories, he would have put the soldiers inside and left the workers outside in the streets, instead he preferred the latter to be inside and to have the security forces in hand. Now, given these ideas, it seems to me that Giolitti doesn't think like us. So we'd have Modigliani who'd come back like one of the Apocalypse. And what are we doing? This is one of those shows you don't put on until you've thought it all out in advance. They say: go away, let us take power and they'd have the republic at once . . . we'd soon have a republic in German style . . . a kind of German-type socialism . . . if this suits us . . .

Milan: It's much less bad than what's happening now! We'd prefer it because what's happening now is going beyond the frontiers of the predictable. Then they'll be thinking about bread, about bureaucrats, about all this mess.

Rome: It's easy to do what they're doing at the moment, but we'd have to see what comes after.

Milan: Let me ask you the question: how do we move forward then?

Rome: No one knows.

Milan: It is tragic!

Rome: I know, there is nothing to be done.

Milan: You must draft a note this evening on the opening of the Senate.

Rome: What do we say?

Milan: That there must be a directive line, that things cannot go on like this, stick to generalities. There is a great political crisis, a crisis of regime . . . that it is imperative to have guidelines etc.

Rome: That's right, the point can be well made. I'll do it at once this afternoon and send it to you promptly.

Milan: Excellent.

Rome: You can't come here at the moment?

Milan: As long as it's not been settled, no.

Rome: All right. What I want to say . . . In my opinion, even if they manage to patch this situation up for the last time, it is the absence of will in the government which has been the burning question from the moment this terrifying problem came up.

Milan: I think that, too. The other day, in a meeting of senators and deputies, I got unanimous agreement on that point.

Rome: But couldn't they call on parliamentary arbitration to settle the procedure?

Milan: It is not a question of procedure, that would be easy. But they say: how can we destroy ourselves on our own territory? That they should impose it on us, this state of things in the factories, material plundered, workers who have manhandled directors . . . We cannot accept it. How can we go back into the factories and not dismiss those who seized directors and foremen by the throat? They, I think, have suffered most: Revetti, for example, says: I have 450 million in goods in the factories, but the 450 million could all go down the drain provided they give in. That's the pitch of exasperation they've reached.

Rome: But isn't it possible to persuade the workers to accept the general idea (since we've reached such a serious point) of asking the CGL to distinguish between a political movement, between what's been a political movement, and an offence against property?

Milan: We are trying but even this CGL counts up to a certain point behind us there are the extremists ready and in ambush.

Rome: I know and for this reason, it's necessary to work politically

It's necessary to say: we'll give you this, that and the other but you must come into government.

Milan: It's obvious. If it were rational, the Chamber would overthrow this government and then it would follow naturally that responsibility would fall to the CGL which would do what it wants . . . But constitutionally, there is no other way out. The Chamber should overthrow this ministry, overthrow it to give the mandate to the Honourable Turati and the Honourable Modigliani.

Rome: But these would at once put up the Constituent!

Milan: But the industrialists don't give a damn about the Constituent.

Rome: But it's necessary to consider the whole country not just the industrialists, and where are we going to end up? Do we want to overthrow the constitution? It's easy to say it, but when we get to the point of doing it, it's not so simple.

Milan: Listen Amendola, nothing can happen worse than is happening now.

Rome: I agree, this is something which takes us into the political field.

Milan: It's obvious.

Rome: Everything that happens is a real calamity, it's frightening.

Milan: I agree.

Rome: This afternoon I'll write the note and send it.

Milan: Goodbye.

Mutual farewells

(ibid, D.13, busta 74, n.2936)

VI.
The Travail of Arbitration

Telephone conversation between the consortium of mechanical and metallurgical industries, Milan, and the consortium of metallurgical industries, Rome

Rome, 17 September 1920, 13.30

Milan: Is that professor Vettori?

Rome: It's not the professor, I'm the secretary.

Milan: Then take down what I say and let professor Vettori have it at once: Professor Vettori is requested to find senator Conti at once and to draw his full attention to what appears in today's *La Stampa*. In that paper, together with a paraphrase of the previously drafted decree of the President of the Council, it is clearly stated that this decree is the result of the full agreement reached on both the question of control and the question of discipline between the CGL and the general confederation of industry, which was represented at the Turin meeting by senator Conti and the Honourable Olivetti. *La Stampa* reports the news of the full agreement between the CGL and the confederation of industry with such assurance that, in its comment, it expresses great surprise at the news reaching it from Milan yesterday that ratification of the agreement was not unanimous and that there was lively argument within the industrialists' confederation; as the CGL was acting on behalf of the entire working class, so the industrialists' confederation, in the persons of senator Conti and the Honourable Olivetti, was acting in the name and on behalf of all the industrialists. It also says that there are industrialists who want to call Giolitti's decree a diktat and *La Stampa* hastens to assert that senator Conti and the Honourable Olivetti cannot fail to speak up against such a fallacious interpretation since they know full well that the decree was simply the product of the agreement reached between the two parties and accepted by Conti and Olivetti in the name and on behalf of the confederation of industrialists. The news in *La Stampa*, probably leaked from the President's cabinet, has created the most painful impression among the industrialists' delegates in the confederation, who absolutely refuse to believe that it corresponds to the facts. The declarations which senator Conti and the Honourable Olivetti made in assembly yesterday, leave no room for doubt in the matter. It is the unanimous opinion of all the delegates that, for the dignity of the industrialist class, senator Conti should categorically deny *La Stampa*'s story, which would signify the worst outcome for our cause.

Rome: Right, I will communicate it at once to professor Vettori.

Milan: Tell him also that the confederation of industrialists meets at 2 p.m. and that this morning there has been a very important meeting at the prefecture between the confederation and the prefects of Milan and Turin.

Rome: All right.

Milan: Many thanks.

(*ibid*, n.2957)

Telephone conversation between professor Vettori, Rome (general confederation of industrialists) and the Honourable Olivetti, Milan

Rome, 17 September 1920, 18.00

Rome: Listen, sir, I have spoken to Conti, he said he leaves it to you to decide whether it would be better to stay in Milan or to come here.

Milan: Right.

Rome: Then he insists, on the question of the decree, that there was no agreement at all. He insists that you make sure a denial is issued to the press because in all the talks with Giolitti there was no agreement at all; it was only that when Giolitti talked about control they expressed their own opinion, that is that the decree represented a diktat which absolved the industrialists' side from expressing their thoughts and opinions, from registering a prior acceptance.

As for the second point, discipline, they were so firm that he stood up and declared that if the President wanted to ruin Italian industry, then he could please himself. In view of these things, he would think it necessary to issue a statement to the press at once.

Milan: All right.

Rome: Note, too, that in the current *L'Idea Nazionale*, there is an article called *Behind the Scenes at a Capitulation*, which is nothing but an attack on you and Conti. It says . . . (*reads the article . . .*)

Milan: I understand . . . hold it a moment . . . look . . . I think I will come down, yes, yes, I'll leave this evening at 8.45.

Rome: Good, so I'll come to the station at 10.55 tomorrow morning.

Milan: Yes, yes, fine.

Mutual farewells

(*ibid*, n.2958)

Telephone conversation between ingegner Toffoletti and, subsequently, senator Crespi (consortium of mechanical and metallurgical industries, Milan) and the Honourable Olivetti (consortium of metallurgical industries, Rome)

Rome, 18 September 1920, 15.35

Rome: Listen Toffoletti, write down what I say and let Crespi have it: I have spoken with Conti, together we have examined every aspect of the current situation in depth and at length. The government's intention is to settle the conflict as soon as possible, because it thinks the working class will not end it until the principle of solidarity with all those who took part in the conflict is recognized, so the government does not intend to give up what it has a mind to do in this matter unless the CGL agrees. We have pointed out to the government that the solution would produce . . .

Milan: Hello, this is Crespi speaking, so talk directly to me.

Rome: Ah, splendid, sir, then I'll sum up the conclusion in a few words, thus: The advice of Conti and myself is this: the alternatives are to submit to the government's measures or to resist to the bitter end. Both have the most serious consequences which we do not conceal, but given the situation we're in, in which the government will ultimately intervene against the weaker party, which is precisely the industrialists, you know our opinion: come to a settlement. In these conditions, we say: it's better to finish it because we're afraid that the industrialists' situation tomorrow might be worse than it is today.

Milan: Wait a moment, did you know that I've had a talk with both parties?

Rome: Yes, I knew that.

Milan: Well, I think there is a chance of reaching a settlement because, thinking things out in full, there are some things which cannot be overcome and if colleagues followed me . . . As for what you say, I think I am still the stronger.

Rome: But . . . the government says the industrialists are the weaker.

Milan: I don't give a damn about the government. I am going on trying to co-operate in a solution which will be fair. Do you know that Giolitti has invited us to Rome?

Rome: I don't know anything.

Milan: It's a fact. There should be a meeting today between us, the two prefects and the CGL; if we manage to find a formula, we'll telephone Rome, otherwise we'll come down, though I don't know whether those gentlemen will want to come.

Rome: I understand. This morning I spoke to Corradini whom I'd asked to intervene. I made him aware of the seriousness of the situation and he said to me, 'If I had the others to hand, I could perhaps get something, but without them, how can I?'

Milan: I see. Then tell Conti this from me: that within half an hour we'll be at the prefecture; I think it will be possible to reach an agreement on the basis which you and Conti discussed at Turin, which should fully satisfy everyone.

Rome: That's fine. How are negotiations going on in engineering?

Milan: They were very close to a solution at two. This evening, I'll let you know something about it.

Rome: Do you think I should come up?

Milan: No, no, stay in Rome because we'll need you if we have to come to the President of the Council, but I repeat, I have never been so hopeful of settling as at this moment.

Rome: That's what we want.

Milan: Thanks, see you soon.

(*ibid*, D.13, busta 74, n.2964)

VII.
The Judgment of an Industrialist

Attilio Bagnara (industrialist of Sestri Ponente) to *Toeplitz* (deputy director of the Banca Commerciale)

Genoa, 20 September 1920

My dear sir,

The recent battle in the metallurgical industry was started by a headless autocracy which, during the disputes, chose delegates who had a mandate only to discuss, not to settle. This point has now been made by *Il Corriere della Sera* as well, in yesterday's article *Controversial issues*. But I pointed out at the time that, for negotiations with the better representatives of the proletariat, the most authoritative representatives of the employers, indeed the industrialists themselves, should have gone. It was said to me then that delegating lesser figures gave more chance to temporize, but I made the point that this was a shabby practice, unworthy of the seriousness of the issue. But I'm a loner, not wanting to get mixed up in the errors of others, and the self-evident truth of what I was saying was either not understood, or if it was understood pointed to a rapid settlement of the dispute with the metalworkers, whereas some people were hoping for political and fiscal gains from prolonging it and making it worse. God knows I don't want to sound like a scandal-monger and I have to say that at this moment, no one can be sure of knowing the truth, the whole truth; on some subjects, there can be only impressions and suppositions.

The iron and steel industrialists took the upper hand and chose *avvocato* Rotigliano as their spokesman. If you don't know him, he is a skilful and forceful talker and was a brave officer during the war when he won several medals for courage. But I also think that he would be honest enough to admit that he has no sense of the realities of industrial life, no understanding of the collective psychology of the masses and none of the needs of proletarians, of the devices used to inflate them etc. So *avvocato* Rotigliano acted out his lawyer's role as best he could, face to face with his opposite number but in the total absence of any presiding magistrate whatever. The metalworkers' representatives asserted – and no one contradicted them – that their people earned less than other workers; therefore they asked for an increase. In effect, they'd proved there was a rising labour market.

The industrialists' representatives tried to prove that industry could not stand wage increases. Obviously, according to the laws of economics, when an industry cannot pay the going price, either for raw materials or for labour, it has to resign itself to a shutdown. But was this really true in any absolute sense?

At all events, by the last phase of the negotiations, the workers' representatives, faced with repeated rejections of their economic demands, were in such a bad way that they would have accepted even modest concessions with great satisfaction.

For a long time I've been arguing that this is the time to restore the cost of living supplements paid for workers' dependants. A family of six people, with four of them out at work, lives in some comfort, but another family of six with only one at work, even at 25 lire a day, cannot feed itself. There are the most miserable inequalities and this measure would have diminished them and deprived the adversary of his most persuasive arguments.

Moreover, there is the law on pensions for workers and employees; but only those who are now young will ever be able to take advantage of it. And I said: let's spontaneously make a contribution to the National Fund for social insurance, to pay a pension, even if only a small one, to the old people we now have.

These two measures would have provided for children and old people, symbols of the dawn and the sunset of this life, which cause us so much tribulation. It would have been balm to the morale of every family. Besides, it was impossible to ignore the inferiority of metalworkers' pay; we'd have to give something, but it would have been much, much less than the figures the papers are bandying about now.

By this time, you'll be wondering why I am writing this letter to you. Here's why: serious mistakes have been made; those who made them are now trying to exonerate themselves by throwing the blame on the government. Now a new scapegoat has been found: the banks. And it seems to me that they are trying to attribute part, if not all the blame to your bank. I did not believe it and I don't believe it.

Yours, affectionately,　　　　　Attilio Bagnara

(Archives of the Banca Commerciale Italiana)

Toeplitz to *Bagnara*

Milan, 28 September 1920

Dear friend,

I found your letter of the 20th waiting on my return after a short absence. Thank you for giving me your views on the recent agitation, doubly interesting to me because of your technical competence.

I am especially grateful to you for demonstrating your solidarity in face of the stupid insinuations levelled these last few weeks against the conduct of the Banca Commerciale and of me personally during the metalworkers' agitation. Our friends in Genoa obviously lose no opportunity to stoke up the campaign against myself!

Warmest greetings,

G. Toeplitz

(ibid)

VIII.
The Evacuation of the Factories

Telephone conversation between Avvocato Rotigliano in Milan and Ceccarelli of Ilva and then the Honourable Olivetti, in Rome

Rome, 21 September 1920, 18.50

Milan: Let me speak to Ceccarelli.

Rome: Hello, who is that?

Milan: *Avvocato* Rotigliano.

Rome: Listen, sir, *avvocato* Jacchia wanted to tell you: *il cavaliere* Muzzerini, Labriola's *chef de cabinet*, came here this morning, asking for the report which you had promised the minister.

Milan: Ah!

Rome: What should we say to him?

Milan: That I'm in Milan, that you'll write to me about it . . . But that I'm very busy and will do my best to let him have it . . . also . . . that I am in Milan and that you will write to me, full stop and finish.

Rome: All right. Listen, this evening's *Il Giornale d'Italia* carries an interview with Crespi . . .

Milan: What does he say?

Rome: He says that Minunni's piece is all lies and slander. What he says about you in particular Rotigliano is this: that the resolution in favour of control was accepted by the industrialists as a free expression of the will of the majority of delegates and then goes on, 'I say majority because in the last days of debate the intransigent current among the delegates grouped around Rotigliano, representative of Ilva and other powerful interests, demanding that all responsibility should be the government's alone.' He says that about you and then goes on to say that there was a moment at which you believed your intransigent resolution would win a majority: he then reports that the conciliatory motion got 21 votes and yours 14.

Milan: Oh well, nothing to say on that. And he says nothing else about me?

Rome: No, he says nothing else about you. *Commendatore* Olivetti has just now instructed me to ask you to make him a short report on the agitation, especially with respect to the opening of the factories, for the administrative council.

Milan: Ah! I understand.

Rome: And about what you were preparing, one should say nothing to him?

Milan: Let him be told that I have made some arrangements about the problem which was discussed last night. So far I have had only *pourparlers*.

Rome: Do you want to speak to *commendatore* Olivetti?

Milan: Yes, let me speak to Olivetti.

(Olivetti comes to the telephone.)

Milan: Listen, I wanted to talk to you about that recommendation you made to me about the financial side. It looks as though our ideas have been well received by our colleagues.

Rome: Good. Now, is there any news of the closure of the factories? What are they doing?

Milan: I have no news. On the contrary, I sent a telegram about what's being agreed at Florence, Milan, Genoa and Turin. Here in Milan there must have been a meeting of engineers and technical *capi* to demand that for this joint commission, choice of delegates should be assigned to the various engineers and technical *capi* and not to the workers' leaders. These people are getting worked up about it and they're right, they say: we want to choose delegates to the commission working out control over firms ourselves . . . it's a matter of their interests. It's fair.

Rome: I see, I see.

Milan: And they're right.

Rome: But do it like that and then we'll be in a minority . . . The question must be studied thoroughly because we could be a majority or a minority . . .

Milan: We could see to it that the election was supervised . . . **But I** think this thing can be fully thrashed out . . . And then there are now going to be discussions on this agreement which is a pretty laborious business. Today there's been a meeting at FIOM when the evacuation of the factories was discussed. There were 103 votes in favour of evacuation and 111 against, but it seems Buozzi will go all out to make sure there is a wholly favourable vote for the liberation of the factories. At the moment, they are still inside and we know absolutely nothing. But this will show you how everything depends on the internal commissions and how uncertain the mood was.

Rome: I spoke to Livorno and they told me the mood has not improved there either; they say if they're not paid for the working days of the occupation, they won't come out of the plants.

Milan: And . . . yes . . . it's not at all to be ruled out, you know, that we're still heading for a crack-up? Then, listen, Ceccarelli told me that Labriola was wanting the report I'd promised him, you know? But I wouldn't give it to him.

Rome: It means that you'll do it again at your leisure.

Mutual farewells

(*ACS, Ministero degli Interni, Direzione generale di PS, Affari generali e riservati*, D.13, busta 74, n.2983)

IX.
The D'Annunzio Peril

Martino (Prefect of Pisa) to *Giolitti*

Coded, Pisa, 22 September 1920, 13.25

Information obtained at various times and places during last few days tends to suggest preparation of imminent nationalist conservative movement in Kingdom with direct intervention D'Annunzio who would assume leadership, relying on solidarity of army and especially detachments in Armistice zone all devoted to him.

This information finds some confirmation in message sent by D'Annunzio to Rome 2 September. Suspect movement could be supported and financed by industry and big banks. The latter after decisions forced by metallurgical dispute which have led to assertion of principle union control over industry could try to escape situation which they think dangerous to their interests by reversing position and staging under pretext Adriatic claims a movement with objectives and methods which completely mask real ends they intend.

Movement would be designed violently to oppose action socialist maximalism and would try to defeat it at a stroke with exemplary repression, for execution of which D'Annunzio would count, not only on insurrection of the bourgeoisie but also on the *carabinieri* and royal guards which he thinks thirsting for revenge on continuous aggressions and demonstrations of contempt by socialist organizations and crowds. I deem it my duty to convey this information to Your Excellency for you to take what notice you will of it.

Respectfully

Prefect De Martino

(ACS, Ministero degli Interni, Ufficio cifra, n.18,525)

X.
Payments and Dismissals

Lusignoli to *Giolitti*

Milan, 22 September 1920, 23.25 (arrived 23 September, 2.10)

Absolute priority over all other absolute priorities

This morning meeting of representatives of industrialist

and workers chaired by me discussed procedure evacuation factories: in general agreement has been reached, stop. Two questions remain unresolved: in plants where full production continued, workers demand assessment amount to pay workers independently retroactive agreement, stop. I have made D'Aragona, Buozzi understand that this claim contradicts agreements achieved and have asked them not to persist, stop. I have reason to believe that congress of workers now assembled to approve action of their representatives will carry resolution which will assert new claim but in such form to make it possible for me to state that agreement must remain unaltered; in special cases I could intervene to facilitate agreements between parties, stop.

Greater difficulty seems will to oppose industrialists who try to resort to arbitrary interpretation Your Excellency's decree on dismissals, stop. To eliminate conflict deriving from industrialists' intention to dismiss from factories workers considered guilty and workers' intention not to accept any dismissal, Your Excellency adopted device of asserting that personnel were to return to their posts, a joint commission to settle measures to take in cases of incompatibility, stop. Your Excellency's thinking evident: measures to be adopted must follow judgment commission, but until this judgment workers remain their posts stop. Now industrialists claim that senator Conti has told them that President of Council verbally acknowledged to him that workers subject to judgment must not re-enter plant but will keep post until judgment made, receiving pay, stop. Now this is in absolute contradiction to concept formulated by Your Excellency and if industrialists were to insist on it, there would be no evacuation of factories, stop.

Therefore I ask Your Excellency to telegraph me that my interpretation of decree is correct; this does not rule out that in determinate cases compromises may be found by mutual agreement, stop. Senator Conti left this evening for Rome, where Your Excellency, I think, could convince senator of his evident error, stop. I have impression he resorts to this expedient to regain trust of industrialists somewhat shaken, stop.

Respectfully
Prefect Lusignoli

(*ibid*, n.18,601)

Giolitti to *Lusignoli*

Coded. 23 September 1920, 22.00

I confirm, with respect to first problem raised – that in plants where full production continued workers' pay to be assessed independently retroactive agreement – that such a solution would not correspond to agreements reached since formula retroactivity was devised precisely to settle disputes that might arise from claim payment wages contested period, stop. You will notify workers' representatives that this was spirit of that agreement, stop. As for interpretation of agreed formula dismissals by which personnel will resume their posts, intended to specify that there should be no dismissals and that institution joint commission must make decisions on inconveniences arising incompatibility parties, stop. Therefore before judgment of commission has been made there must be no dismissals, stop. It is certainly true that senator Conti had made fuller proposals but it is equally indisputable that formula senator Conti was not approved, stop. I therefore consider your interpretation correct, the more so in that it does not rule out acceptance of compromises by mutual agreement.

President of the Council of Ministers Giolitti

(*ibid*, n.18,605)

Corradini to *Lusignoli*

Coded. Rome, 23 September 1920

Please deliver following telegram to Honourable D'Aragona: By unanimous consent all parties including most advanced, acceleration by all possible means of settlement of situation achieved by agreements reached considered extremely urgent. Situation at this moment bristles with difficulties and can give rise to a series of serious incidents which might possibly distort conditions so laboriously achieved, stop. I therefore urge you to work as hard as you can so that demobilization of factories begins quickly and a rigorous halt is called to any further invasion of plants, since public opinion no longer understands how, after agreement has been reached, there still continue in places unjustifiable acts of violence which must be absolutely forbidden, stop. In other words, it is essential to give the impression that we are definitely passing to the re-establishment of de facto peace as the logical corollary of the agreements reached, stop.

All local authorities cannot fail to be convinced that it is their imperative duty to prevent new violence and that state of mind which can lead to conflict and the creation of de facto situations prejudical to a swift pacification which is in everyone's mind and which, in the opinion of all parties, is reasonably to be expected, stop.

It appears, further, that workers' quarters in Milan plan to stage a mass assembly to celebrate the agreement reached, stop. Now you must agree that in the state of mind which has been created, such a demonstration can lead to excesses which are always dangerous but which at the present moment must be totally avoided, stop. I rely on your clear perception of events and on the desire which there is in everyone to get out of the present situation quickly and without further complications, stop. I would be grateful for your views on the present situation and your agreement on a line of conduct which makes further excess impossible and does not conflict with the parallel line of the government.

Yours

Under-secretary of State for the Interior Corradini

(ibid, n.18,704)

XI.
An Interview with Toeplitz

Sketch of an interview with *Le Matin* composed by Giuseppe Toeplitz (French)

The statements attributed to M.Pogliani, director of the Banca Italiana di Sconto, in an interview he gave the special correspondent of *L'Excelsior* have had considerable echo in Italy, where *L'Idea Nazionale*, well-known organ of the bitter enemies of the Banca Commerciale Italiana, has been prompt to give them full prominence.

In France, too, people are understandably fascinated by this conflict between two banks which is also a conflict between two different systems and two contrasting policies. This is why we wanted to interview M.Toeplitz, deputy director of the Banca Commerciale Italiana, who is openly accused of having lent a hand to the strikers and the bolshevizing socialists: which is a rare and exceptional charge to level against a great bank. M.Toeplitz acceded gracefully to our request and told us, with a firm and tranquil smile, what we summarize here.

'I already knew the statements attributed to M.Pogliani from *L'Idea* though I no longer have the text of *L'Excelsior* to hand at this moment. I will not conceal from you the fact that I was astonished to see that *L'Idea* had evidently obtained a first draft of the interview even before its publication in the Parisian paper, since it had taken the opportunity to bring it out in Rome in its Thursday edition which carried Friday's date.

'By happy chance, I had occasion to meet my eminent colleague M.Pogliani the morning after publication. He formally declared to me, in person, that he had never said or caused to be said such things, so remote from the truth or even from any plausibility. He was waiting, as I was, to see the text of the Parisian paper, finally to give the lie to fantasies unmistakably bearing the trade-mark of their inventor, manufactured no doubt in those very factories, or to be more precise, in those shipyards which are the source of this war without quarter which has been waged for years against the Bank which I have the honour to direct. It is to be hoped that this correction will have better luck than another addressed by M.Pogliani at the time to *L'Idea Nazionale* which took great care not to breathe a word of it.'

'But,' we asked M.Toeplitz, 'what exactly was the role of the Italian banks and above all the Commerciale, during the recent metalworkers' agitation?'

M.Toeplitz answered us briskly: 'Banks as such must not play politics; and the Banca Commerciale exerted no pressure in any sense. But it had to be in the know and its directors were able to give advice to their friends in the general interest of the country. This advice, which followed government policy, might have contributed to the solution of the serious situation created by the occupation of the factories sponsored by extremists; but I challenge the enemies of the Banca Commerciale to produce one single shred of evidence of pressure exerted or material aid given to any tendency whatever during the struggle between owners and workers in the metallurgical industry.

'The line of conduct of the Banca Italiana di Sconto and of M.Pogliani personally was exactly the same as that of the Commerciale and of the very modest role which I personally was called upon to play on that occasion. M.Pogliani was in perfect solidarity with our attitude, which was absolutely identical to his and which, given the circumstances, could not have been other than it was. We let ourselves be guided by that commonsense which in Italy always manages to overcome all difficulties; and commonsense has been the only victor in the violent struggle: you may rest assured that the great majority of the industrialists and even the workers, here in Italy, at bottom ask only one thing: to be quickly restored to a position in which they can buckle down to serious work. The sense that our only salvation lies in work is happily general throughout all classes of the Italian population.'

'And the role attributed in all this to German industrialists?'

'Listen, sir,' said M.Toeplitz, rising to his feet, 'the Boche phantom is a kind of fairytale ogre, and when they talk about our bank, they agitate endlessly to stir up Italian nationalists against us: seeing that this no longer works with us, that the gaff has been blown, they try to use it to inflame French chauvinism, well-known to be tempestuous. But these tales of ogres and the Wicked Fairy are good only for children, indeed I doubt even that from what I know of post-war children. Here, everyone knows that German influence, if it ever existed in the past, no longer exists anywhere in any Italian bank – do you hear me? No German influence, no German capital, no German men, no German ideas. As for our Banca Commerciale Italiana in particular, I am proud to add that not only is it not now nor ever will be subjected to German influence, but it is impervious to every foreign influence, no matter what the country of origin. It is Italian in its name, Italian in its spirit and Italian in its action. And no one knows that better than its enemies and detractors who are always the same: their voices strikes that false and cracked note which is easily recognizable whether the gramophone record is played in Genoa, or Rome, or even Paris.'

(Archives of the Banca Commerciale Italiana)

Index

Proletarian Order

Gwyn A. Williams

Gwyn Williams analyses the development
of Gramsci's revolutionary theory up to
the founding of the Communist Party in
Italy – through the crisis of Italian
socialism 1911-21, the growth of the
revolutionary movement 1919-20, the
factory council movement in Turin and
the occupation of the factories.

**Pluto Press, Unit 10 Spencer Court
7 Chalcot Road, London NW1 8LH**

The Bolsheviks
and the October Revolution

Central Committee Minutes of the Russian
Social-Democratic Labour Party (Bolsheviks)
August 1917 – February 1918

Translated from the Russian by Ann Bone

Revolution in Russia, October 1917, meant
that posterity was to inherit a new society.
What remains are the notes for the Bolshevik
Central Committee, hurriedly pencilled on torn-
out sheets of paper.
Captured in these notes is the deep division
that lay between revolutionaries and routinists on
the central committee, between men terrified to
lose and men terrified to grasp the opportunity to
change the pace of history.
The minutes are extensively supplemented
by documents, the official notes of the Institute of
Marxism-Leninism, Moscow, together with
additional notes and comments for this edition.

**Pluto Press, Unit 10 Spencer Court
7 Chalcot Road, London NW1 8LH**